IMAGES
of America

AFRICAN AMERICANS IN COVINGTON

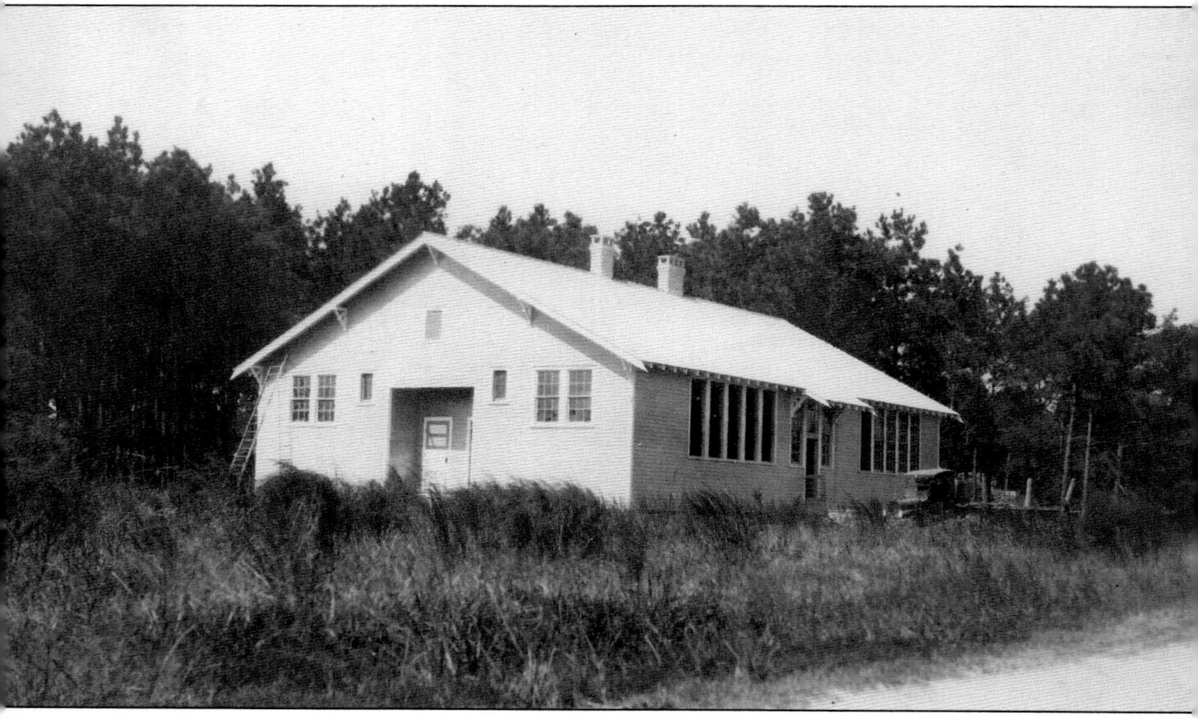

First Rosenwald School. The first Covington Rosenwald School building stands completed in 1927. African Americans raised $1,000, the Rosenwald Fund granted $1,100, and the St. Tammany Parish School Board's $5,000 came from a district bond issue. Prof. James Harrison served as principal. Located in the heart of the African American community, the school coalesced as a meeting ground for many community events. (Courtesy of Fisk University, John Hope and Aurelia E. Franklin Library, Special Collections.)

On the Cover: Mrs. Conerly's Class. Ruby Conerly stands with her second-grade students at Covington Rosenwald School for their 1965–1966 class picture. By the 1950s, a larger and more modern building replaced the first "four-teacher type" school. Covington Rosenwald closed at the end of the 1966 school year, replaced by Pine View High School and Covington Rosenwald Middle School for African American students and teachers. (Courtesy of Ruby Conerly.)

IMAGES
of America

AFRICAN AMERICANS IN COVINGTON

Eva Semien Baham
with a foreword by Rev. Mallery Callahan

ARCADIA
PUBLISHING

ISBN 978-1-4671-1396-0

Published by Arcadia Publishing
Charleston, South Carolina

Printed in the United States of America

Library of Congress Control Number: 2014954337

For all general information, please contact Arcadia Publishing:
Telephone 843-853-2070
Fax 843-853-0044
E-mail sales@arcadiapublishing.com
For customer service and orders:
Toll-Free 1-888-313-2665

Visit us on the Internet at www.arcadiapublishing.com

This record is both because of and for Covington's African American forebears, whose tenacity, courage, and integrity made many possibilities for their descendants.

Contents

Foreword

I was fortunate to have this "village" raise me. My family is representative of many, welded with the hand of God in spite of the harsh realities of Jim Crow. After I was born in New Orleans in 1952, my parents, Alfred and Verna Callahan, brought me home to Covington. My father was a janitor at BellSouth (now AT&T) for 35 years. He tried to advance himself, but the installation position was not open to "colored" men. My mother worked for a white family as a domestic, like many African American women, including my grandmother.

Known affectionately and respectfully as "Miss Virginia," my grandmother worked for the Meyers family at their summer home on Jahncke Street in Old Covington for $4 a day. As an adolescent, I worked in their yard during summers, happy to earn pocket change. However, I could not go inside to eat, relegated instead under a shade tree. My grandfather, "Mr. George," a robust man, loved the outdoors and was an avid fisherman. He worked for the railroad for $1.50 a week. Nonetheless, my grandparents purchased several acres of land, two of which I live on today.

I attended Covington Rosenwald School, which closed on extremely cold days for lack of heat. Our secondhand books arrived tattered. Teachers received little pay but gave immensely to educate us. My first-grade teacher, Mrs. Ida Prielou, taught us how to say, "can't," while telling us never to use it. She said, "You either don't understand or you need help."

We celebrated life. Saturday broadcasts of prizefights, Sunday church, and other events added quality to our lives. We were good citizens, albeit within racially infused politics. Most candidates only visited our community during elections.

Optimism and determination kept our setbacks as secondary traveling companions. We worked through segregation to integration to improve Covington. We overcame great odds, graduated from college, and honored our elders' sacrifices by fulfilling their dreams for us. Our hopes and efforts are like theirs: greater progress by our progeny.

Though I have been blessed to travel the world, Covington will always be my home.

—A native son, Rev. Mallery Callahan

ACKNOWLEDGMENTS

A crowd dedicated to the message of Juneteenth stood in Louisiana's humidity and heat at Atkins Park to hear, once again, the story. The assemblage heard the speaker connect freedom to the local community's quest for education. The diligence of 1920s African Americans in Covington imbued a core group who were on a quest. Planning for Covington's bicentennial was underway, and they made their case to the speaker for help with their community's history.

Ella Selmon, Mary Ann Pierre, and Jerome "Bo" Elzy initiated this work in 2012. They formed a committee, including Jerry Coner and the quiet presence of Jessie Richardson. With roots extending far into this community's past, they canvassed the town. A year of work culminated with a successful program and led to another year, producing this text.

Small-town African American history is multifaceted but generally begins with the church. Pastors lead, but within the congregation is a human spirit with great diligence. Ida Thomas James and James "Gus" Davis, Bethel Reform Methodist Church; Brenette Garrett Allen, Doughty Chapel African Methodist Episcopal Church; Jackie Elzy, Greater Starlight Missionary Baptist Church; and Teresa Henry Alston, the First Missionary Baptist Church, are by all local accounts critical to the operations of their churches. They lived up to their reputations in this endeavor.

More than 100 years of segregation did not keep Covington's white and black communities completely separate. Many white Covingtonians were generous in uncovering important information, including Emily Diamond's children, HJ Smith's Son's heirs, Peggy Sharp, Fr. Jonathan DeFrange, Ruth Prats, Robin Perkins, Mayor Mike Cooper, Lee Alexis, Howard Nichols, and many others around town.

This story found its way to New Orleans. Rev. Otto Duncan, pastor of the historic St. James African Methodist Episcopal Church, and Kathleen Rhodes Astorga, whose prominent (Rhodes) family has a foundation in Covington, are excellent detectives. In Houston, Melanie Garrett Allen keeps the story of White Settlement alive and well.

Additionally, appreciation extends to all who shared their photographs.

Technology often eludes historians. Les Baham's expertise keeps the historian in his family in the right century.

Introduction

The saga of the Broxton and Maples families offers a glimpse into slavery in Covington. Philip Broxton traveled to Louisiana as Nathan Maples's slave in 1807. Maples joined a wave of white South Carolinians who, in the early 1800s, moved west. Opportunity existed in territory opened by the Louisiana Purchase in 1803. However, Maples appeared to be on the very low echelon of slave owners, as Philip Broxton seemed to be his only slave. To remedy that, Maples returned to Sumter County, South Carolina, in 1807 and purchased Broxton's wife, Jennie, and their children, Matilda ("Mitty") and Sarah, and brought them back to Louisiana.

In 1820, Maples owned five slaves: Philip, Jennie, Mitty, Sarah, and the Broxton's young son, Philip Jr. Freedom came for Jennie in 1825 and for the elder Philip in 1826, although not for their children. Broxton bought property in Covington and lived with his family until his death in 1838. Jennie and extended family members purchased her children and grandchildren from the Maples family: her daughter Mitty and Mitty's son Joseph Robigo in 1831, and other daughter Sarah and her three children, Arabella, Susan, and Mary Jane, in 1840. Jennie Broxton appeared before Judge Lyman Briggs in Covington, and the required advertisement to purchase her slave children appeared in the Covington newspaper, the *Advocate*. The sale was recorded in 1842. That should have sealed Broxton family freedom. It did not.

During the 1850s, the Maples children filed a legal complaint against the free Broxton children. They claimed that their father, Nathan Maples, who died in 1841, did not have command of his senses when Jennie Broxton tricked him into selling the remaining Broxton family members. In the district court of St. Tammany at Covington, the heirs of Nathan Maples petitioned for the revocation of all sales of the Broxton family, including that of the deceased Philip and Jennie. This would return the Broxton children to the Maples children as slaves and force the Broxtons to pay market rates for their deceased parents, Philip and Jennie. The jury from the district court sided with the Maples family. Jesse R. Jones, one of the founders of Covington, represented the Broxtons and filed an appeal with the Louisiana Supreme Court.

In *John A.P. Maples, et al. v. Mitty and Sarah, f.w.c.* [free women of color] (1857), the state supreme court rejected any consideration to revoke the freedom of Philip and Jennie because "both of those persons were dead at the time of the institution of the suit." To the remaining issue of the sale of Jennie's children and grandson, the court found no evidence of "simulation"—that is, deception—when Jennie transacted this sale with Nathan Maples and his wife, Mary. The same day, January 31, 1840, that she bought her children for $800, the supreme court noted, Jennie "exchanged" property in Covington with Nathan and Mary. In essence, Jennie Broxton gave the Maples family cash plus property for her children and grandson. The supreme court even noted that Jennie might have overpaid, given the combined value of the property and the cash. Because both Nathan and Mary were parties to the sale, the court could not find in favor of their heirs. "Here, the proof leaves no doubt on our minds," the court held, "that there was a real *bona fide* consideration for the sale of *Sarah* and her children, passing from *Jenny Broxton* to *Nathan Maples*." This reversed the lower court's decision and set the Broxton children and grandchildren free at last.

This saga from slavery to freedom describes historical experiences of antebellum African Americans in Covington. Permanence did not always define enslavement or guarantee freedom, both of which had long histories in St. Tammany Parish. Among the French, Spanish, and British who claimed this region at one time or another, Spanish slave laws gave the most rights to slaves and the most opportunities to gain their freedom. Historian Gilbert Din recorded that under both French and Spanish rule, Catholic priests "denied blacks extreme unction," or last rites. That was a moral aberration compared to death for a slave for stealing animals or striking a free person. British law made emancipation "difficult" and "punishment . . . severe." Under Spanish law, however, "slaves could buy their freedom . . . and owners could free slaves for any reason before a notary." Din notes that the Spanish "did not view enslavement as a permanent condition." However, slaves were chattel under all the regimes, and slave owners and governments protected their property.

For example, in 1821, Louisiana's legislature empowered parishes to police slaves. St. Tammany Parish had little interest in slave patrols before 1821, as there were very few slaves in the parish. According to historian E. Russ Williams Jr., only Terrance Carriere of Mandeville "owned a significant number of slaves," and he had only 29. There were 631 total scattered over the parish, held by "numerous small-scale slave-owning families." After 1830, with an increase in slaves to a total of 1,360, fear of slave rebellions "became more acute." Terrence Carriere now had 69, and Terrance Cousin owned 37. No one in Covington came remotely close to those numbers. Most whites owned no slaves; those who did possessed between one and twenty. Despite so few slaves in Covington and the parish at large, Russ notes, "the police jury found reason to implement the state's patrol ordinance of 1821." Poor, non-slaveholding whites—simple farmers, for example—found work as patrollers.

St. Tammany's forested terrain accounted for its few slaves. Slaves, as early as the 1730s, provided long-term labor in nearly every aspect of the timber industry and in brick manufacturing. Parish historian Judge Frederick Ellis recorded that slaves sawed trees and that French rulers encouraged industries associated with timber. Acres of pine forests, complicated by crisscrossing rivers with connecting and nearly impassable bayous, prohibited large-scale commercial crop plantations. Instead, slavery in St. Tammany Parish survived because of a strong market, particularly in New Orleans, for its natural long-leaf yellow pine forests and its by-products, tar, pitch, and turpentine. Brick making and kilns, where a large number of slaves worked, necessarily accompanied this process. Male slaves worked as skilled laborers: brick makers, blacksmiths, locksmiths, masons, carpenters, sailors, and rowers. Female slaves often worked fields and small gardens to supply food; they also cooked, cleaned, and made clothes. Since slavery was small-scale, proximity defined relationships between masters, slaves, and free people of color.

The families of Adeline Hosmer Terrell and Duplin and Zoe Dupere Rhodes illustrate this master-slave relationship in Covington. Adeline's husband, Elijah Martin Terrell, died during the 1840s, and she lived in Covington near what is now Florida Street. In 1850, Zoe, illiterate and going by the last name Rhodes, acquired "two unimproved lots . . . adjoining the town of Covington, taken from the land of the said Mrs. Adeline Terrell" for $20. Although Zoe, born free in 1834, lived in Algiers with children Mary, Peter, Alfred, and Julia through 1860, Duplin, her husband, a skilled and literate carriage maker and slave, lived in Covington near the Terrell property. Five years after the end of slavery, Terrell sold property to Zoe. This time, the sale included Zoe's "X" and Duplin's signature.

Many French and Spanish men who took African women as their wives and mistresses freed the women and the children they had together, or sometimes just the offspring. There were, however, slaves who bought freedom for themselves and their families. Loren Schweninger recorded that free people of color managed farms, raised crops and animals, were tailors and carpenters, and engaged in other areas of work for their survival. Free people of color in 1850 Covington included the Taylor, Cutveyer, Baham, Terrell, Garrett, Parent, Maples/Broxton, and Lemore families, as well as Mary Ann Pierre, Joseph Vie, Eliza Mitchell, and John and Jane Reed (parents to several children, including Ishom).

In Covington, and St. Tammany Parish at large, some free people of color owned slaves. The majority of these were family members, whose emancipation ultimately came when a relative, as in the case of Jennie Broxton, bought a child, a mother, or siblings. Statistics of African American slave ownership in this area show that free people of color often owned one to no more than five slaves. Philip Broxton's family of four included one slave. Cassimer Popelous had eight family members, including one slave, while Voltaire Baham owned one slave and Roselle Maxon's eleven total family members included seven slaves. Anecdotal family storytelling in this area likely discusses family slave ownership. Indeed, Rhodes family lore holds that Zoe Dupere Rhodes bought her husband, Duplin, out of slavery.

This was the case for Charles and Patience Doughty. He founded the first African Methodist Episcopal church in New Orleans and Covington. Doughty, a slave brought from Virginia to New Orleans, was freed by Francois Hébrard in 1818. Two decades later, Doughty purchased Patience and petitioned the court in New Orleans for her freedom. Afterward, they were married.

Buying and selling human beings and owning them as chattel came to a halt as talk of the Civil War loomed. Prices plummeted, even as Louisiana initially dismissed the coming of a rebellion. Charles Dew pointed to Louisiana's economic dependence on the Union in 1860. New Orleans was the South's "most cosmopolitan city," with "financial activities closely associated with the major eastern ports, New York in particular." Toward that end, Louisiana governor Thomas O. Moore answered an October 1860 query from South Carolina governor William H. Gist as follows: "I shall not advise the secession of my state . . . and I will add that I do not think the people of Louisiana will ultimately decide in favor of that cause."

The push came from Governor Moore's political patron, US senator John Slidell, "the master manipulator of the state Democratic organization," who accused the Irish and Germans in New Orleans of being "at heart abolitionists." Delegates from St. Tammany Parish voted against secession in 1860. Although some charged that the vote to secede was suppressed, and that Louisiana did not vote to leave the Union, the state went to war.

St. Tammany Parish faced devastation, particularly after New Orleans fell to the Union during the spring of 1862. Grim reports prevailed that the Northshore economy was squashed by the loss of its major customer, the Crescent City. A military officer quoted in Judge Ellis's text reported seeing "wretchedly poor families." He further noted, "We did not see over a dozen men on these bayous, and they were nearly all old persons, but few negroes . . . and not more than six or eight families of women and children." Mercifully for St. Tammany Parish, the war ended in April 1865.

The declaration that ended the Civil War also ended 140 years of enslavement in St. Tammany Parish, but only 65 years in Covington. Jacques Dreux posted his Spanish land grant in 1803. A decade later, he sold it to John Wharton Collins. On July 4, 1813, Collins, Jesse R. Jones, Jonathan Gilmore, and a lone African American known only as Collins's slave, Tom, stood at the fork of the Tchefuncte and Bogue Falaya Rivers and called the town Wharton, later renamed Covington. There is little doubt that other African Americans preceded Tom in the area. His presence serves as record that African Americans had a stake in the foundation of the town. For all the people that the Broxtons represent in their fight to be free and to remain free, Tom, though a slave at the founding, solidifies African American roots in early Covington.

This text is their story, from that earliest moment to the present. It is a survey of their experiences, how they lived as second-class citizens, how they met those challenges, and how they built their lives with dignity and perseverance in their town. Each chapter has a brief overview, followed by images donated by families to demonstrate the chapter's theme.

This is also the story of institutions, whose recurring references are abbreviated as follows: African Methodist Episcopal (AME), St. Tammany Parish School Board (STPB), Mount Zion Pilgrim Baptist Church (MZPB), Doughty Chapel African Methodist Episcopal Church (Doughty Chapel), Greater Starlight Missionary Baptist Church (Greater Starlight), Bethel Reform Methodist Church (Bethel Reform), First Missionary Baptist Church (FMBC), and the National Association for the Advancement of Colored People (NAACP).

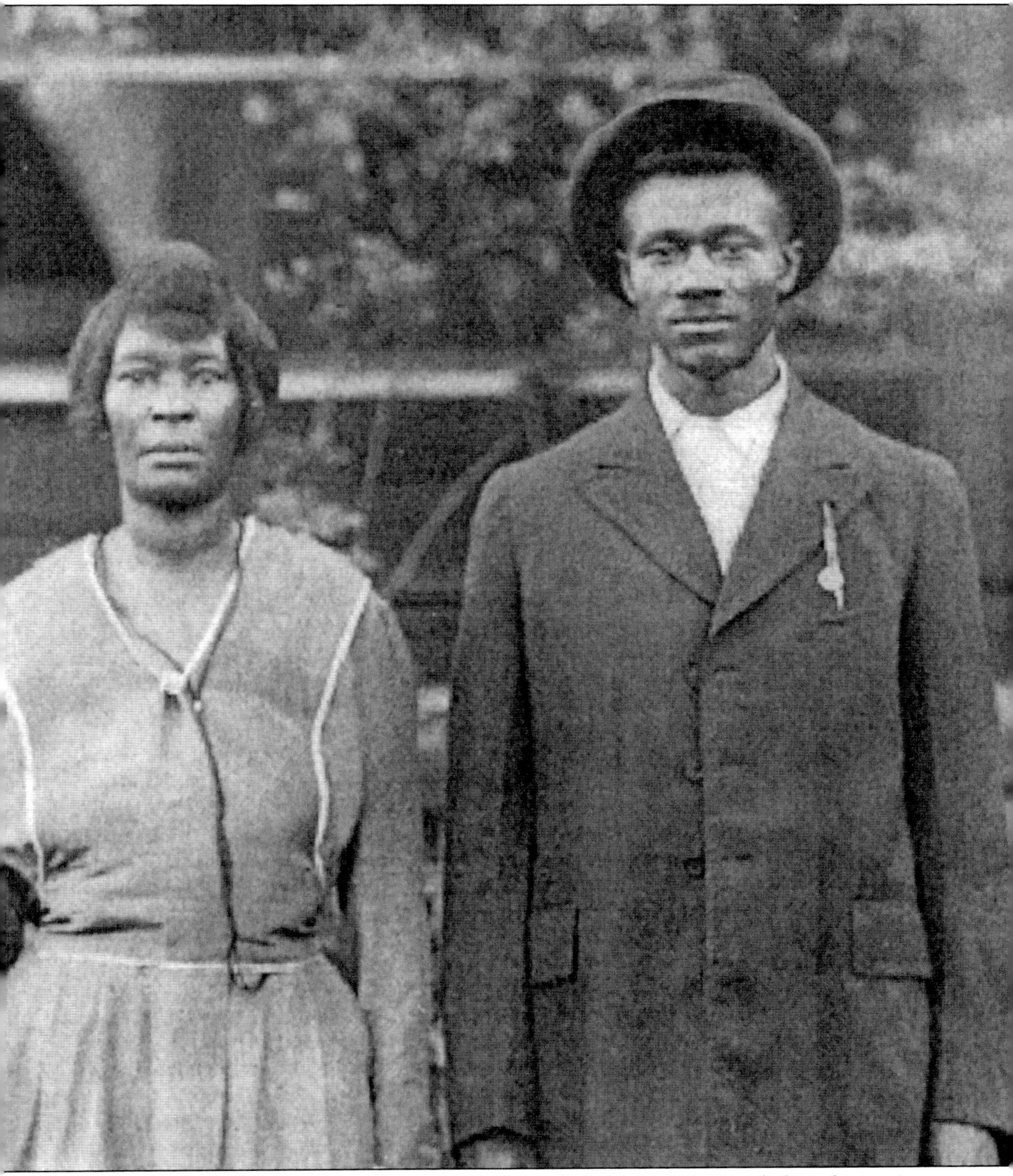

IDA HARVEY THOMAS AND WILL E. THOMAS, 1920. Traveling photographers made formal portraits available to local families. Homemaker Ida, like many women, added to the household income as a domestic worker. Will was a general laborer, although he also listed "baseball player" as his line of work. He played in a local league. They were photographed at their home on Guillot (renamed Claiborne) Street. (Courtesy of Ida Thomas James.)

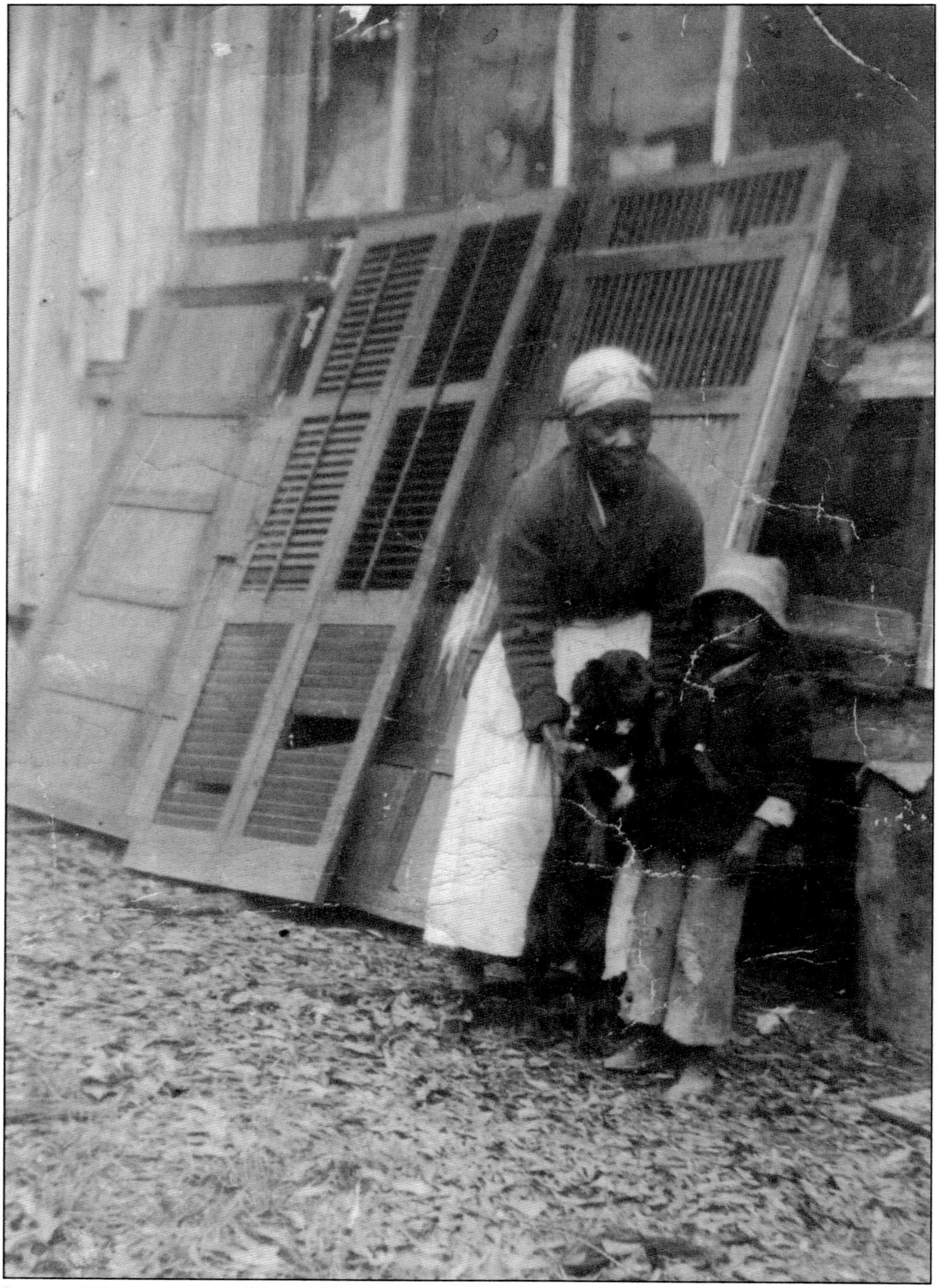

Luella Williams with Willie Walter Louis Davis, c. 1940. Living on Military Road near Covington, Luella Williams entertains her grandson, about three years old, on his visit. She was a domestic. The boy's father, Willie Sr., was a painter, cement finisher, and local "medicine man." His mother, Clothilde, was a cook for a prominent family, and his sister Ella Davis (Selmon) became a civic leader. (Courtesy of Ella Davis Selmon.)

One

FREEDOM AND FAMILIES

The end of the Civil War brought freedom. Constitutional amendments applied to all; however, the 13th, 14th, and 15th were aimed at former slaves. The 13th prohibited slavery and "involuntary servitude," the 14th guaranteed citizenship and "equal protection under the law," and the 15th prohibited voter discrimination based on "race, color, or previous condition of servitude." Although civil rights were critical, African Americans began their free lives by solidifying their families.

Louisiana's African American legislators were "intent on removing various social discriminations" of slavery, historian Charles Vincent noted. Therefore, they passed the Act Relative to Marriage, which, in 1868, "validated all private or religious marriages contracted before it passed." Additionally, legislators recognized the legitimacy of children born of slave unions with an 1870 act "to authorize natural parents to legitimate their natural children." Two Covington families, among 80 percent of African American households with both husband and wife, are illustrative.

Joseph Daniels, 39, and Caroline Ash, 38, married December 25, 1867; on November 1, 1870, they legitimized "one child, a boy, named James Edwards Daniels," born December 26, 1860. Duplin Rhodes and Zoe Dupere legalized their marriage December 24, 1868. In 1870, they legitimized their children, Macedonia, Robinson, Willis, Joseph, James, and Mary Elizabeth.

Many families fled postwar violence. Thomas Wharton Collins, the son of Covington's founder, wrote in the 1879 *Morning Star and Catholic Messenger*, "If the negroes move to Kansas . . . they will find themselves ground up fine in the mill of competition." Others were less grim.

The *St. Tammany Farmer* referenced former slave Gabriel Parker, noting, "it is not necessary for a black man to go to Kansas to get rich." Parker and his business partner, Frank Jackson, purchased over 800 acres in 1869 for $4,000 and owned a prosperous brick-manufacturing facility in Covington. Other men were teamsters, like Green Watkins; carpenters, like Richard Waddles; shoemakers, like Albert Leroy; merchants, like Thomas Lacroix; and sailors, like Frank Bowers. Women worked as domestics or as laundresses and seamstresses in their homes. Anna M. Dumas became the first African American woman to head a post office, from 1872 to 1885. African Americans founded churches, educated children, and bought property.

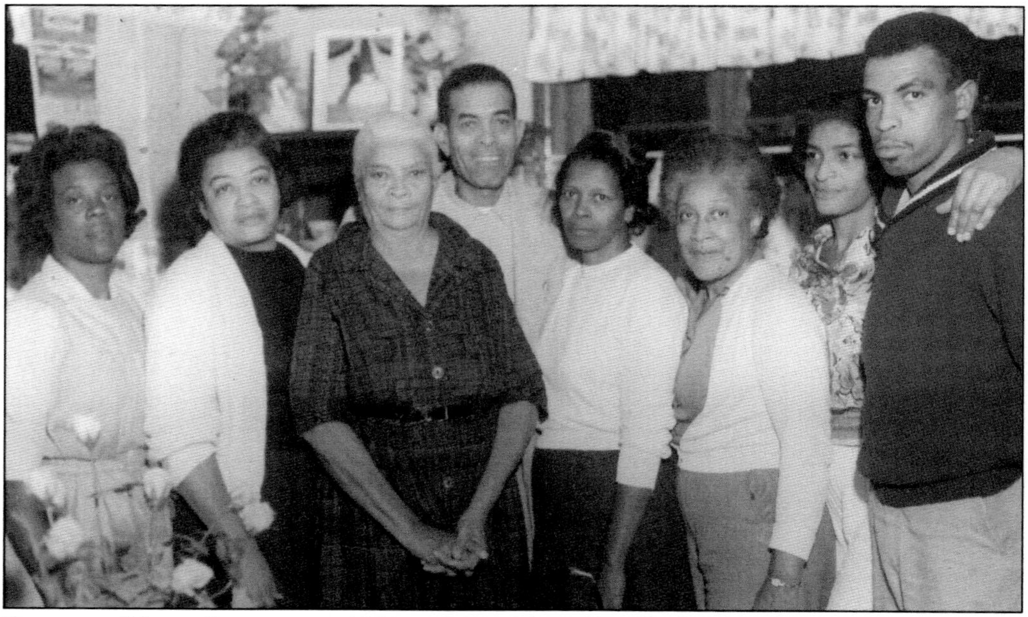

Family of Marie Randle, c. 1950s–1960s. Marie Randle, homemaker and widow of Rev. Henry G. Randle, headed a typically large family that included many active community leaders. Pictured at a family gathering are, from left to right, daughter-in-law Grace, daughter Mable, Mrs. Randle, brother Sidney Daniels, two unidentified, daughter Alvera, and son Milton. Son Henry (not pictured) was a professional photographer. (Courtesy of the Randle collection.)

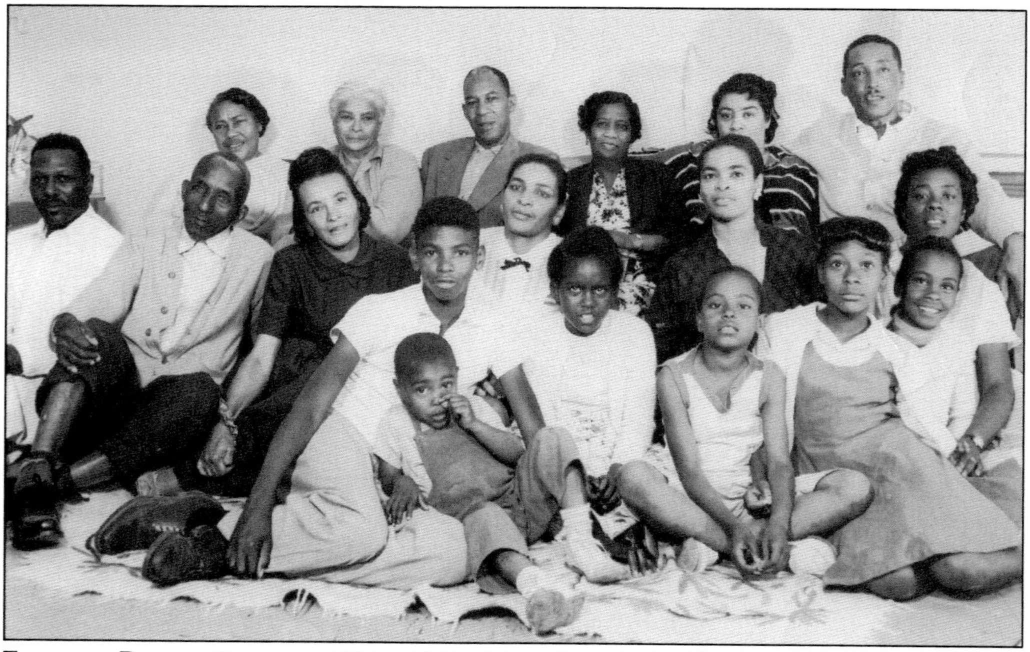

Extended Randle Family, c. 1950s–1960s. Marie Daniels Randle, the matriarch of the Randle family, poses with her children and their spouses, her grandchildren, and other relatives. This is a good example of family life in the African American community during this period. Generational families were deeply rooted in Covington, with grandparents, aunts, uncles, and siblings living nearby. (Courtesy of the Randle collection.)

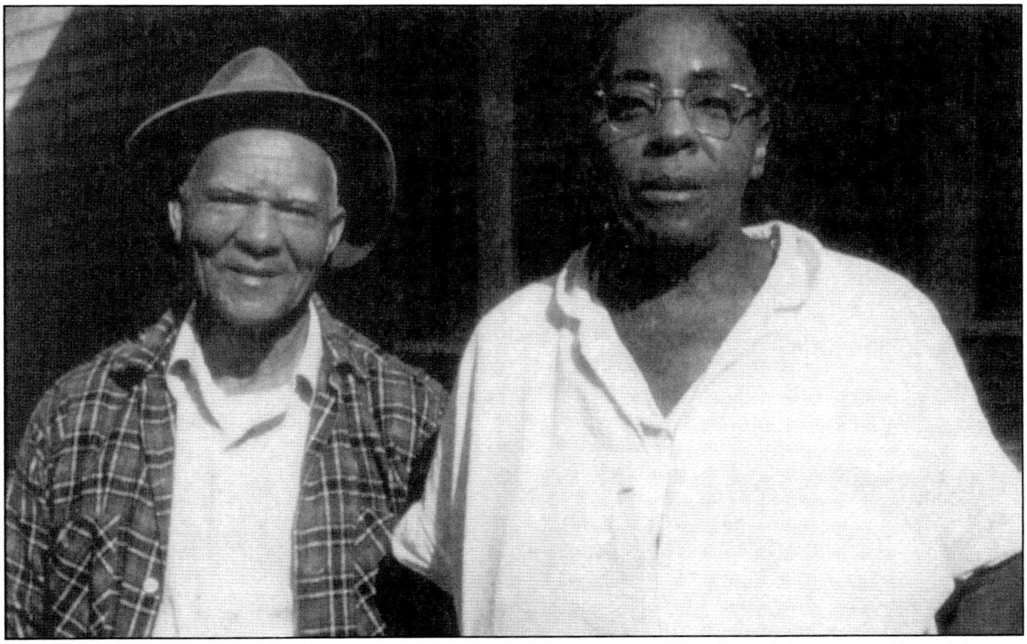

WILLIE AND ENDA SHERIDAN, C. 1960S. In 1930, Willie supported his five children as a farm laborer. Although he and wife Enda did not live on a farm, they owned their home. Enda, a homemaker, also worked as a domestic. By the 1960s, Willie owned a mechanic business, and Enda worked as an operator for South Central Bell (now AT&T). (Courtesy of Sharon Sheridan Wilcox.)

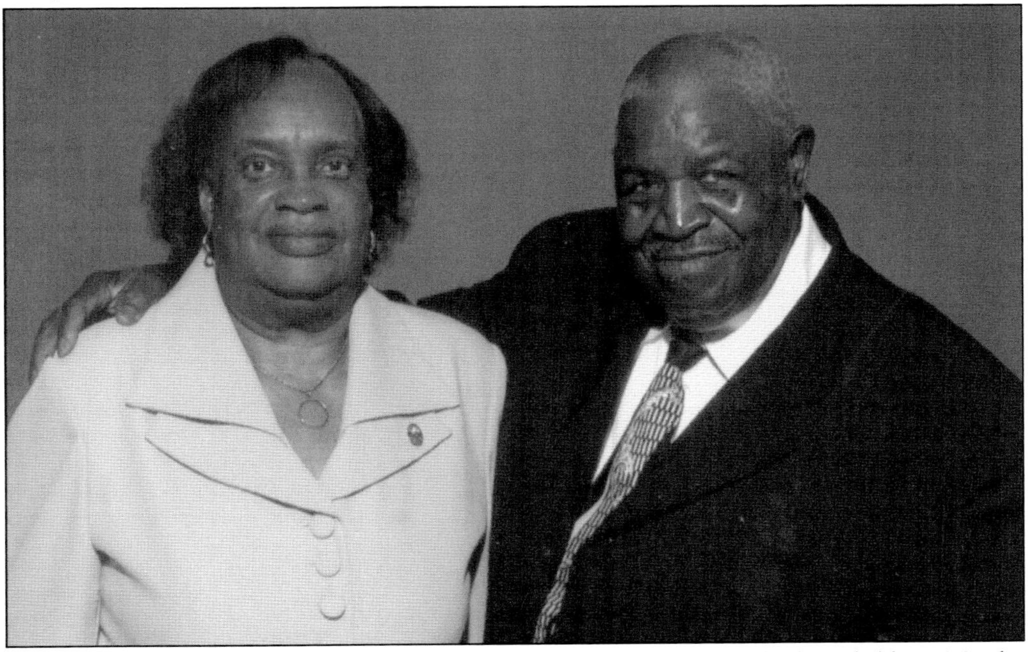

MERTHE D. AND GEORGE GROOVER. This couple married in 1962 and had 10 children. Merthe Groover worked at Revere's Café and the Southern Hotel. She provided childcare in her home for over 40 years. George Groover retired after 30 years with the city. The Groovers made their family life in Covington, where marriages and long-term (65 years) membership in a local church demonstrated stability and high moral standards. (Courtesy of Merthe D. Groover.)

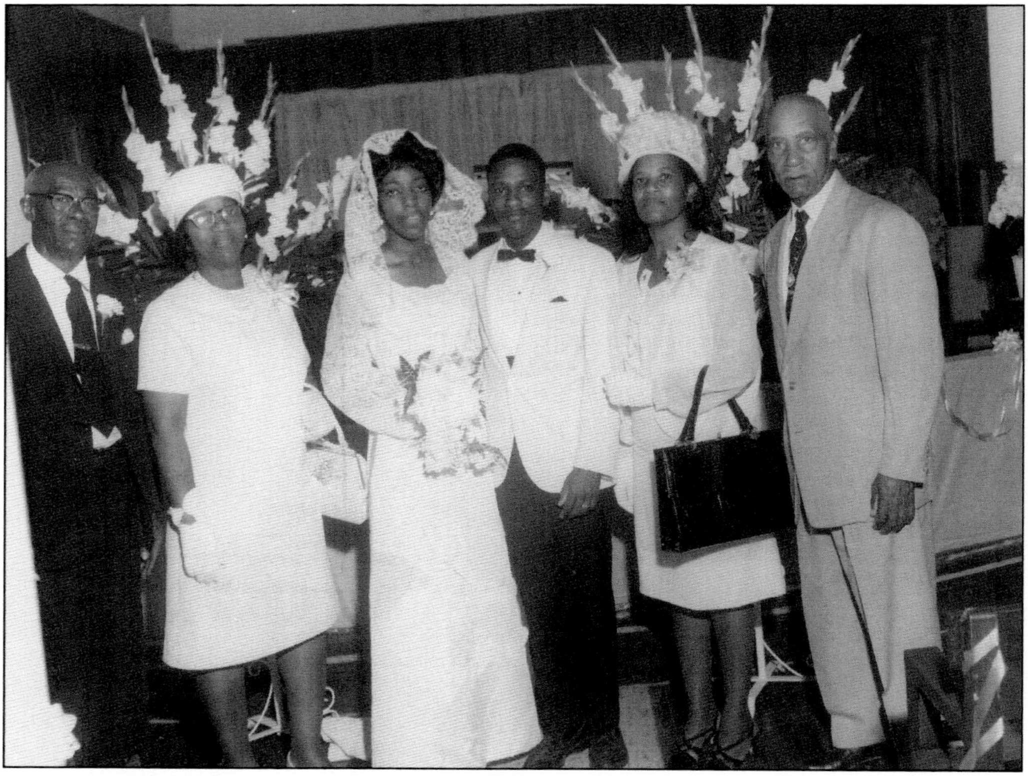

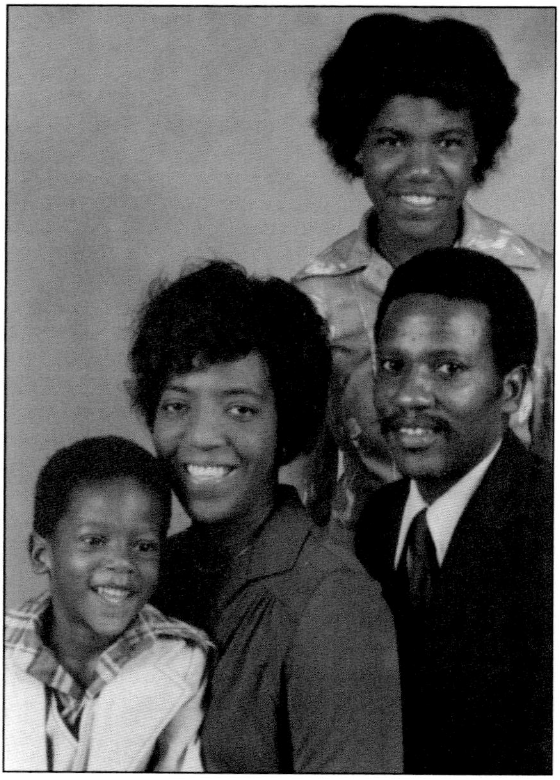

WEDDING OF IDA THOMAS AND JOE JAMES, 1969. Rev. Peter Atkins, Bethel Reform Methodist, officiated this wedding ceremony. Kinship was important. Pictured are, from left to right, Alex Coner (Ida's godfather, who stood in for her father, who died in 1959), Eula Mae "Honey" Thomas (mother of the bride), Ida and Joe, Jessie James (mother of the groom), and Earnest Richardson (Joe's grandfather, who stood for Ivery James Sr., who died in 1968). (Courtesy of Ida Thomas James.)

THE JAMES FAMILY, 1977. Eight years after their wedding, Ida and Joe's family sat for a portrait. From left to right are Jonathan, Ida, Joe, and Karen. They lived near their extended families, involving themselves in their church and community affairs. Joe's father, Ivery James Sr. (who died in 1968), owned many rental properties and the neighborhood grocery store. (Courtesy of Ida Thomas James.)

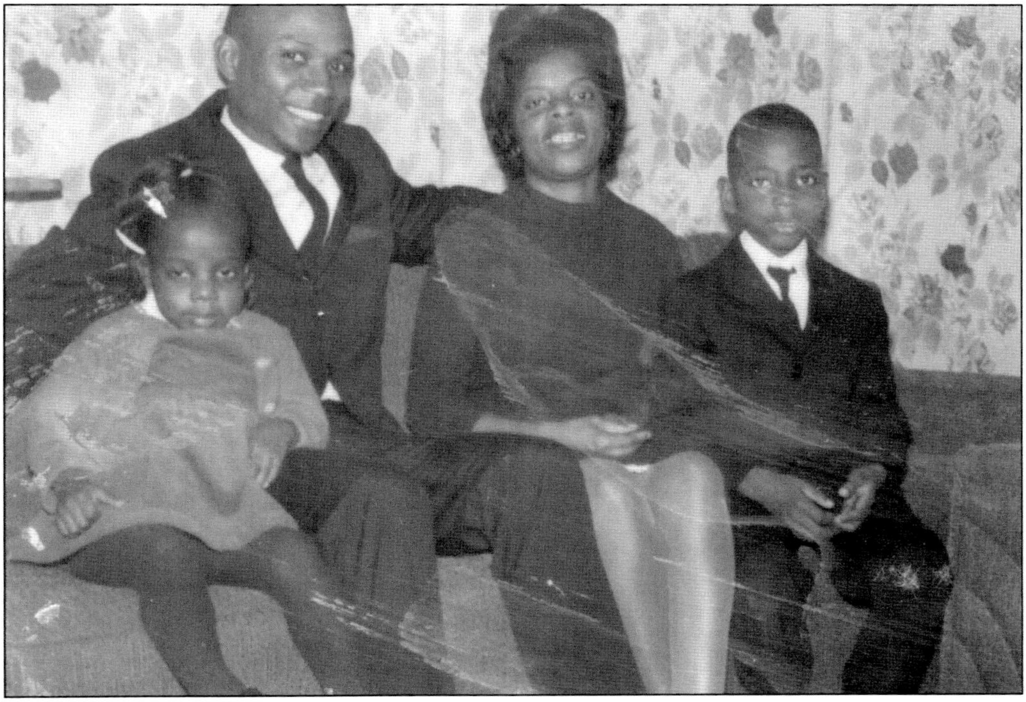

THE BRADFORD FAMILY. Sentiment regarding Burnell Bradford Sr. held that he "could plant a seed on concrete and it would grow." He served Covington by voluntarily planting flowers throughout the city, a program he began in 1976. City government and numerous organizations honored him for his contribution to area beautification. He is joined in this portrait by his daughter, Ann; wife, Shirley; and son, Burnell Jr. (Courtesy of the Bradford family.)

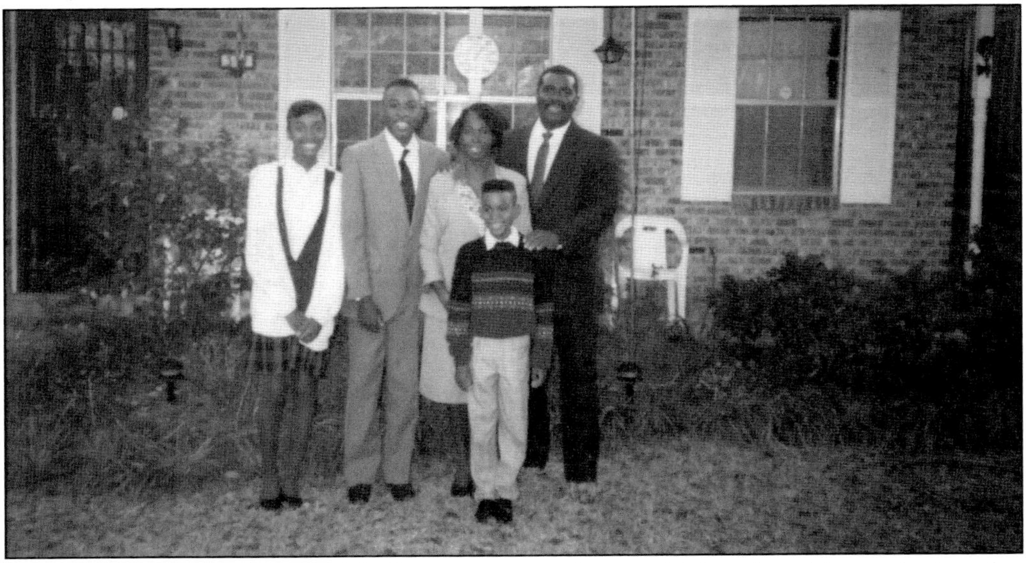

HAROLD AND BEVERLY RAMSEY. The Ramseys pose with their children, from left to right, Latasha, 13; Harold Jr., 16; and William, 9, in front of their home. The family was affiliated with the First Missionary Baptist Church, whose pastor, Rev. Otis Brumfield, remains a close friend. Church membership is a recurring theme among African American families. It gave stability and offered coherence among families and the community at large. (Courtesy of Rev. Otis Brumfield.)

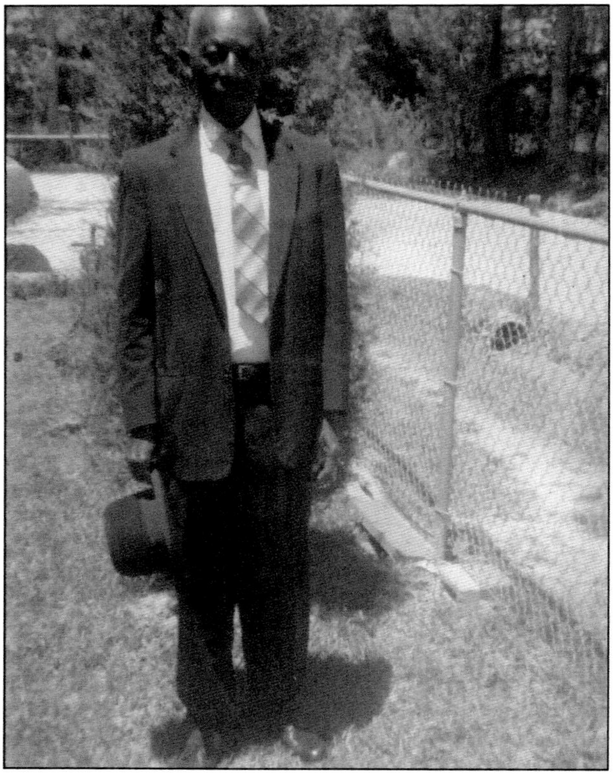

Larciner Pierre, 1892–1974. Delta Pine Oil, the successor to the Mackie Pine Oil Company, employed African American men such as Larciner Pierre. The work was hazardous, as it produced Tung Oil, uses of which include furniture oil and coatings for waterproofing. The industry flourished in southeast Louisiana from the 1930s until the late 1960s. Pierre and his wife, Daisy, kept a small farm just outside the city. (Courtesy of Mary Ann Pierre.)

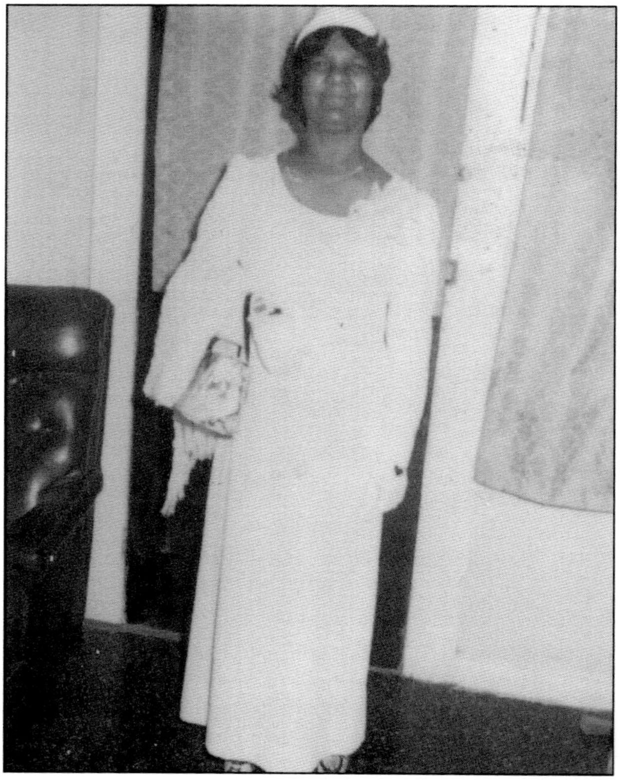

Daisy Harris Pierre, 1909–1984. President of the Stewardess Board, Missions Band, and Communion steward at Mount Zion Pilgrim Baptist Church, Daisy Pierre worked in several venues to help her husband, Larciner, support their family. She worked at Young's Sanitarium on Jancke Street, as a domestic for Sen. Jesse McLain, and at the St. Tammany High School cafeteria in Slidell. (Courtesy of Mary Ann Pierre.)

Isaiah "Sonny" and Doris M. Robertson. Sonny, a native of Port Allen, Louisiana, arrived in Covington to visit his mother after returning from World War II. He met Doris Magee and stayed. They were a powerhouse couple. Their successful nightclubs featured popular R&B groups. Sonny managed the Dew Drop Inn, and Doris, Dot's Ponderosa. Their philanthropy supported nearly every charitable organization in the community. (Courtesy of Rev. Kenneth Robertson.)

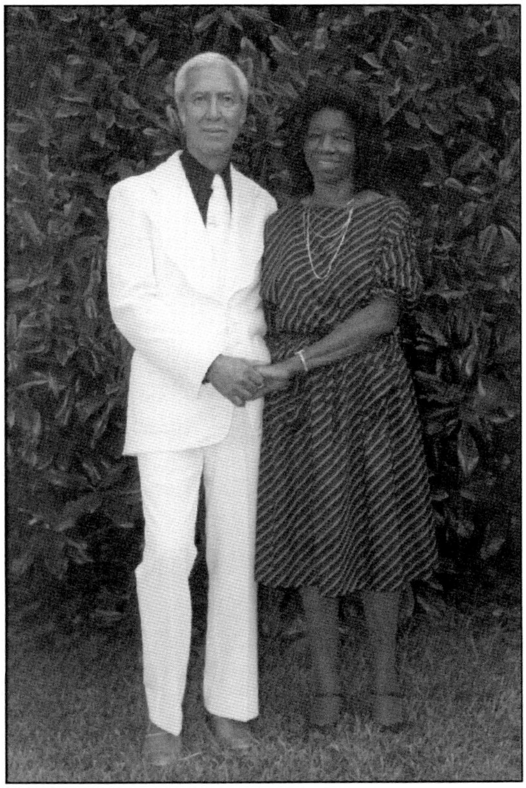

Graduation from Southern University, 1964. Hildreth Atkins received her undergraduate degree with proud parents Rev. Peter and Mrs. Hazel Atkins attending the ceremonies. Hildreth noted that they were advocates for higher education. Reverend Atkins's church offered scholarships to students. African American college students in Louisiana generally attended either Southern University in Baton Rouge or Grambling State University in north Louisiana during segregation. (Courtesy of Hildreth Atkins Crawford.)

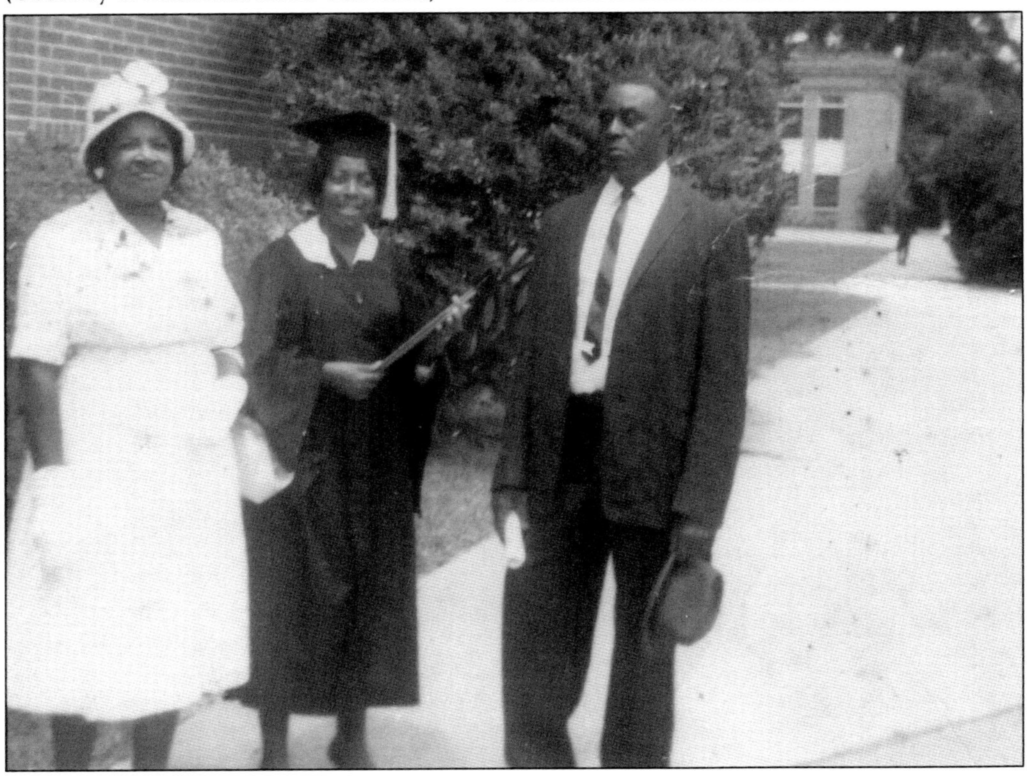

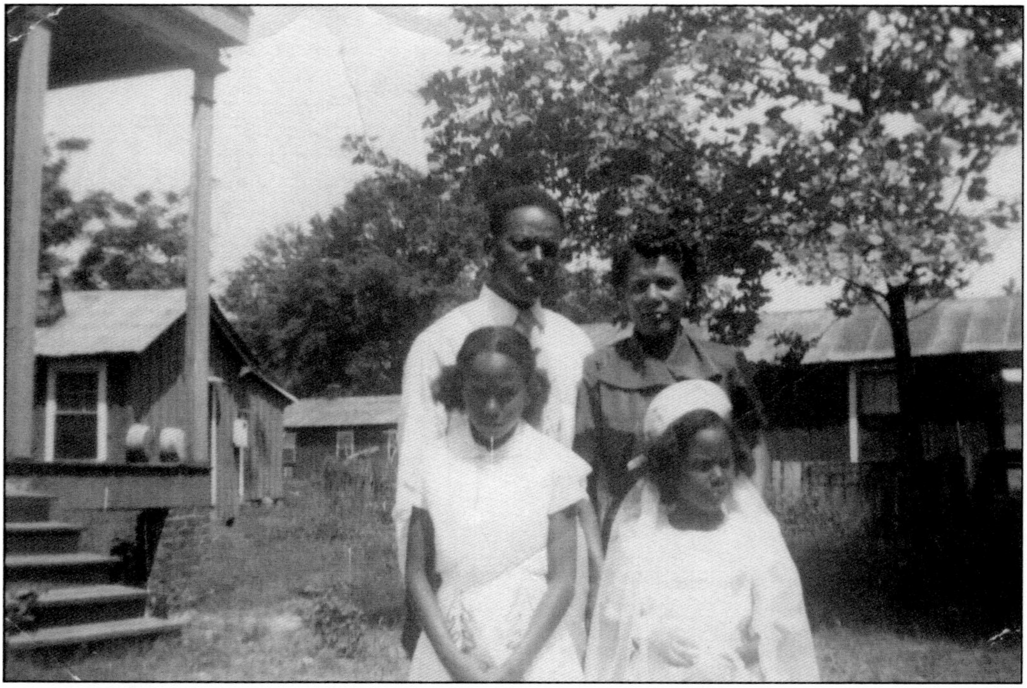

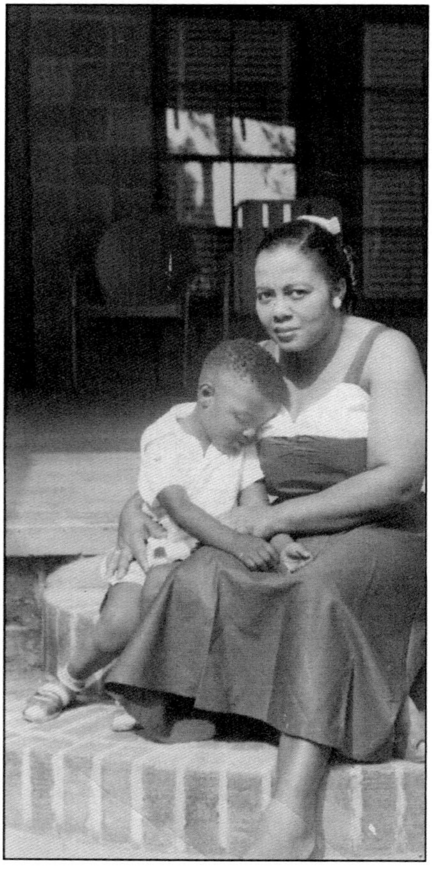

The Royal Family, 1950. Lena Mae Royal, daughter of Stanley and Margaret, made her First Communion at Holy Family Catholic Church in Covington. Also standing with the family is daughter Sammie Lou. They are in front of their aunt Naomi Pierre's home on Columbia Street. It was common to visit relatives or have celebrations in honor of momentous occasions. (Courtesy of Lena Royal Whittaker.)

The Hamler Family, 1952. Outside the frame of this photograph sat James "Jim" Hamler and older son James "Butch." Shown are Marie and younger son Donnie. "Mr. Jim" owned a trucking business, and "Ms. Marie" was a beautician. The family lived across from the cemetery on Florida Street, near Doughty Chapel African Methodist Episcopal Church. (Courtesy of Ida Thomas James.)

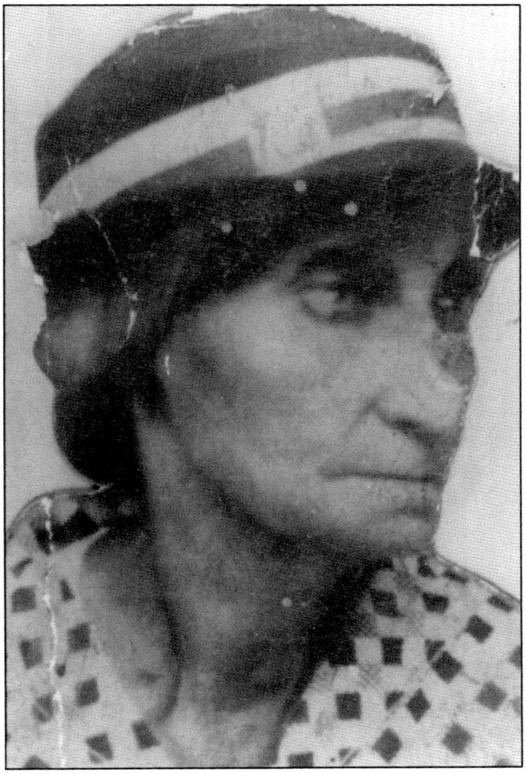

Tillie Hutchinson Richardson, c. Early 1900s. John and Tillie Richardson married during the late 1800s. She was a housewife, rearing five children: Earnest, Robert, Fannie, Laura, and Thelma. John Richardson hauled tree stumps and logs to train beds. The couple first lived in Goodbee, Louisiana, west of Covington, then moved early in the 1900s to Covington, where they lived on Tyler Street and Thirty-first Avenue. (Courtesy of Jessie Richardson James.)

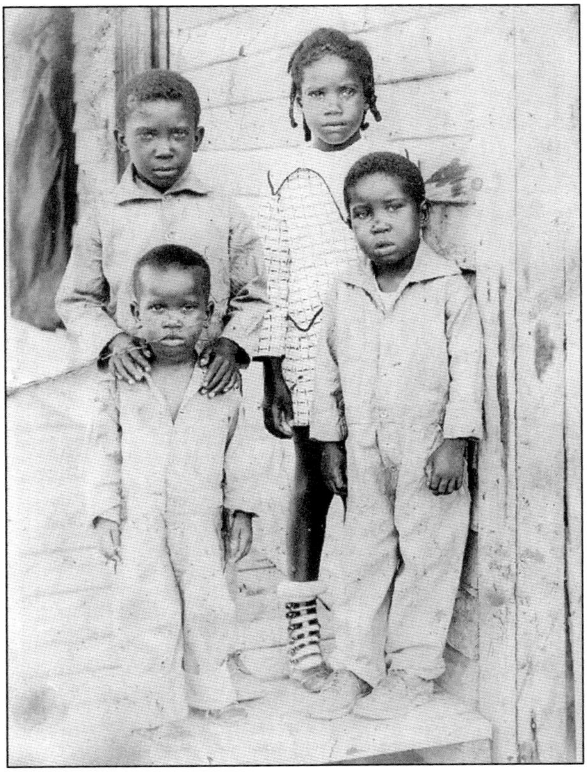

Earnest and Lutie Williams Richardson's Children, 1930. A traveling photographer captured this image of the Richardson children, who had been playing in the yard. They had to go inside to put on their shoes and get their hair combed and brushed for the portrait. They are, from left to right (first row) Percy, 2, and Frankie, 4; (second row) Charlie, 10, and Jessie Irene, 8. (Courtesy of Jessie Richardson James.)

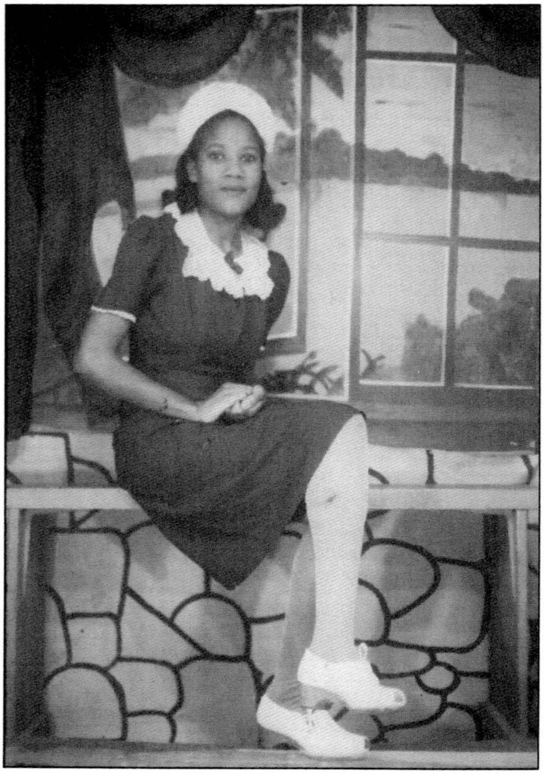

Jessie Irene Richardson, 1942. Jessie, 20, married Ivery James in 1942. They had five children. She was the school bus driver when segregation prevented bus service for African American children. Her route included Lee Road, Stafford Road, and Three Rivers Road. She picked up children to attend Covington Rosenwald. Few parents had cars; therefore, without Jessie's bus service, most children walked long distances to school. (Courtesy of Jessie R. James.)

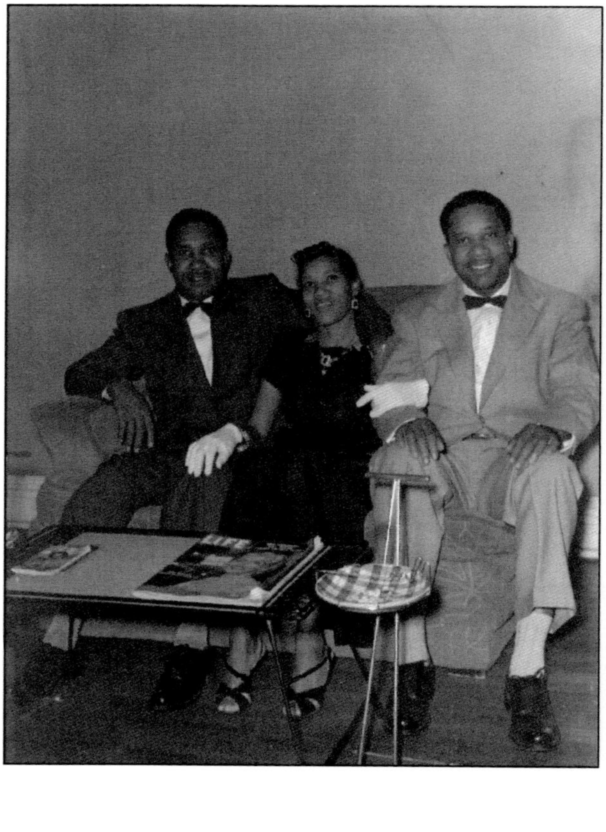

All Grown Up, 1956. Jessie Irene Richardson, now James, visited with her brothers, who moved to Chicago for better opportunities than those available in Covington. After Frankie's discharge from the Army, and Percy's from the Navy, they utilized the GI Bill to further their education. Frankie completed a course in tailoring, and Percy received certification in tailoring and radio and television repair. (Courtesy of Jessie R. James.)

ALBERT AND DOROTHY WILLIAMS, 1955. The Williamses were active in their church and community. Dorothy was a member of the Band Boosters Club and worked as a domestic, and Albert lived on the premises of a wealthy family as a caretaker while maintaining a separate home for his family. He was a World War II veteran and lived to be 91 years old. (Courtesy of Gwendolyn Williams.)

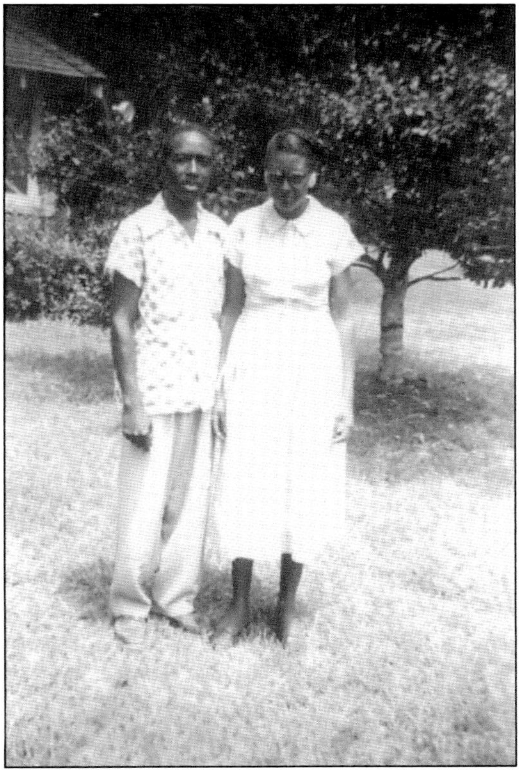

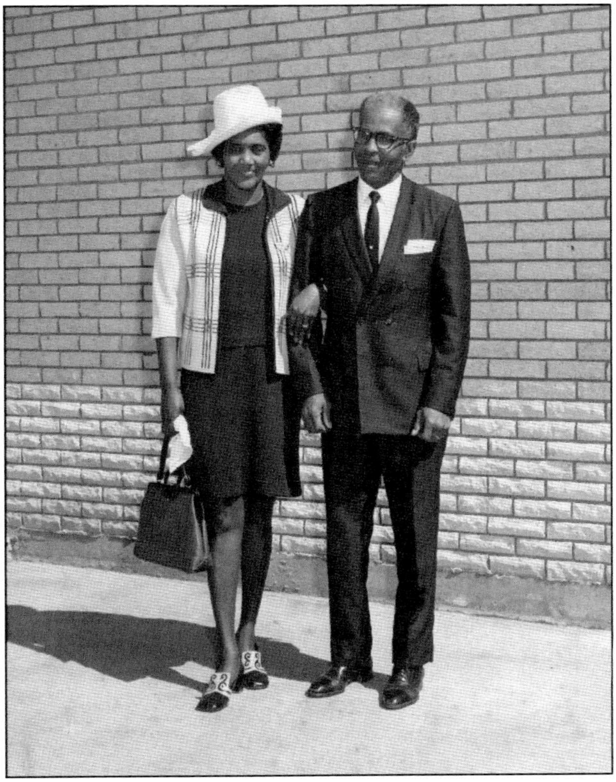

HELENA B. AND ALEX SHERIDAN. The Sheridans provided leadership in the Order of the Eastern Stars, Prince Hall Masons, Bethel Reform Methodist, NAACP, Boy Scouts, and Band Boosters. Helena was an usher and missionary; Alex, a trustee at their church. She led the Naomi Youth Fraternity No. 104 and worked with the Good Neighbor Club. He also helped with maintenance at Head Start. (Courtesy of Sharon Sheridan Wilcox.)

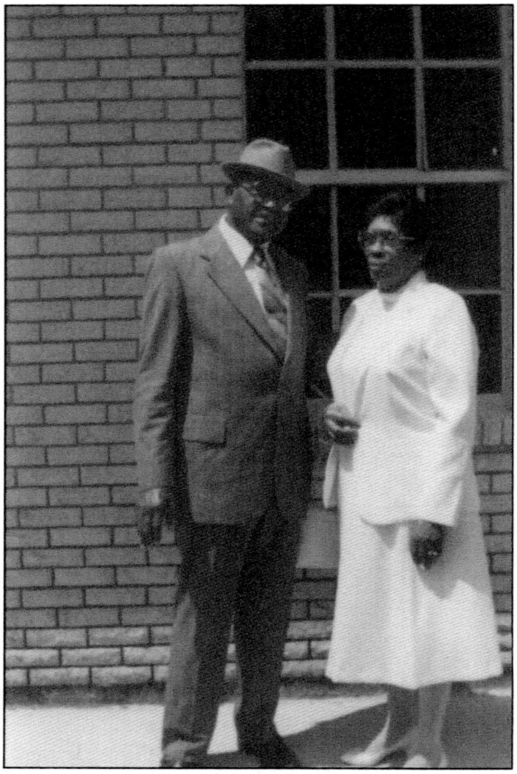

Willie and Altha Mae Moore. Affectionately known as "Mr. Willie" and "Ms. Mae," the Moores are members of Bethel Reform Methodist Church. She sang in the choir and was a Sunday school teacher and also worked as a domestic and as an independent beautician. He worked for the City of Covington and was a trustee at Bethel Reform. (Courtesy of Ida Thomas James.)

Wedding Day, 1964. Jimmy D. and Bertha G. Magee, both 23 years old, engage in an age-old tradition of cutting the cake at their reception on January 25, 1964. Jimmy taught sixth grade at Covington Middle School. He retired after 30 years. Bertha was assistant secretary at Bethel Reform, where they were married by Reverend Atkins. (Courtesy of Shawn Magee Route.)

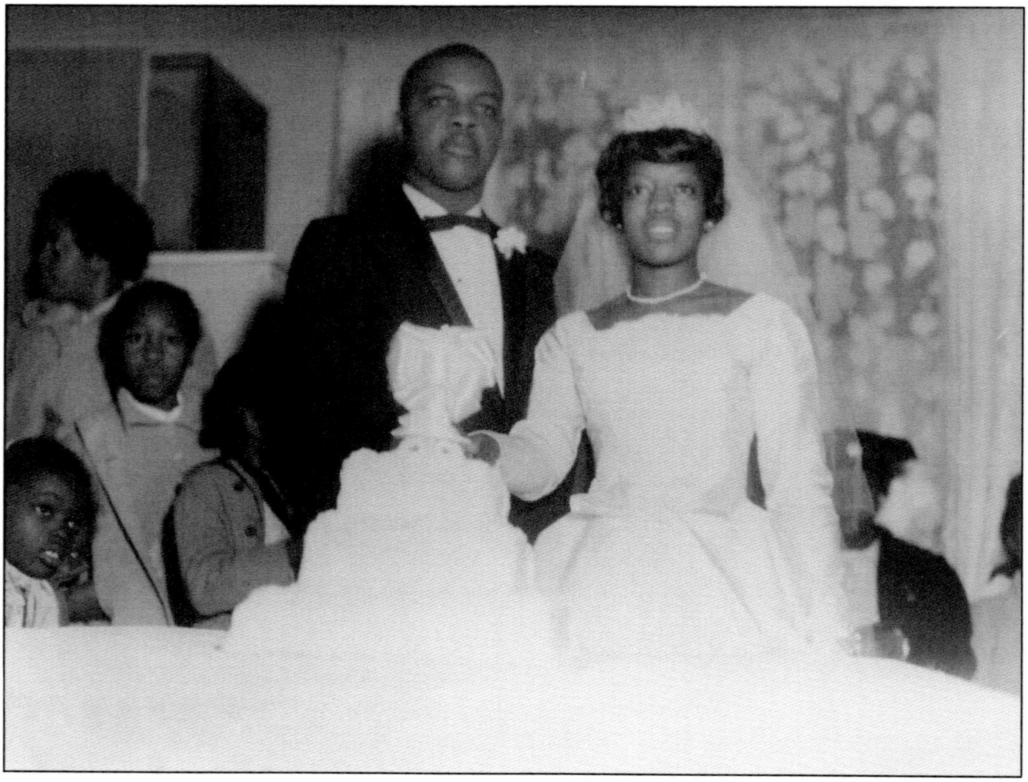

THEODORE R. HAYES JR. Hayes's "first passion was architecture." Because of limited opportunities for African Americans, he became a teacher of industrial arts. A native of Baton Rouge, he migrated to the area to teach at Chata Ima High School, in Lacombe. His son Michael owns the architectural firm Universe Design in Covington and designed the multipurpose building at Greater Starlight. (Courtesy of Michael M. Hayes.)

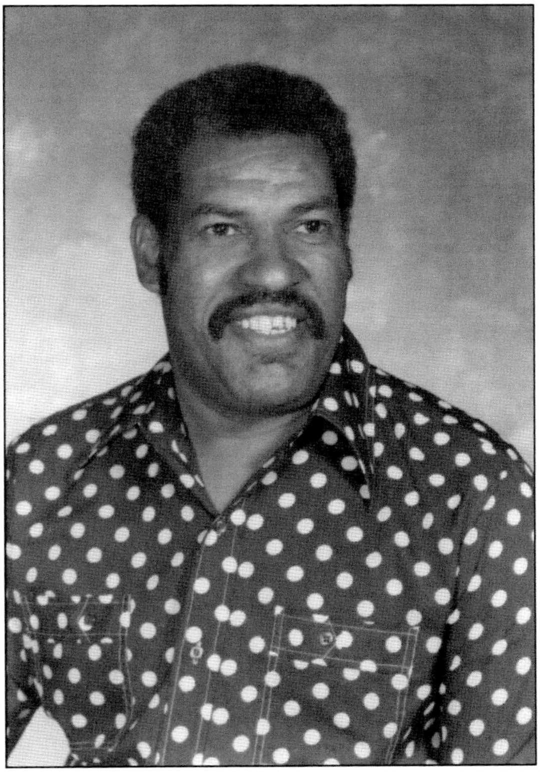

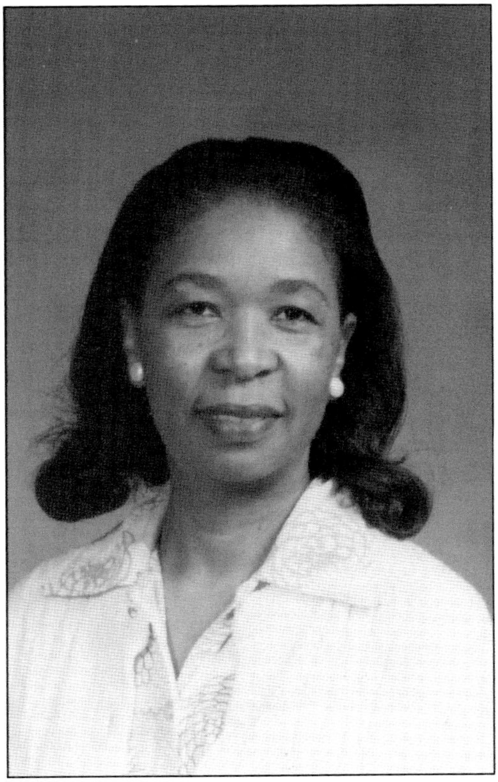

MARY LOUISE DENT HAYES. Formerly of Baton Rouge, Mary Louise Dent Hayes first taught in Delhi, Louisiana. She began teaching in Covington just as the transition was made from segregation to integration. She taught at Pine View High, Covington Middle, William Pitcher, and Covington High. As a member of Greater Starlight, she directed the children's choir and junior mission and sang in the senior choir. (Courtesy of Michael M. Hayes.)

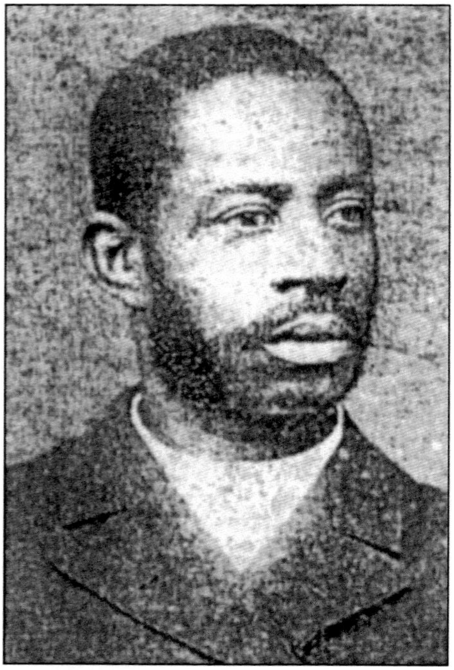

Rev. Charles Doughty, c. 1860s. Freed in 1818, Doughty later met Rev. Jordan Early, who introduced Doughty, a Methodist, to the African Methodist Episcopal Church. Doughty founded the historic St. James AME Church in New Orleans in 1841. By 1848, the church held a charter with the state. He founded the Covington AME Church, which bears his name, in 1854. Reverend Doughty died in 1868. (Courtesy of St. James AME Church.)

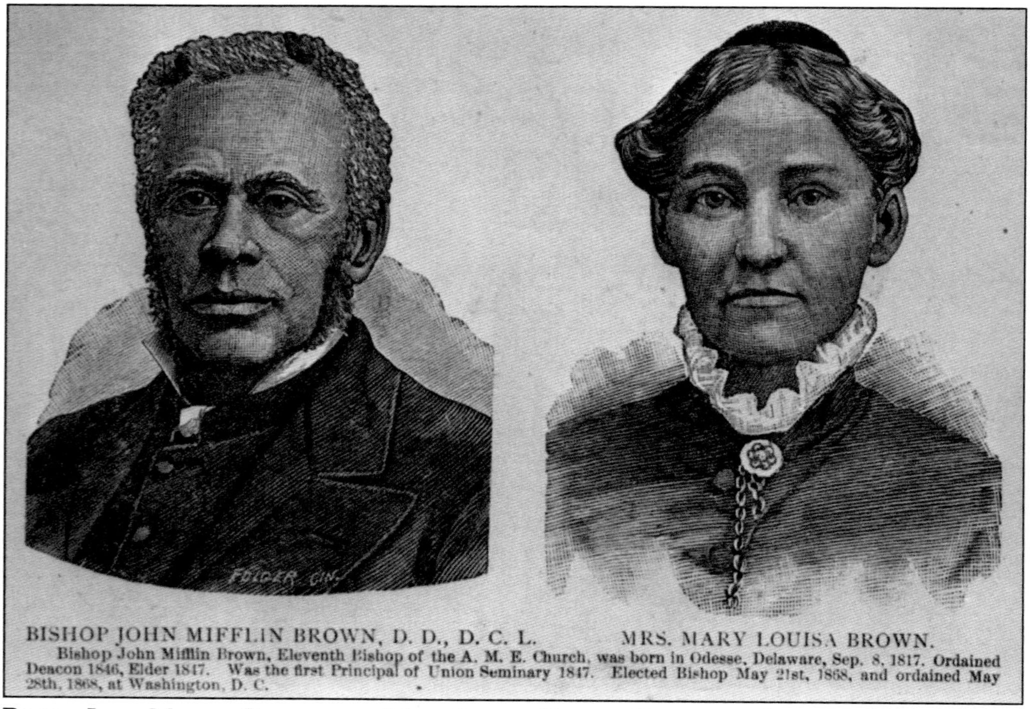

Bishop John Mifflin Brown and Mary Louisa Brown. Brown was the second pastor (1852–1857) at St. James AME. Where Doughty was marginally literate, Brown was classically and theologically educated at Oberlin College, the first college to admit students without regard to race or gender. (Dartmouth College admitted the first African American male.) Under Brown's leadership, Doughty petitioned the Indiana Conference for Covington's affiliation. (Courtesy of State Archives of Florida, *Florida Memory*, http://floridamemory.com/items/show/154687.)

Two

The Church as One Foundation

Jennie Broxton, free woman, reportedly attended Covington's First Methodist Church during slavery, sitting in a second-floor gallery for "negro servants." In 1854, Rev. John Mifflin Brown of New Orleans sent Charles Doughty to Covington to found an African Methodist Episcopal (AME) mission. Doughty was fit for the job since he founded St. James AME (New Orleans) in 1841. Covington AME became the town's first church for African Americans. It received a state charter in 1866, purchased land from former slave owner Adeline Terrell, and dedicated its first building. Doughty died in 1868. Rev. James Harper became pastor and officiated marriages of former slaves.

Doughty Chapel incorporated in 1870 with trustees Duplin Rhodes, Thomas Brown, and Gabriel Parker. Signers included Henry Johnson, Frank Jackson, Samuel Porter, John Adams, Alfred Duncan, William Hall, and Judge Perce. Except for Rhodes, all were illiterate.

The second African American church, founded in 1891, was First Missionary Baptist, the first recorded Baptist presence in Covington. In 1898, Rev. J.W. Daniels, Alex Alexis, and Wallace Benjamin signed to purchase property on Twenty-eighth Street for $25. It received its charter the same year.

Many of the remaining African American protestant churches evolved from either Doughty Chapel or First Missionary Baptist. Deacon George Washington, a member of First Missionary, founded Mount Zion Pilgrim Missionary Baptist Church in 1907.

Women held significant roles in the African American Church, although not as pastors. Laura Douglas, Ida Magee, and Lou Watts joined Rev. J.A. Henry to organize the Greater Starlight Baptist Church in 1931. After meeting in a little red two-story dilapidated lodge hall by the tracks, Annie Mae Roberts played a critical role in buying a house on Twenty-eighth Avenue that became the new church.

Bethel Reform Methodist Church sprang from Doughty AME. Rev. Peter S. Atkins led Doughty Chapel until the AME Conference planned to transfer him to another town. Some of Rev. Atkins's members petitioned him to stay in Covington, which gave rise to Bethel Reform Methodist in 1949. Those five churches formed the core of the historical African American religious experience in Covington.

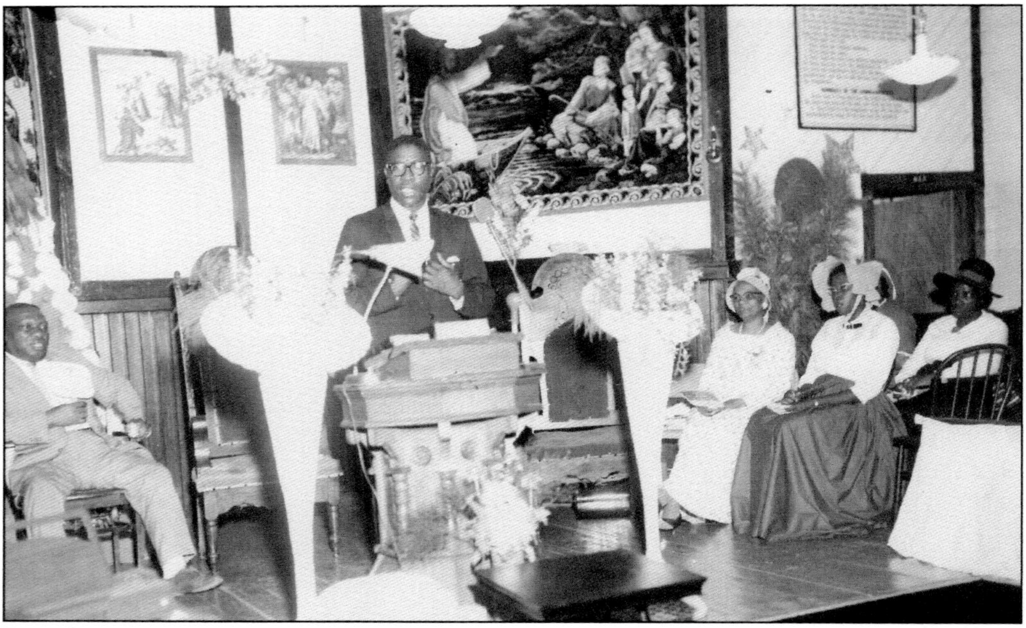

Rev. Coleman Callahan, 1966. Hopewell Baptist Church, Madisonville, celebrated its 100th anniversary with Reverend Callahan as pastor of the church. He was also the second pastor of the Greater Starlight Missionary Baptist Church, Covington, from 1939 to 1940. Standing and speaking at the pulpit is Rev. Percy Simpson. The ladies seated at right are, from left to right, Ophelia Tillman, Mable Sheridan, and Hazel Weeden. (Courtesy of the Randle collection.)

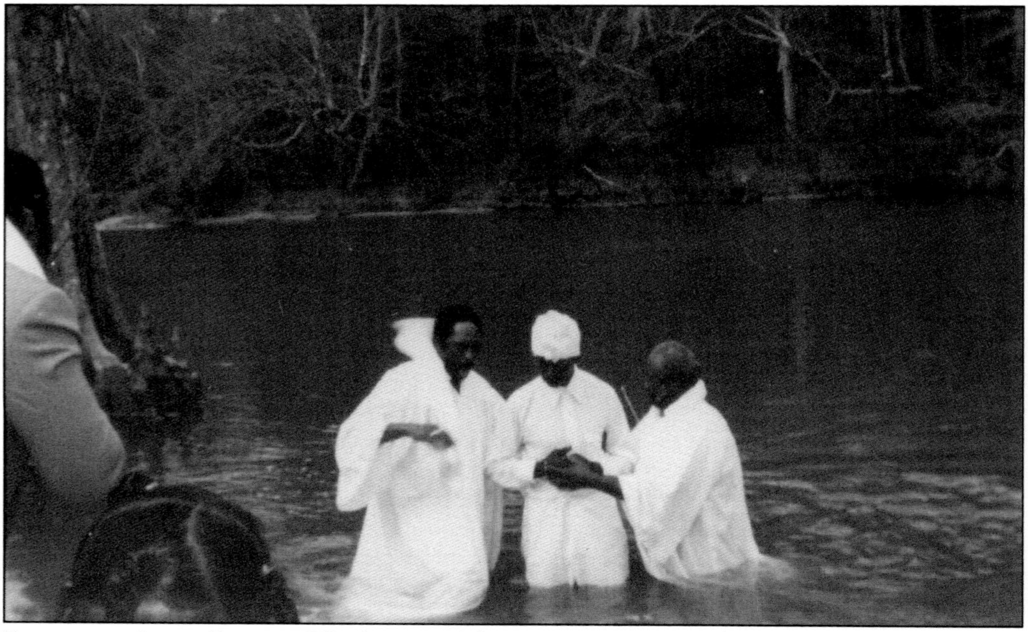

Baptism of James Barney. The historic African American churches all recall baptism at the Columbia Street Landing on the Bogue Falaya River. According to Teresa Henry Alston of the First Missionary Baptist Church and Ella Selmon, a procession marched down Columbia Street and through town to the landing. Generally, several people from different churches were baptized with full immersion. (Courtesy of Ella Selmon.)

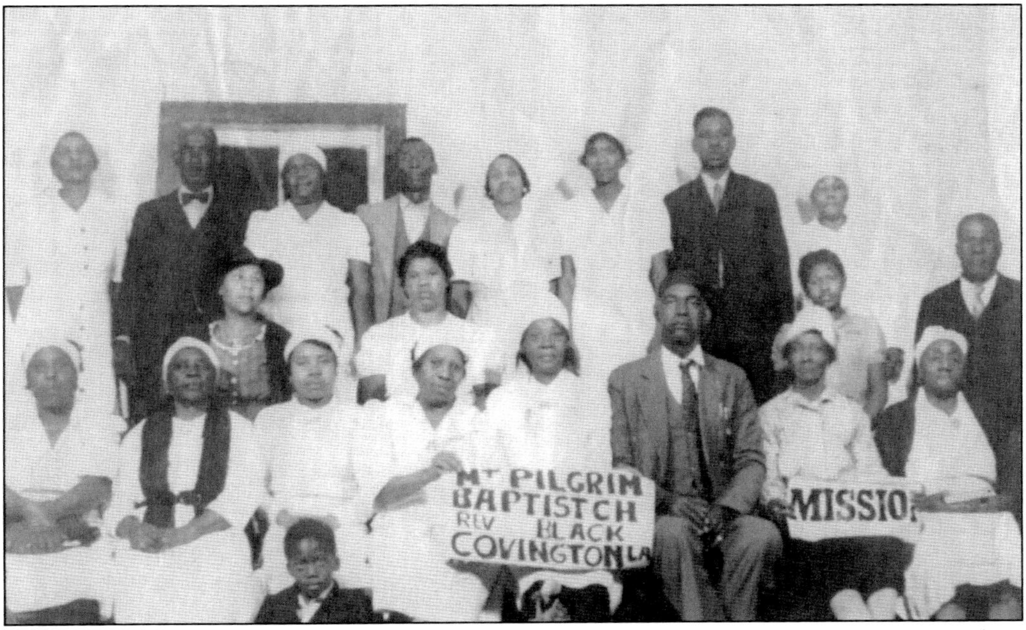

MOUNT PILGRIM BAPTIST CHURCH. Rev. H.B. Black, a native of Beaumont, Mississippi, sat for a portrait with members of his church during the mid-20th century. The First Church of God in Christ, located nearby, took a similar portrait with the pastor and members holding signs with the church's name. It is referred to as Quillen Temple, after its prophetic bishop, Howard Quillen Sr. (Courtesy of Ella Selmon.)

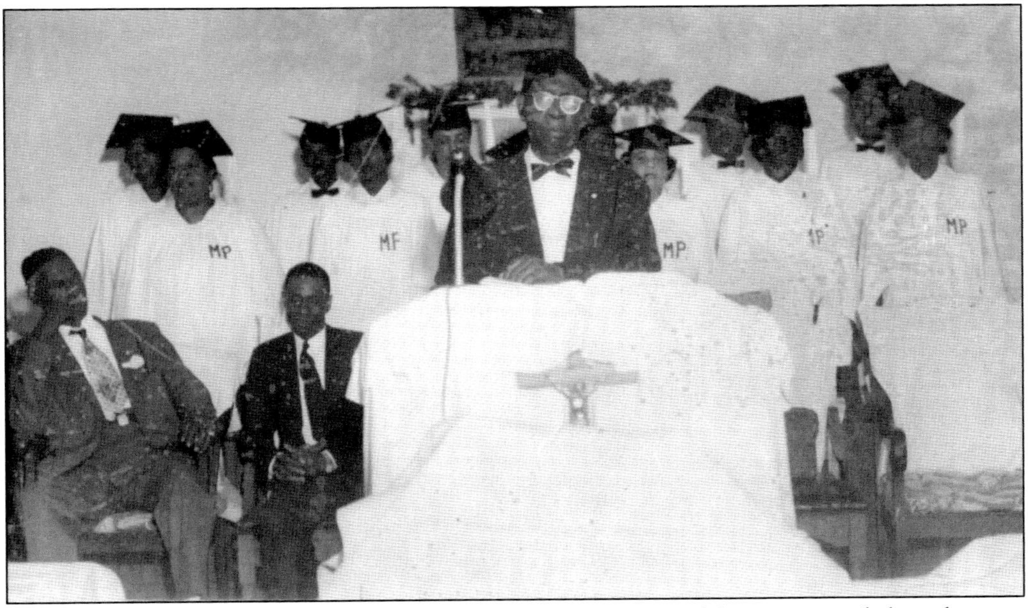

MOUNT PILGRIM BAPTIST CHURCH. This image provides a view of the pastors and choir during a regular church service. Rev. J.W. McCoy stands at the pulpit, and Rev. Eli Washington (left) and Rev. Piget Grim (second from left) are seated. The choir members are, from left to right, (first row) Rosanna McCary, Victoria Williams, Mrs. Freddie Hill, Daisy Weary, and Lucille Robinson; (second row) Lillie Bemann, John Demley, Lorena Arrington, unidentified, Roosevelt Polk, Hollie Clark, and Lester Dunn. (Courtesy of Ella Selmon.)

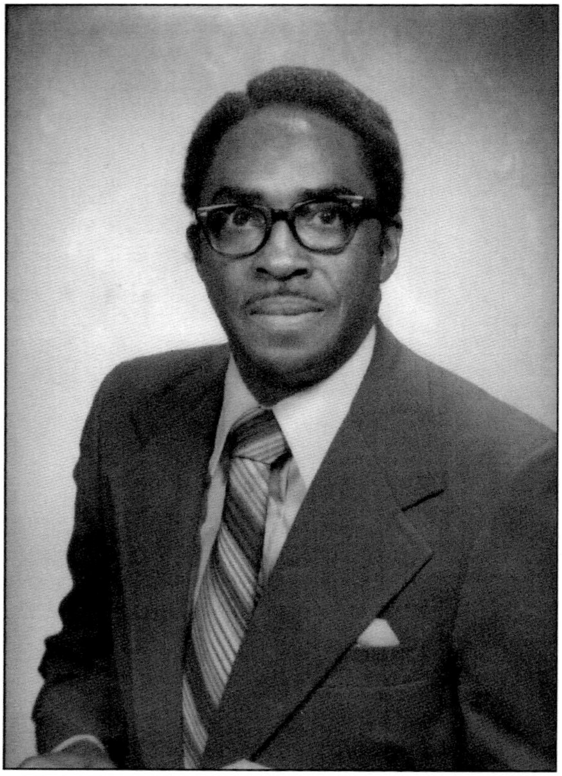

REV. JOE BECK. The First Missionary Baptist Church elected Reverend Beck as its pastor in 1965. He served the church until 2000. Under his leadership, the church underwent renovations for the fourth time in its history. Joseph Kelly led completion of the church's fellowship hall. Reverend Beck leaves a spiritual and tangible legacy. (Courtesy of Rev. Otis Brumfield.)

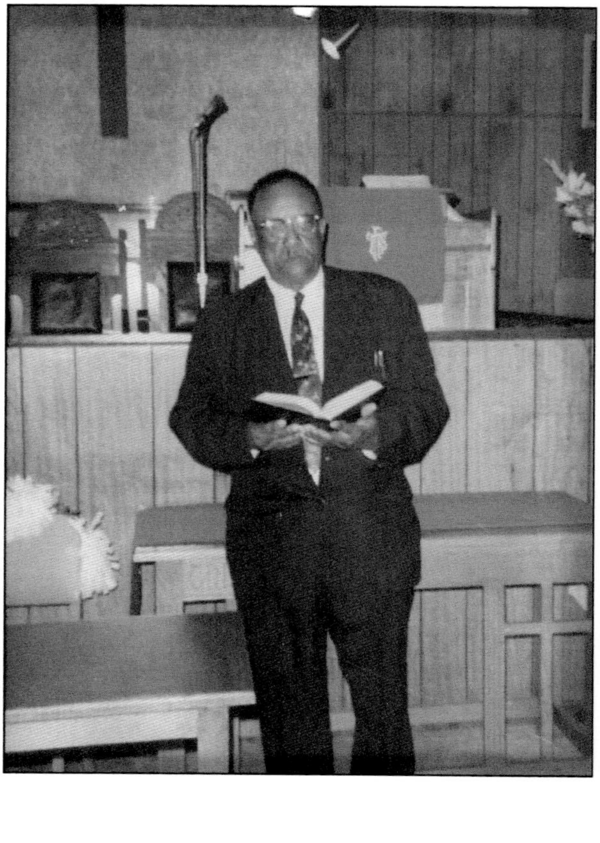

REV. ZACK DOAKES. Another well-regarded pastor of First Missionary Baptist Church, Reverend Doakes led at two different intervals, first in 1956 and then in 1963. At the seventh anniversary of Rev. Joe Beck's ministry in 1972, Reverend Doakes conducted services. African American protestant churches observe special days by inviting other congregations to participate. (Courtesy of Rev. Otis Brumfield and Victoria Johnson Trevigne.)

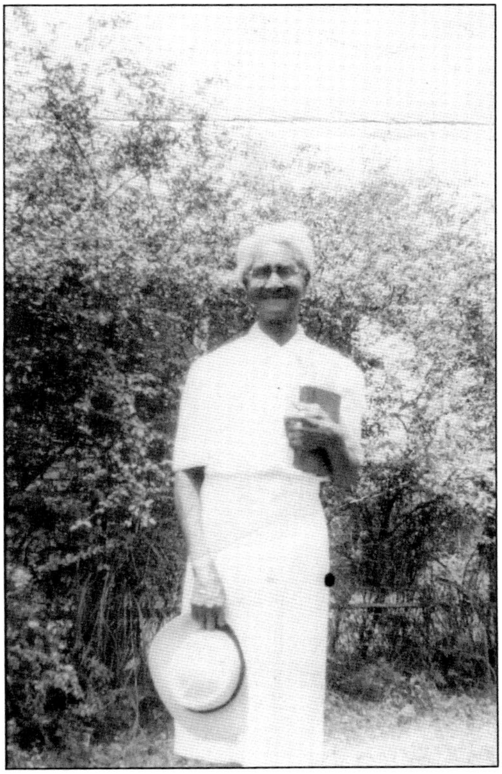

Georgia Plowman. Georgia Plowman returns from service at Bethel Reform Methodist with her hat in her hand and a Bible wrapped in her arm. She and husband William reared their family of nine children, Mitchell, Charlie, Oreta, Albertha, Alice, Ruth, Elizabeth, Magdalene, and Evelyn, at their home on West Twenty-eighth Avenue. (Courtesy of Elizabeth Plowman Steele.)

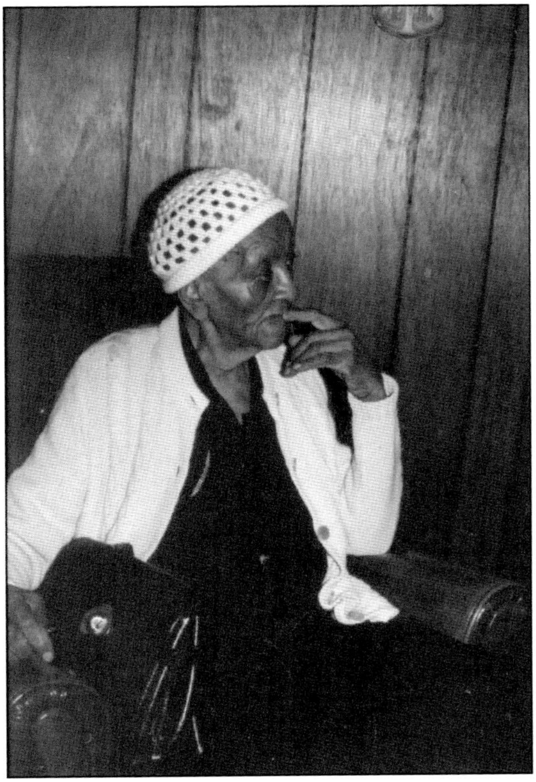

Lydia Richardson. Some African American churches honor older women who exemplify piety, integrity, caring, wisdom, sacrifice, and other characteristics of moral standards. They are given the title of Mother of the Church. Lydia Richardson, whose life was a model of virtue, received that honor from Greater Starlight Baptist Church. (Courtesy of Irma Penn.)

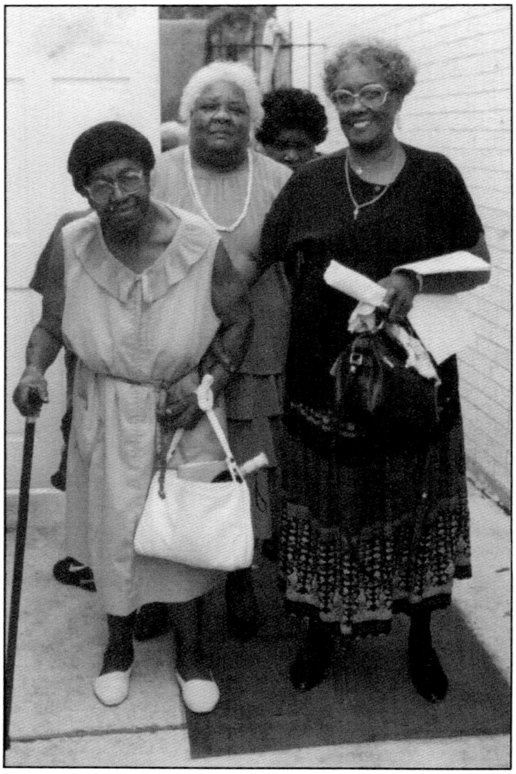

Valued Women. Pictured from left to right, Irene McCoy was a domestic by day as well as a noted soloist and worker with Senior Mission at Greater Starlight. Lucille White was an active member of Mount Pilgrim Baptist Church. Lubertha White and Mary Etta Green both served on Senior Mission at Greater Starlight. Green also sang in the choir. (Courtesy of Irma Penn.)

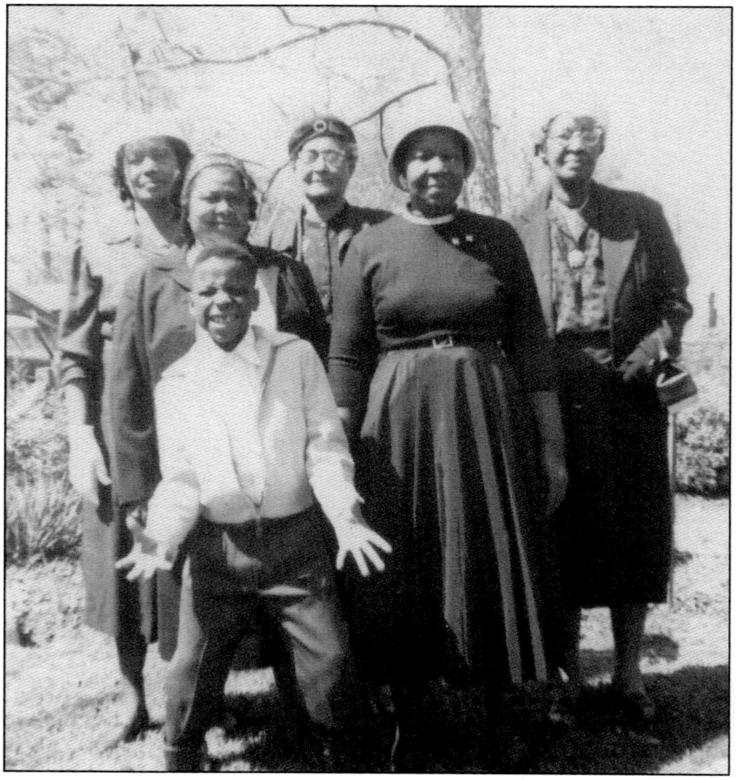

Dressed for Church, 1959. Curtis Ray Davis lightens up the scene as these ladies prepare to leave for Sunday church services. Pictured behind him are, from left to right, (second row) Lucille Butler and Curtis's grandmother Willie Luteal Thomas-Davis; (third row) Nettie Butler, Katie Hooks Butler Randle (Nettie's mother), and Curtis's great-grandmother Ida Harvey Thomas Bell. (Courtesy of Ida Thomas James.)

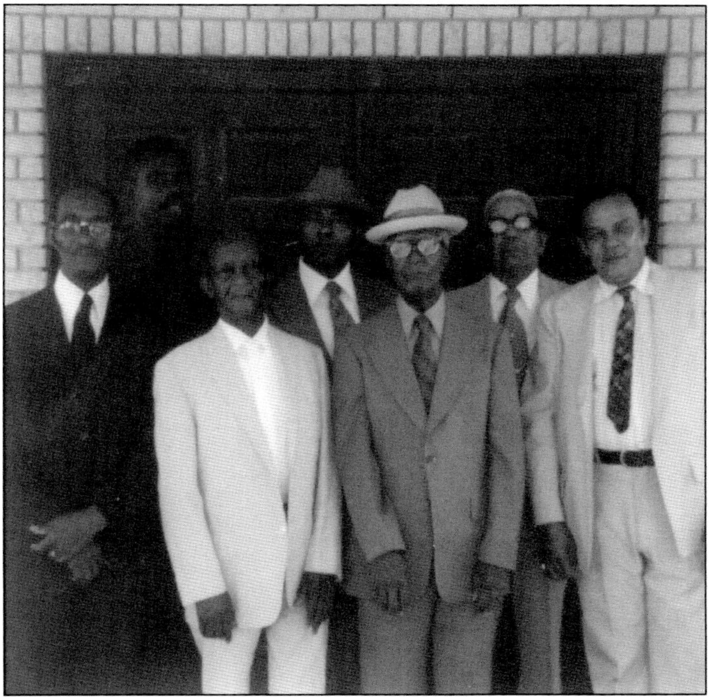

Bethel Reform Methodist Trustee Board. Effective and responsible leadership characterize those selected as trustees for most religious institutions. Standing at the entry of the church are, from left to right, (first row) Rigley Martin Sr., unidentified, Willie Scott, and Leroy Baham; (second row) Horace Martin Sr., Willie Moore, and Thomas Silvan. (Courtesy Ida Thomas James.)

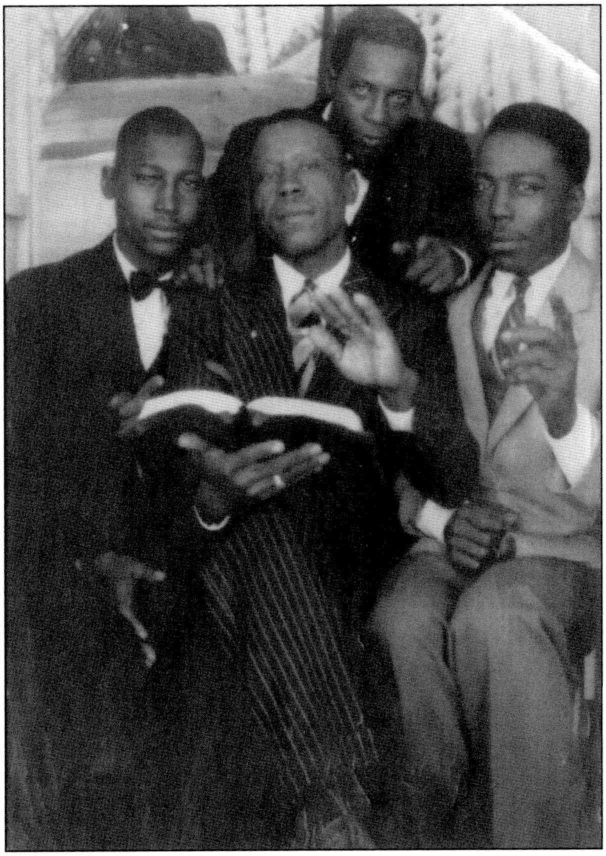

Pilgrim Travelers. This group had its origins in their home church, Mount Zion Pilgrim Baptist Church. They were among several gospel groups singing throughout St. Tammany, surrounding parishes, and Mississippi. From left to right are Henry Williams, Eddie "Sweet Baby" Hill, Henon Cyprian, and Richard Russell Sr. (Courtesy of the Randle collection.)

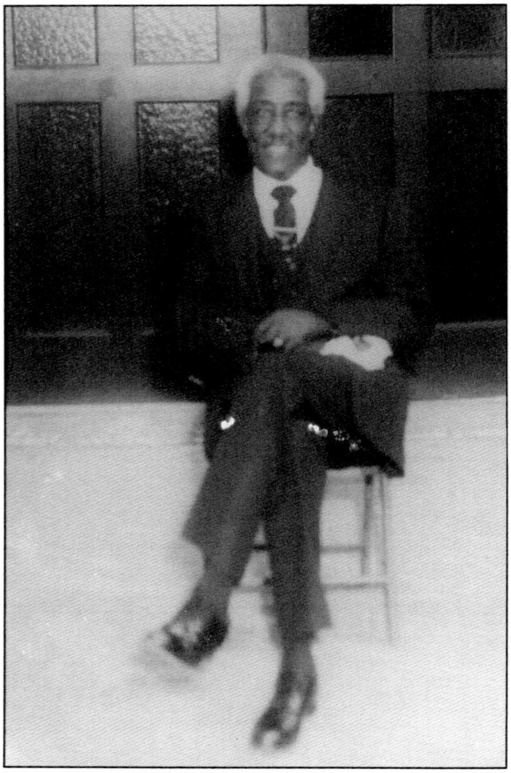

Rev. Wilker Neal. In 1975, Neal became the 14th pastor since the founding of Mount Zion Pilgrim Baptist Church in 1903. Reverend Neal previously served churches in Metairie and New Orleans but stayed in Covington for 12 years. Church history states that he "instituted many needed changes" and was beloved. He resigned in 1987 to return to New Orleans, and died in 1992. (Courtesy of the Randle collection.)

Mount Zion Association Banquet, 2000. Attending this event were, from left to right, (first row, seated) Henry and Grace Randle; (second row) Ella Selmon, Jessie Richardson James, Katie Laurent, Helen Alexander, and Roosevelt Polk; (third row) Mattie Lou Thigpen and J.D. Thigpen. All were members of Mount Zion Pilgrim Baptist Church. (Courtesy of the Randle collection.)

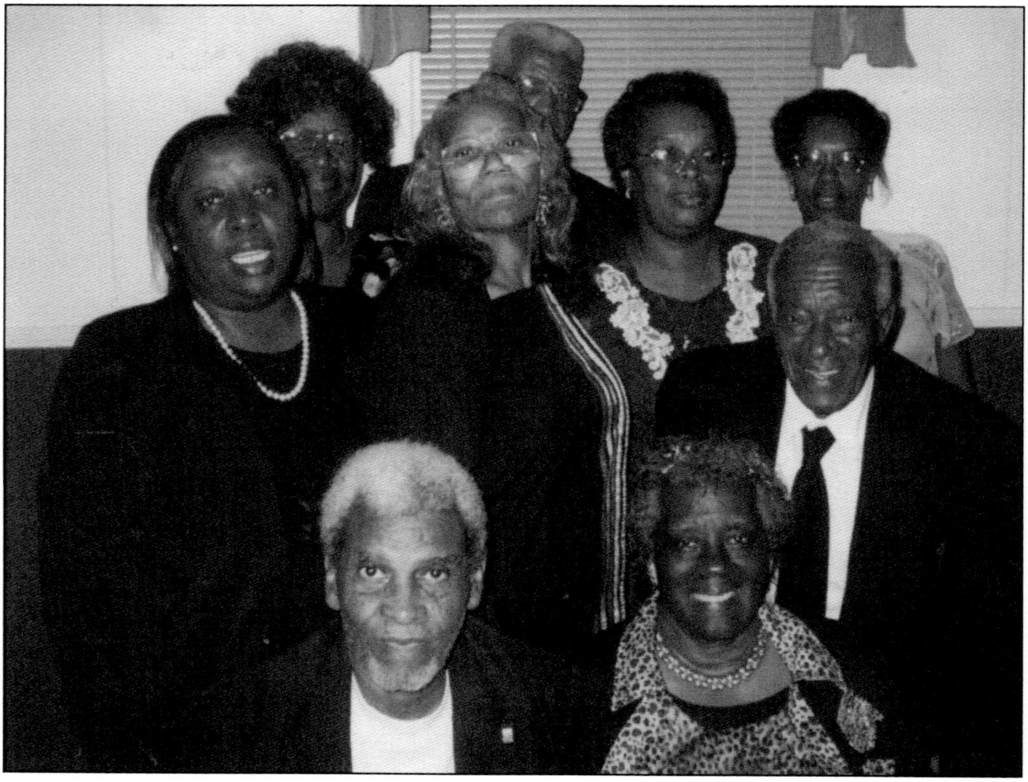

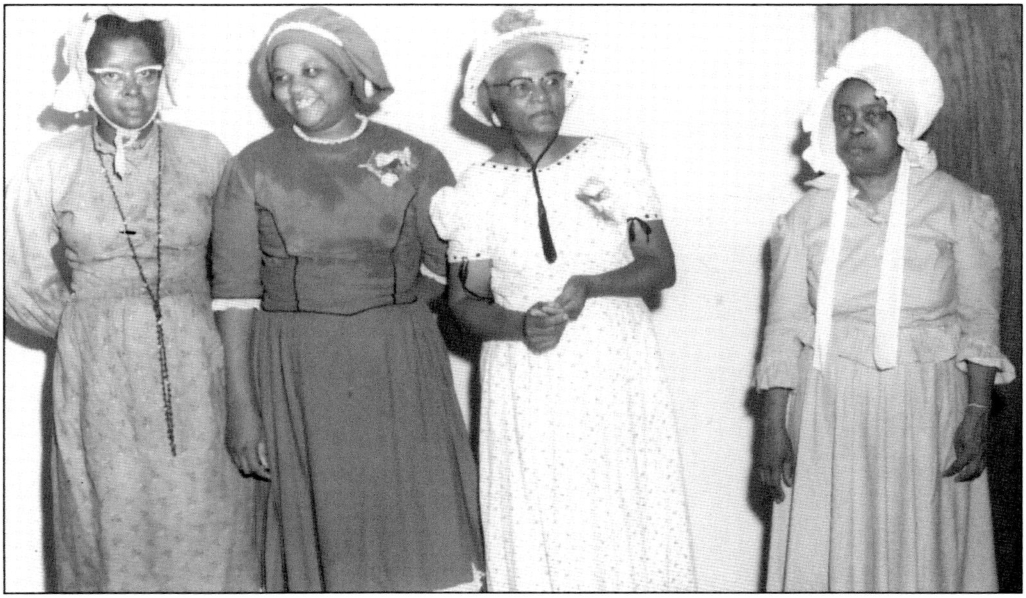

Old-Fashioned Days, 1966. Congregations from around Madisonville, including Covington, observed Hopewell Baptist Church's 100th anniversary. Members of Rev. Coleman Callahan's church, Greater Starlight, in Covington, joined (from left to right) Mable Sheridan, Doretha Clark Page, Ophelia Tillman, and Westerly Williams in the observance. Events such as this connected African Americans across towns and protestant denominations. (Courtesy of the Randle collection.)

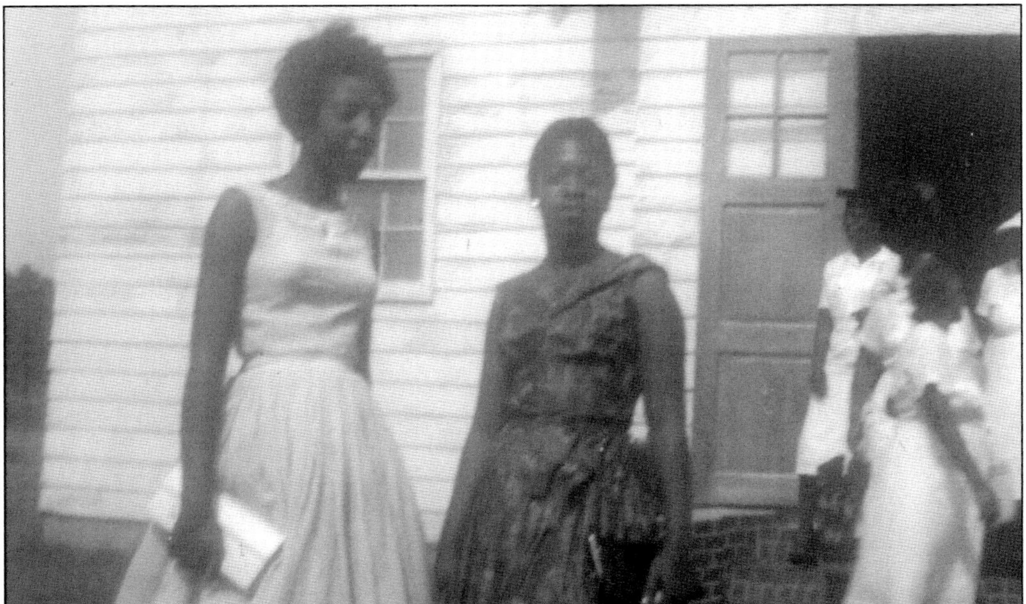

After Church, c. 1960s. Ida Ruth Thomas and Bertha "Fruitie" Guidry socialize after services at Bethel Reform. This photograph offers a glimpse of the original church. Reverend Atkins purchased an Army church, dismantled it, and moved it from Camp Claiborne in Alexandria, Louisiana, to Covington. The congregation met at the Love & Charity Hall until the Army church was reassembled at West Twenty-ninth Avenue.

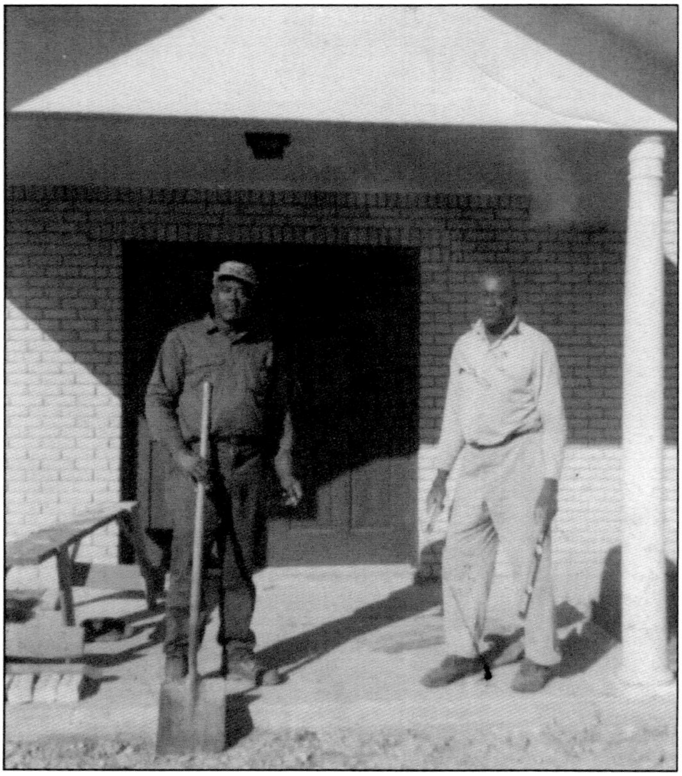

Completing the New Church, 1970. Willie Moore (left) and Rev. Peter Atkins prepared and poured the concrete for the walkway and sidewalks at the entrance of Bethel Reform. The congregation held services, once again, in the Love & Charity Hall until the new church was completed in 1971. (Courtesy of Ida Thomas James.)

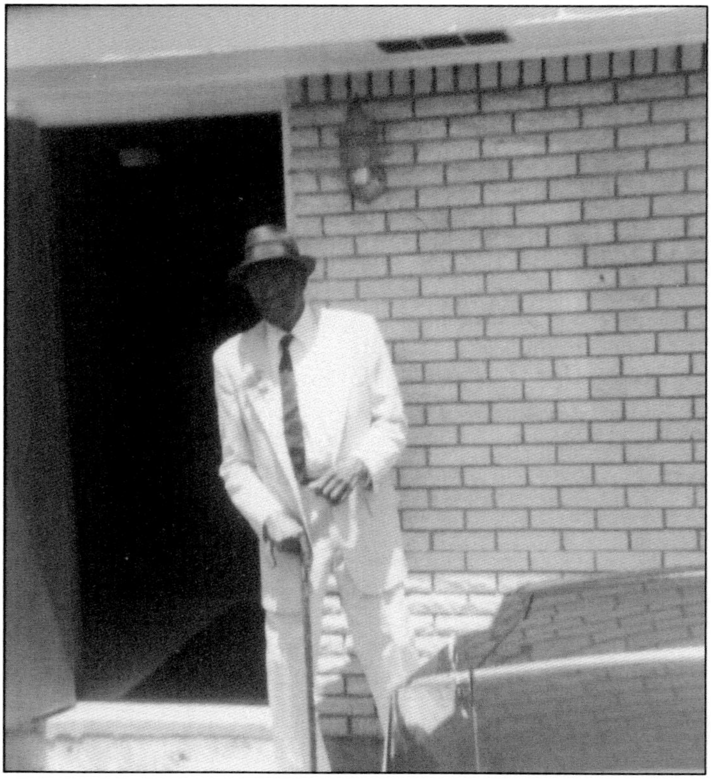

Rev. Peter Sylvester Atkins, 1976. Here, progress made with church construction is evident. The area next to the building enabled the pastor and congregants to utilize off-street parking. Most of the African American churches are nestled in neighborhoods among residences. Reverend Atkins is pictured departing after the regular Sunday worship service. (Courtesy of Ida Thomas James.)

Church Ladies in Church Hats. On any given Sunday, some African American women may be seen in their church hats. This is illustrated by Ann Mae Robert (standing) and Lillie Walker of Starlight Missionary Baptist Church. Church hats may be a fashion statement or a reference to 1 Corinthians 11:5, where Paul enjoins women to wear head coverings. More often, it may be both. (Courtesy of Ella Selmon.)

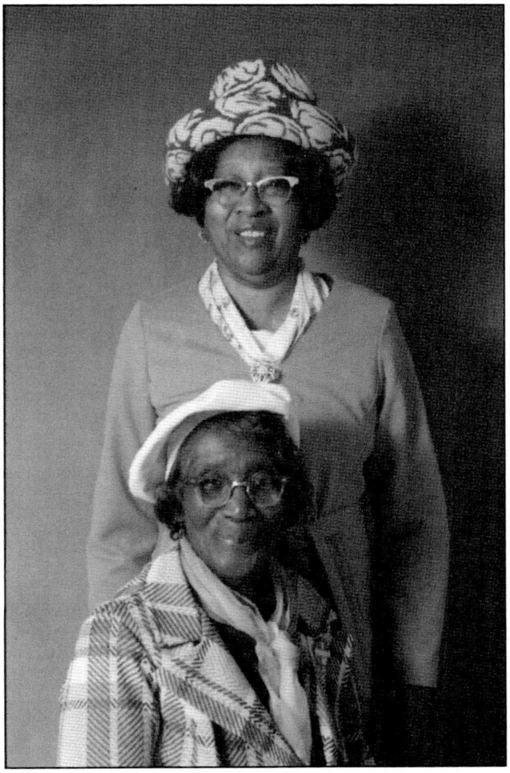

Bethel Reform Methodist Senior Choir, 1977. Members of the choir included, from left to right, Bernie Jean Frick, Evelyn Steele, Hazel Atkins, Altha Mae Moore, unidentified, Doretha Silvan, Shirley Henderson, Barbara Harper, and Lillie Gordon. (Courtesy of Ida Thomas James.)

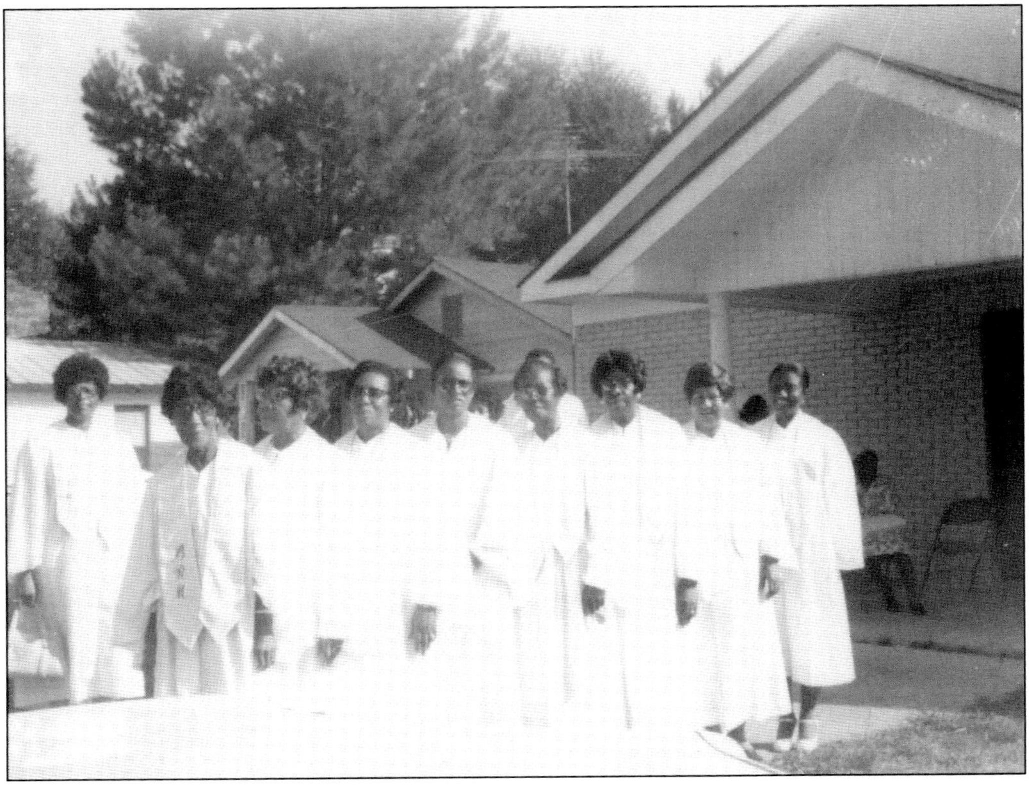

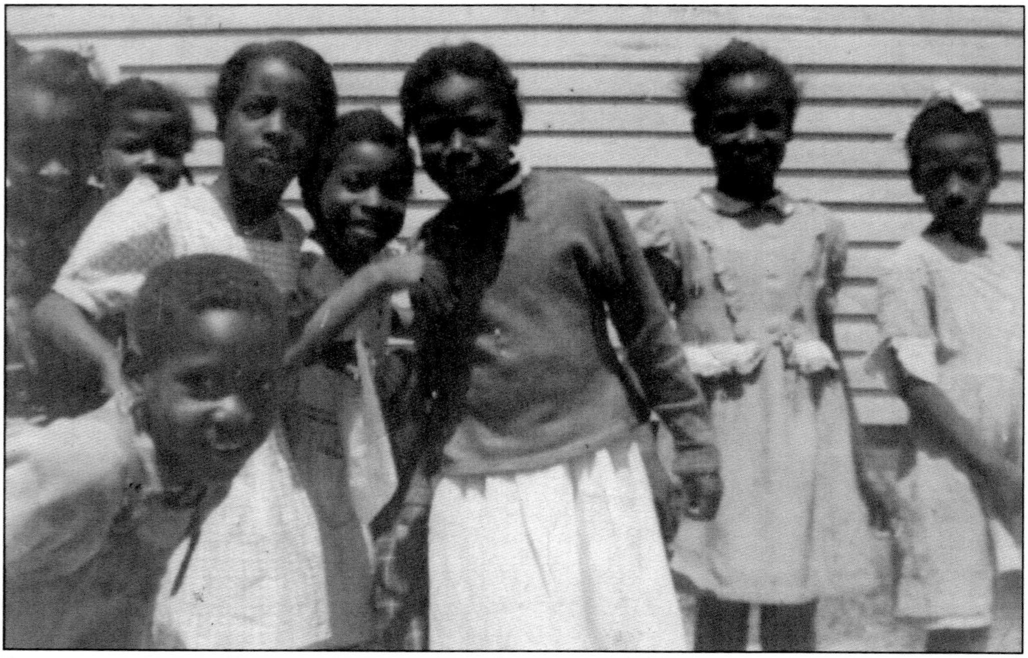

Schoolchildren at Play, 1949–1950. A teacher captured the curious expressions of Rosenwald children during recess. Classes met in the wood-frame building constructed for opening day in 1927. According to a former teacher, Rosenwald was a "wooden building with a pot belly stove." Teachers cleaned their classrooms because there were no janitors. (Courtesy of Matthew Wilson.)

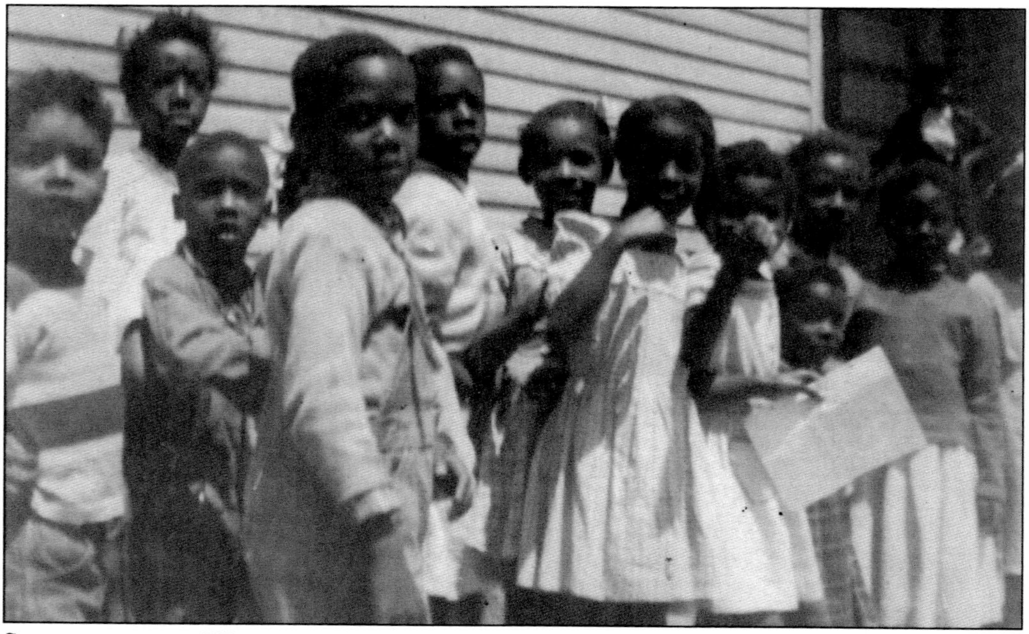

Schoolchildren Waiting in Line, 1949–1950. Curiosity turns into wonderment as these children, identified as being between kindergarten and second grade, respond to the photographer's promptings. Their teacher stands ready at the door. Free public education with state laws governing school attendance and monitoring by parish school boards increased attendance. (Courtesy of Matthew Wilson.)

Three

Origins of African American Education

Census entries in 1870 and 1880 noted many African American school-age children "at school." Long denied, many sought education for their children. Some attended private home schools, although by 1880, there was a public school in Covington for these children. From 1896 to 1911, Fr. Joseph Koegerl of St. Peter operated a Catholic school for African Americans.

The Board of Public School Directors' June 1880 meeting outlined the following: Teachers needed a certificate of competency, pay equaled "one dollar per head per month" for only three months, and no school approved for a ward with insufficient funds. At its July 1880 meeting, the board appointed Anna M. Dumas, the daughter of the head of the post office, the "colored school" teacher. The board deferred on applications for white teachers. At its March 1881 meeting, the board renewed Dumas's appointment and named a Miss K. McDougall as the teacher for the white school. A complaint lodged in 1890, however, demanded that Covington needed a white public school, noting, "The colored people have a school building of their own."

Dumas submitted a letter of application again in 1886. There were applications from out of state. One letter of application arrived October 1887 from "colored" teacher W.H. Wilson, a well-traveled native of Missouri who wanted to relocate to Covington.

House Bill 235, starting in 1880, required a census of educable children in each parish to determine apportionments. Enumerators traversed the parish and listed each child by name and age. Among those in early 1900s Covington were Hester Brumfield, 13, and Aristine Callahan, 6. Siblings Warren and Zina White were among children in White Settlement. By 1900–1901, statistics revealed increased school attendance and additional income for the school board. In the African American school, teacher Ida Bell reported 75 percent attendance for her school, and Anna Olsen reported 100 percent attendance at the White Settlement school.

Three-month school terms ended by 1919. School superintendent Elmer Lyon announced that Louisiana now required nine months of school. Compliance also helped the school board and the African American community apply to the Rosenwald Fund.

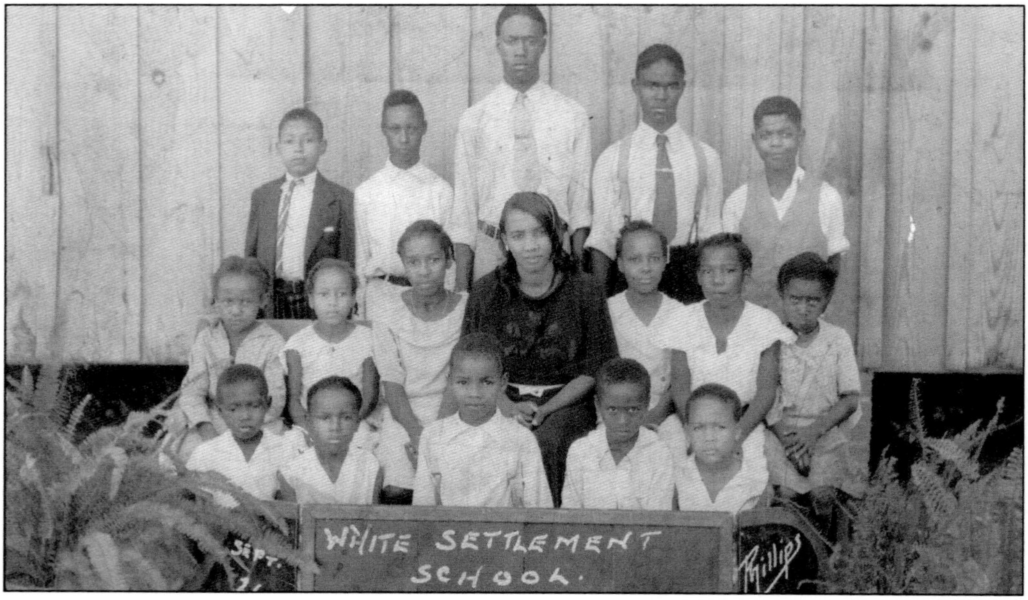

WHITE SETTLEMENT SCHOOL, 1944. Teacher Ivory Parker Williams poses with her students. Although Williams was a native of nearby Madisonville, the majority of White Settlement inhabitants comprised interconnected families of Whites, Russells, Petersons, and Andrews, many of whom are represented among these children. The small community, located just outside of Covington, is closely and culturally associated with the African Americans in the city. (Courtesy of Cynthia Russell.)

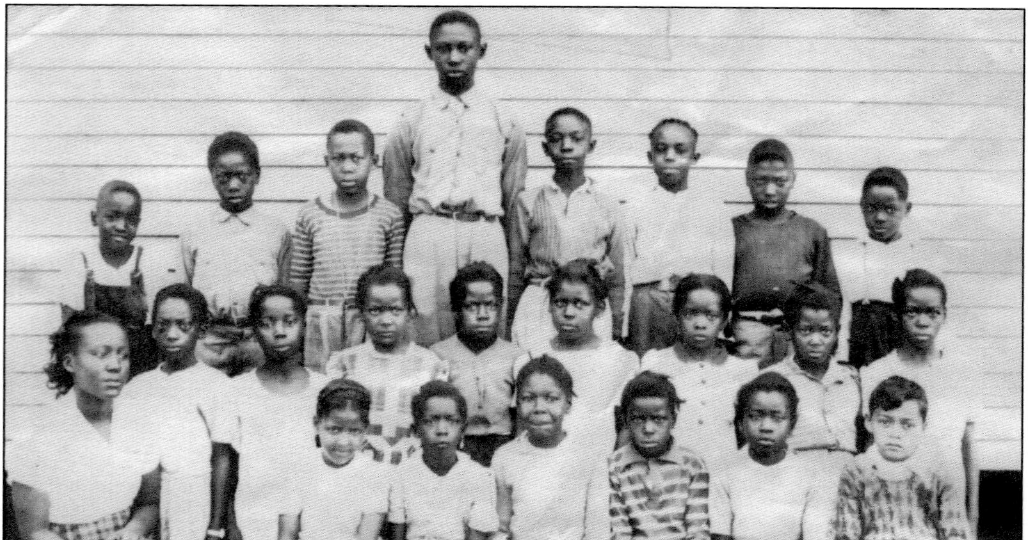

COVINGTON ROSENWALD SCHOOL, 1944. Henri Ella Clayton, the teacher, is pictured at far left. Her students are, from left to right, (first row) Rosetta Frick (whose mother, Helen, also taught), Shirley Weaver, Joyce Batiste, Aline Elliott, Irene Martin, and Henry Duncan; (second row) Ruth Mae Alexander, Odeal Jackson, Wanda Lee Frick, unidentified, Yvonne Callahan, Barbara Jean Strong, Margie Washington, and Marian Duncan; (third row) Eugene Elzy, Gilbert James, Herbert Stewart, Curley Adams, Arthur Martin, Ben White, Wherley James, and unidentified. (Courtesy of Matthew Wilson.)

ROSENWALD TEACHER, 1949–1950. This teacher, identified as Ms. Simmons, and her students are captured during recess. Her husband also taught at Rosenwald. Many teachers arrived as couples. However, single female teachers frequently married local men who were laborers and skilled workers. Single male teachers married local women who were not in the profession. The marriages, among other factors, lessened community emphasis on economic class distinctions. (Courtesy of Matthew Wilson.)

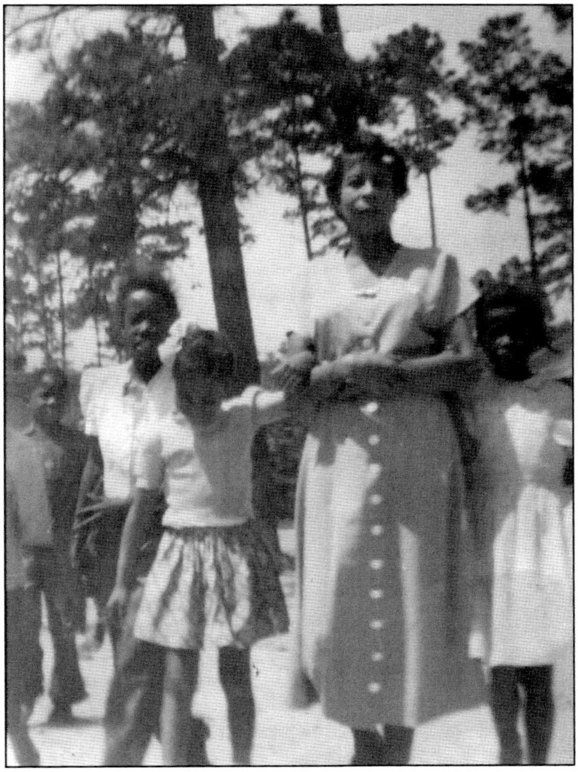

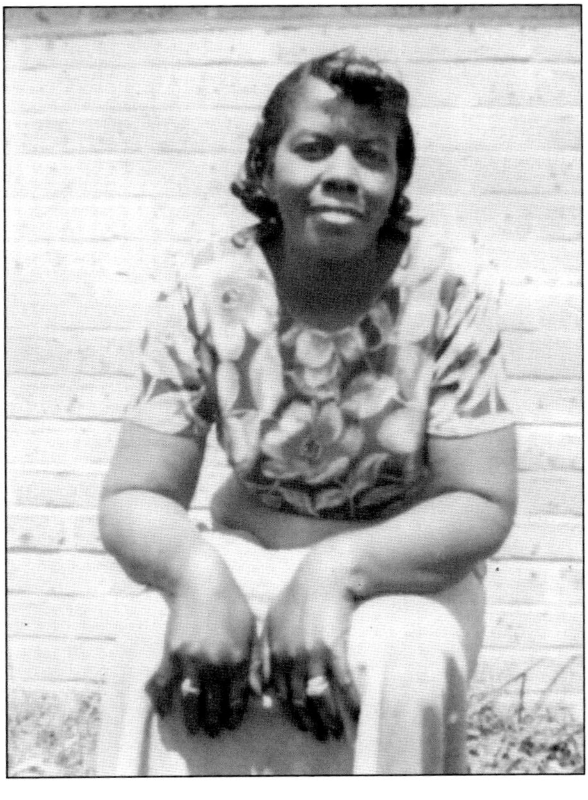

POSING AT ROSENWALD, 1949–1950. This unidentified woman appears to be faculty. By 1950, the old school building was used for some lower grades, while some elementary students and the high school students were housed in the new building. (Courtesy of Matthew Wilson.)

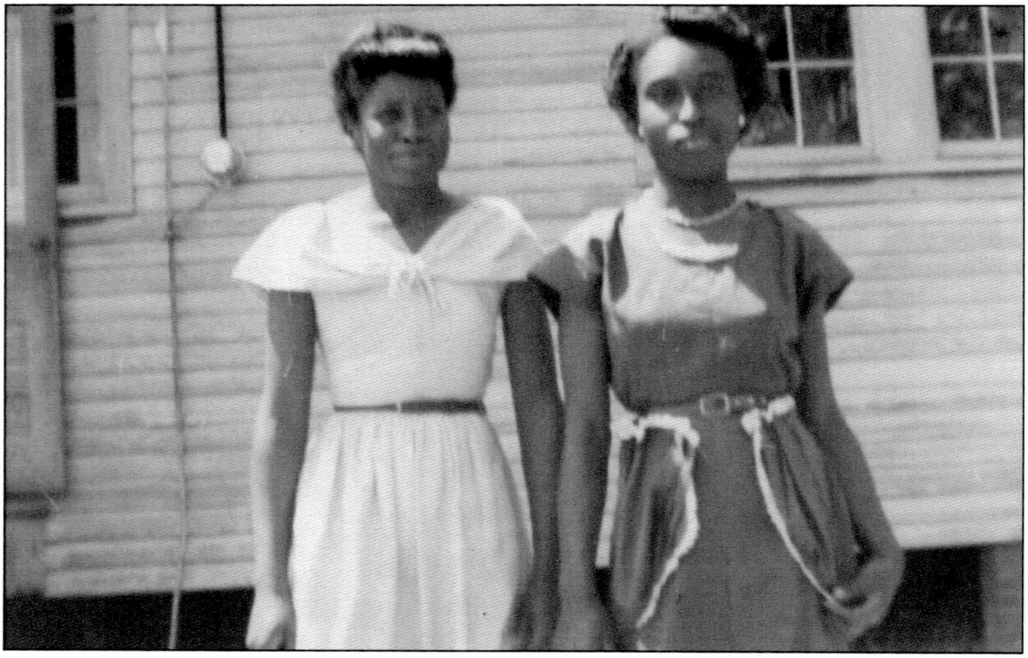

Students at Rosenwald, 1949–1950. Beatrice Clark, right, hailed from a family of pastors and gospel singers. She was the eldest of her siblings, with whom she formed the Rose Hill Gospel singers from the church of the same name in Lonesome Pine, near Covington. She married Calvin Prioleau. The student on the left is unidentified. (Courtesy of Matthew Wilson.)

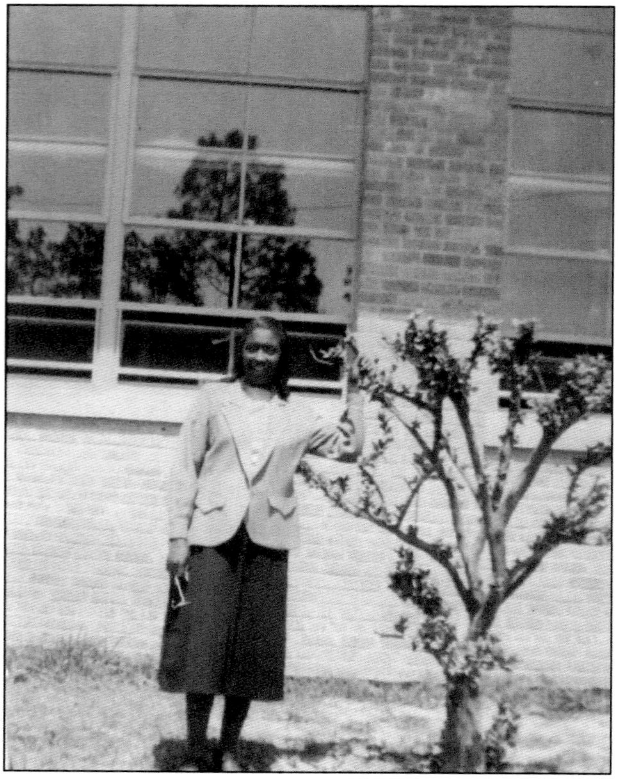

Lillie Mae Zoll Gordon, 1949–1950. Gordon taught history and often taught dance for student programs. She began teaching fifth grade in 1949 and later taught high school. Native to Covington, the Zoll family was immersed in community life. Family members attended local churches Doughty Chapel, Mount Pilgrim Baptist, and Bethel Reform. Lillie married Ellison Gordon. (Courtesy of Matthew Wilson.)

Four

"Rosenwald, Oh Rosenwald"

"The excuses have always been that the colored man does not own property or pay taxes to help in the building of school houses. In this case . . . they are willing to do their part towards the cost of this building," Elmer Lyon, superintendent, admonished the 1919 school board. He had $800 cash from African Americans in Sun and Madisonville, fulfilling their commitment to secure grants from the Rosenwald Fund. Additionally, Lyon reported that the "colored Baptist association" promised land to build in Madisonville and receipt of the title for the Slidell "colored" school was in hand. He urged the St. Tammany Parish School Board to fulfill its financial match.

Julius Rosenwald collaborated with Booker T. Washington, combining his philanthropy with Washington's expertise to educate African Americans. The plan was simply to improve the educational status of this group with African American investment to build schools. Financial support from school districts was equally critical. Southern University sent John Sebastian Jones across Louisiana to explain and to convince African American communities to make that commitment. The catch for them included turning over their monies and donated land to white school boards. Jones reported that he met challenges, but overall, the labor was productive.

The effort by African Americans in Covington came to fruition, as reported at the January 1923 meeting of the school board. At the October 1925 meeting, the superintendent reported, "I take pleasure in stating that the patrons of the Covington Colored school have finished raising the $1000.00 to be placed in the building fund, and now it is up to this Board to keep their promise by adding $5000.00 . . . making application to the Rosenwald Fund for $1100 and the building of a new school." African American laborers, domestics, and menial workers, giving additionally at their churches, raised the money.

Prof. James Harrison, in Covington since 1924, became principal when Covington Rosenwald opened in 1927. Helen Simon Frick recalled registering more than 100 students in two grades on her first day in 1934. Rosenwald became a high school in 1950, Professor Harrison retired in 1957, and the school closed in 1966.

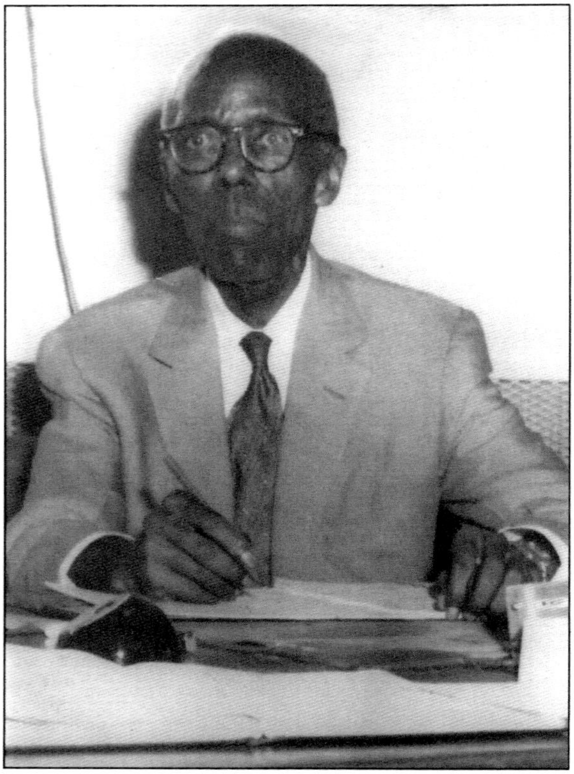

James A. Harrison, Principal, 1924–1957. "Professor," as Harrison was known, arrived from Mississippi in 1924 with wife Lubertha, a teacher, and sons Elton and Lincoln. Professor's parents and their 11 children were literate (according to the 1900 census). His sister Hester was a teacher, one brother was a salesman, and others were farmers. Professor Harrison, a mathematician, emphasized academic rigor and decorum at Rosenwald. He retired in 1957. "I admired that man," remains a common refrain. (Courtesy of Joyce Bledsoe Harrison.)

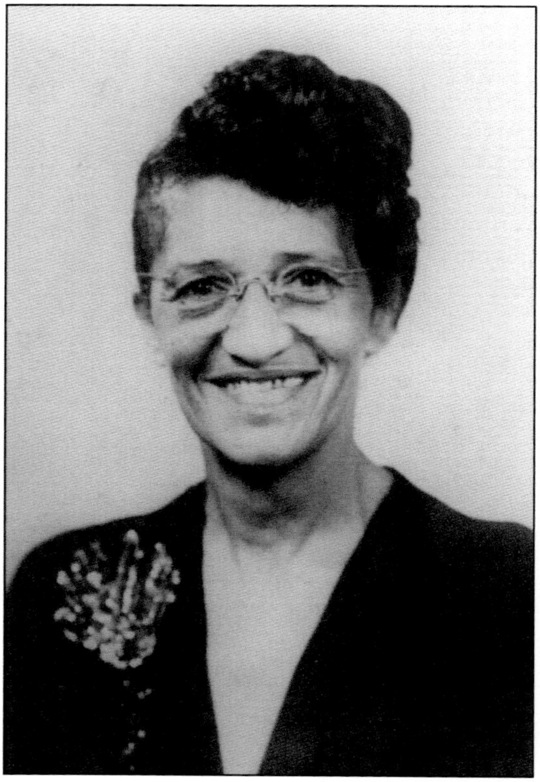

Mrs. Lubertha Lundy Harrison. She traveled from Fayette, Mississippi, with her husband, Professor Harrison, and two young sons, Elton and Lincoln, to lead Covington Rosenwald in the 1920s. Warm memories of a talented music teacher and church musician accompany her name. Her music room was the scene of many enjoyable evenings of entertainment by the students for the community. Doughty AME Church remembers her as their pianist. (Courtesy of Joyce Bledsoe Harrison.)

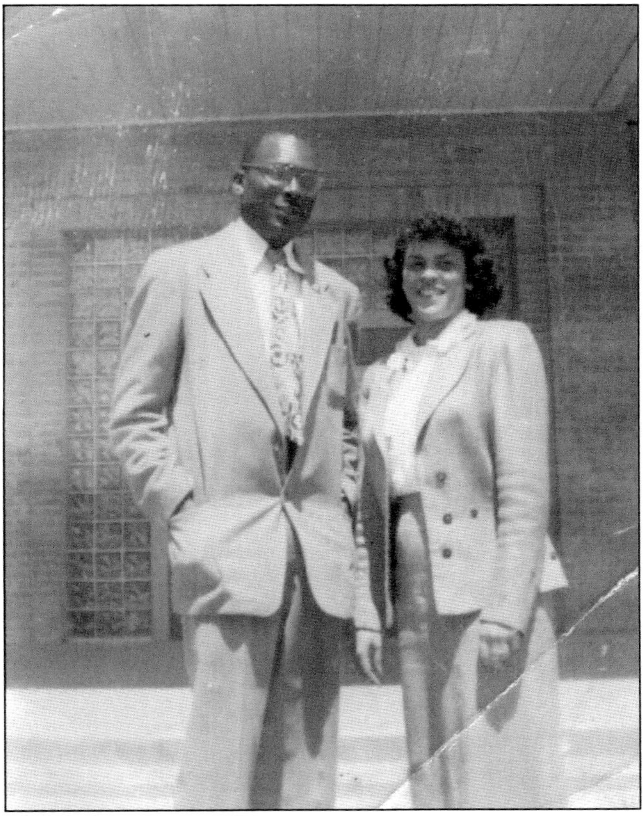

Pete and Marguerite Anderson, 1949–1950. The Andersons married later in their careers while at Rosenwald. According to local anecdotal history, marriage, although not required of teachers, connoted stability and responsibility among them, reassuring parents who expected the transmission of those values to their children in preparation for adulthood. (Courtesy of Matthew Wilson.)

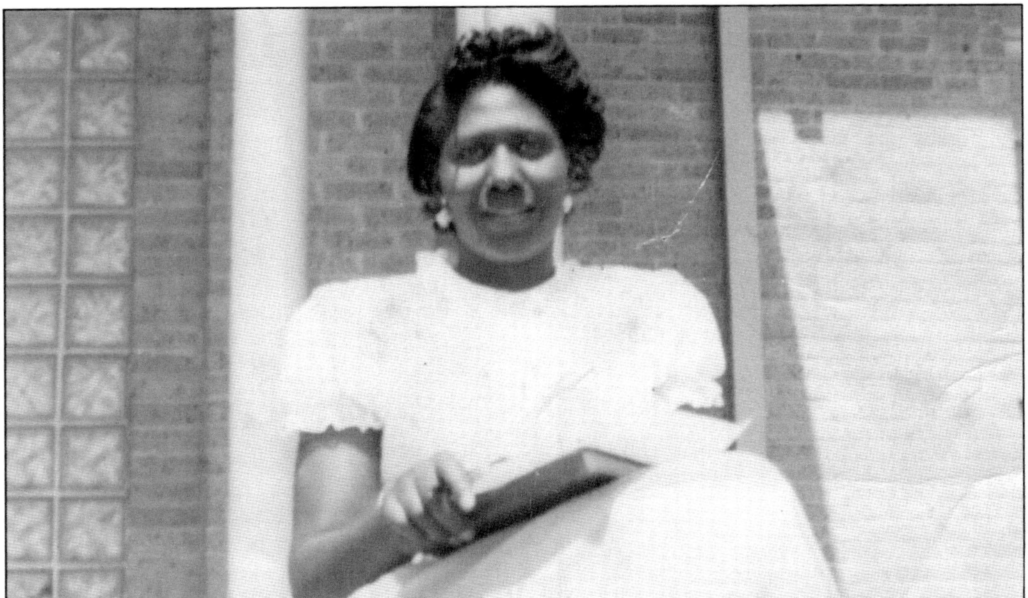

Southern Belle, 1949–1950. Almetta Route sat with elegance during her senior year at Rosenwald High School. Photographed to depict student and faculty life at the school, students such as Almetta dressed for picture day and posed to demonstrate that they used their free time wisely. (Courtesy of Matthew Wilson.)

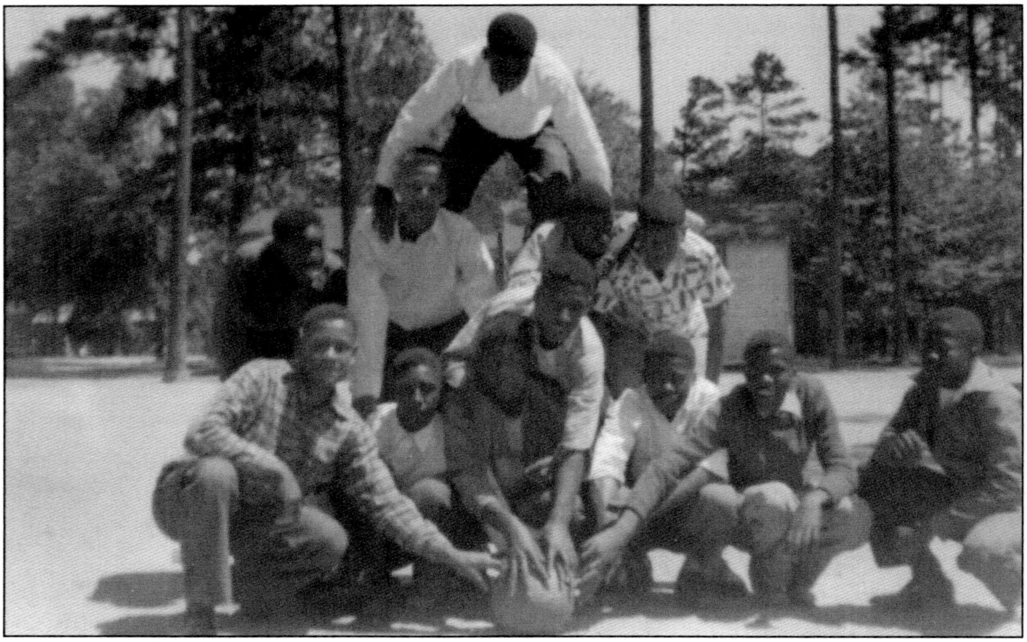

HIGH SCHOOL BASKETBALL, 1949–1950. Young men demonstrate their athletic prowess and their interest in basketball. Star players, according to Nathaniel Johnson, included Herman and Raymond Williams, as well as Earl Christy. During this period, there was no gym; the dirt court served the purpose. The 1950s and 1960s teams included twins Helen and Hattie Williams and Mable and Hazel Williams. Nathelda Naylor was a star in the 1960s. (Courtesy of Matthew Wilson.)

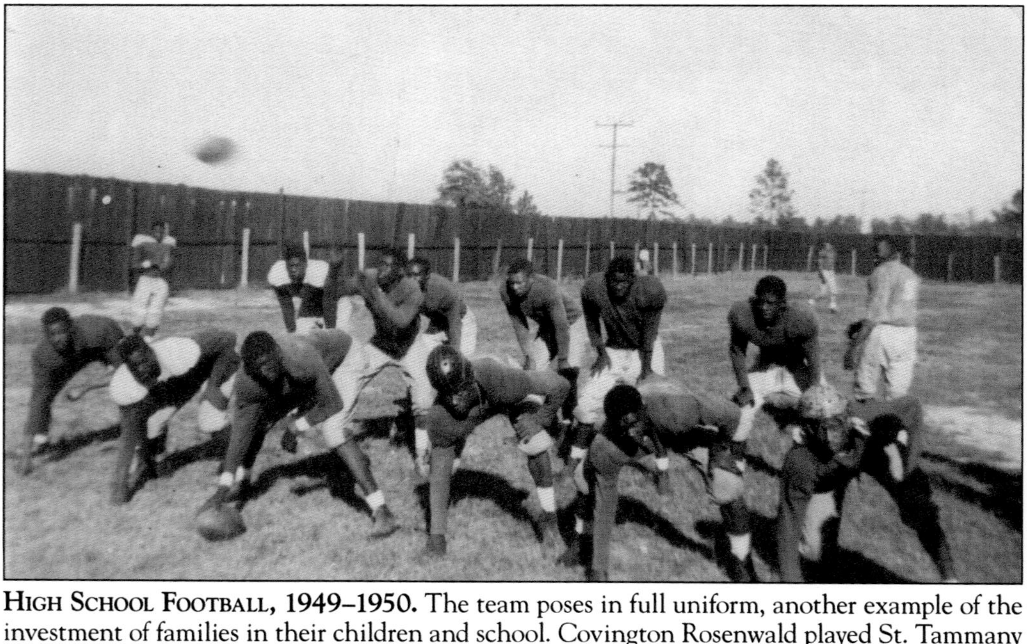

HIGH SCHOOL FOOTBALL, 1949–1950. The team poses in full uniform, another example of the investment of families in their children and school. Covington Rosenwald played St. Tammany High School, the other African American high school in the parish. Opponents included teams from nearby parishes. Students looked forward to playing with the Southern University or Grambling College football teams. Rosenwald and Holy Family shared the same field. (Courtesy of Matthew Wilson.)

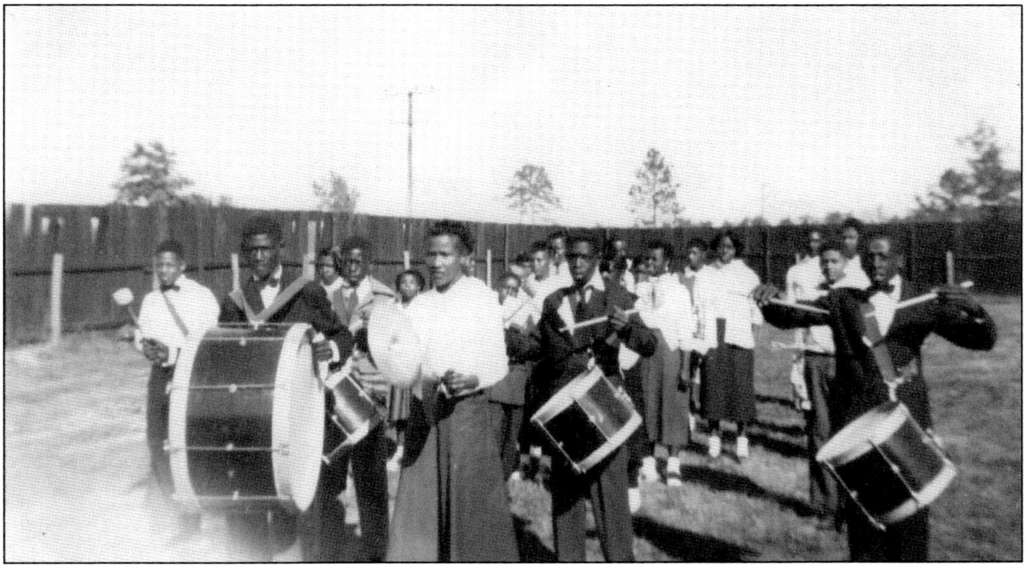

Covington Rosenwald Band, 1949–1950. The marching band, whose members had uniforms and instruments, also demonstrates community involvement. It is a representation, former faculty reported, of the school's efforts to encourage a versatile curriculum and develop well-rounded students. Lubertha Harrison played piano and taught music. Matthew Wilson, hired for one year to substitute in English, notes that his quartet won the parish musical competition in 1950. (Courtesy of Matthew Wilson.)

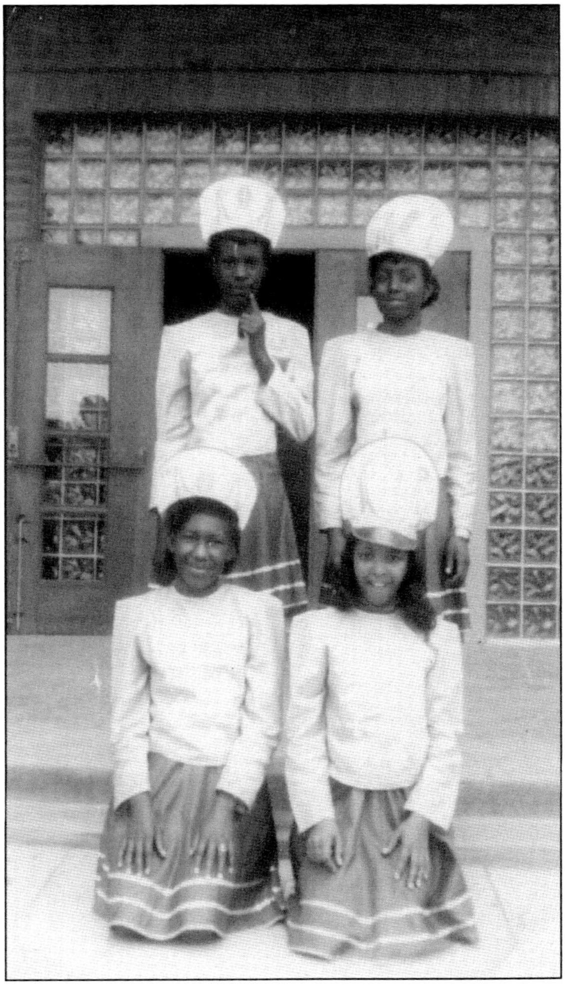

Majorettes, 1954–1957. Rosetta Frick (later Silvan), kneeling at right, was the lead majorette (noted by the bib on her headdress) during her sophomore, junior, and senior years. Standing are Lillie Mae McCormick (left) and Lucille Sheridan (Moore). The girl kneeling at left is unidentified. Parents and seamstresses made uniforms for majorettes, band members, and other groups. (Courtesy of Matthew Wilson.)

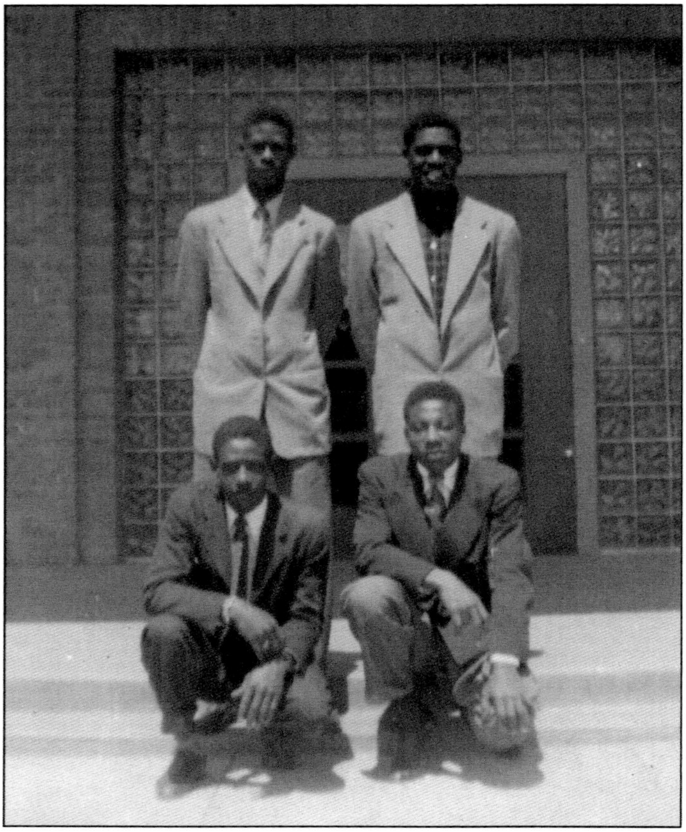

Representative Men, 1949–1950. These students, according to former teacher Matthew Wilson, dressed for picture day. Although the organization is not known, they were members of a high school club. The young men were seniors and graduated in the first class in May 1950. (Courtesy of Matthew Wilson.)

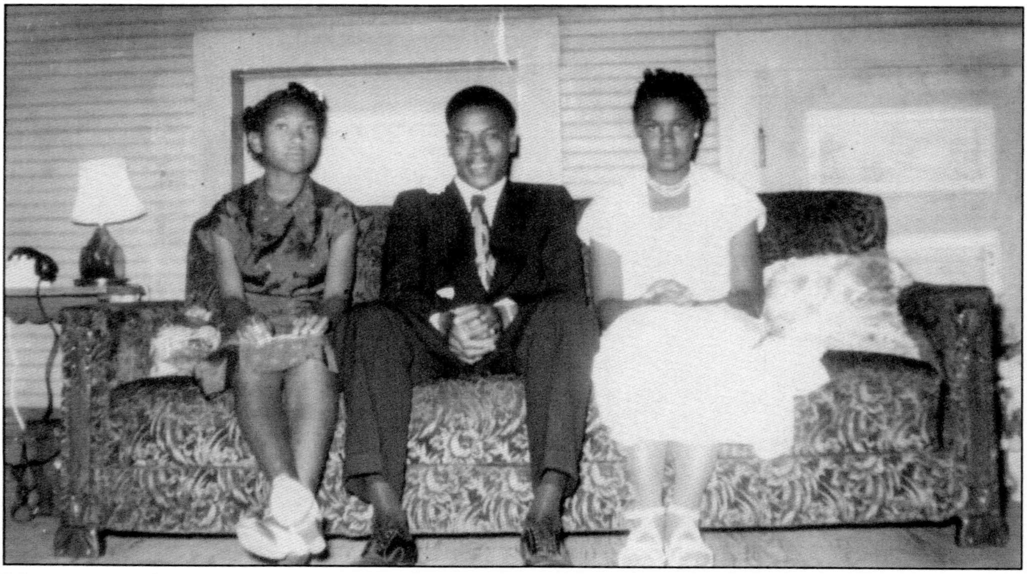

Waiting for School Dance, 1949–1950. Herman Williams poses with Bobbie Kelly (left) and Rose Bud Edgerson, dressed for a school function. Among the varied activities at Rosenwald, dances and banquets promoted shared experiences. Additionally, former teachers explain, the functions involved lessons intended to teach and develop proper dress and behavior in formal settings. (Courtesy of Matthew Wilson.)

DRESSED FOR THE SOCIAL, 1949–1950. Students sat for a picture before the big event. Among them are Willie Laurent (seated third from left) and close friend Joseph Vaughn (fourth from left). Joseph's sister, Marion Vaughn, said that the two young men left high school and joined the military together. They were stationed at Lackland Air Force Base and completed high school requirements as young soldiers. (Courtesy of Matthew Wilson.)

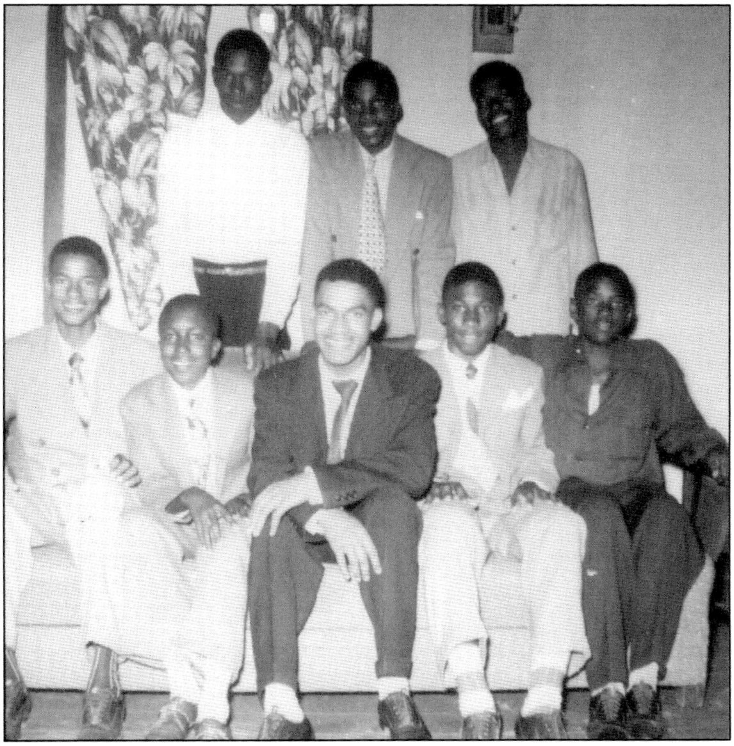

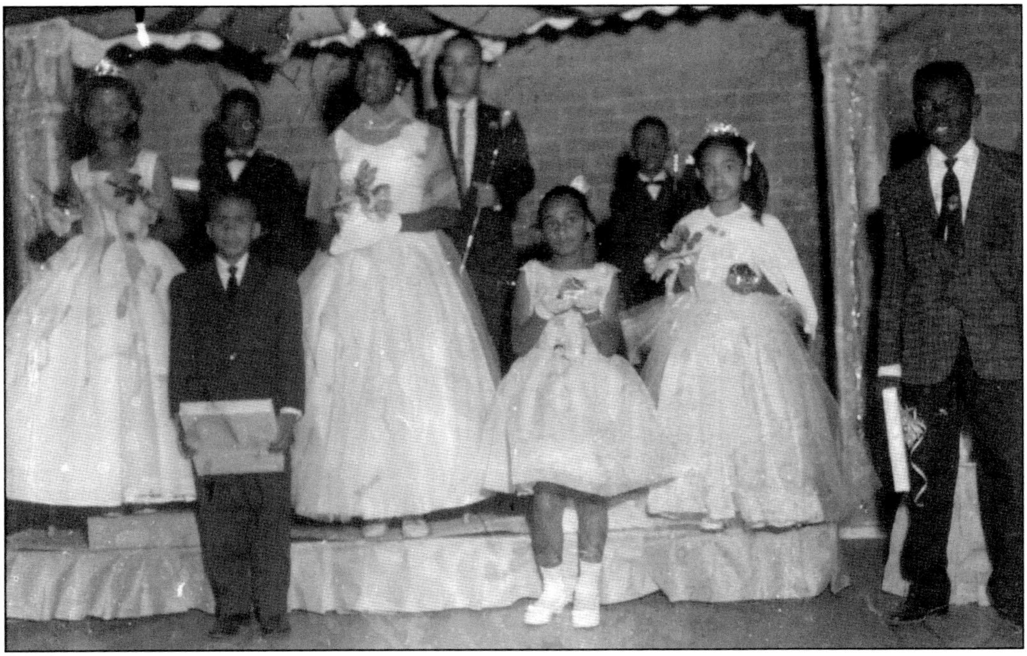

SCHOOL PAGEANT, C. 1950S–1960S. Covington Rosenwald held fundraising competitions that culminated with a pageant. Students, families, and supporting neighbors and organizations raised money for students vying to become "royalty." Kings, queens, princes, and princesses were selected based on the amount of money raised. Community camaraderie and financial support for differing school needs were the outcome. (Courtesy of the Randle collection.)

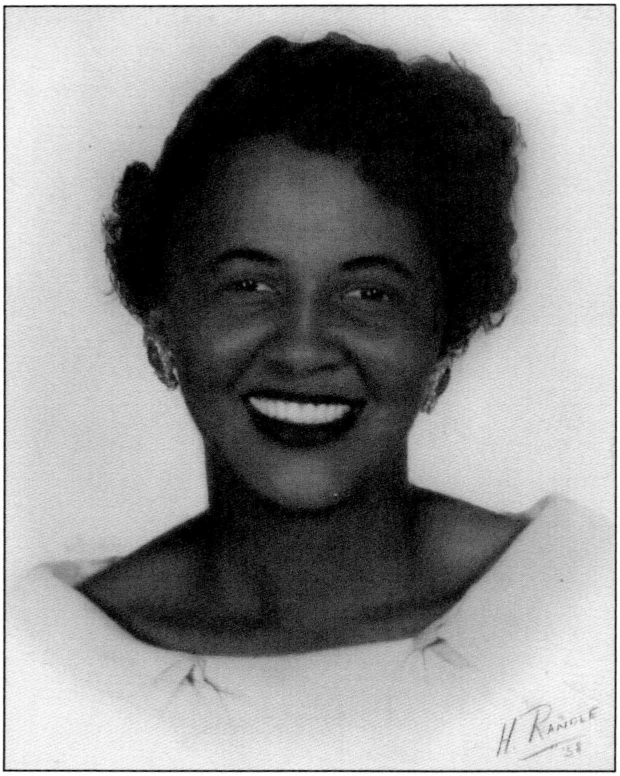

RUBY JOHNSON DIAZ, 1958. Diaz was a teacher when, according to Helen Simon Frick's account of the school, Covington Rosenwald "became a full-fledged High School with Athletics, Band, Home Economics, Industrial Arts, and Sciences," and boasted liberal arts courses as part of the curriculum. An elementary teacher, Diaz also taught at Madisonville and Mandeville schools. (Courtesy of the Randle collection.)

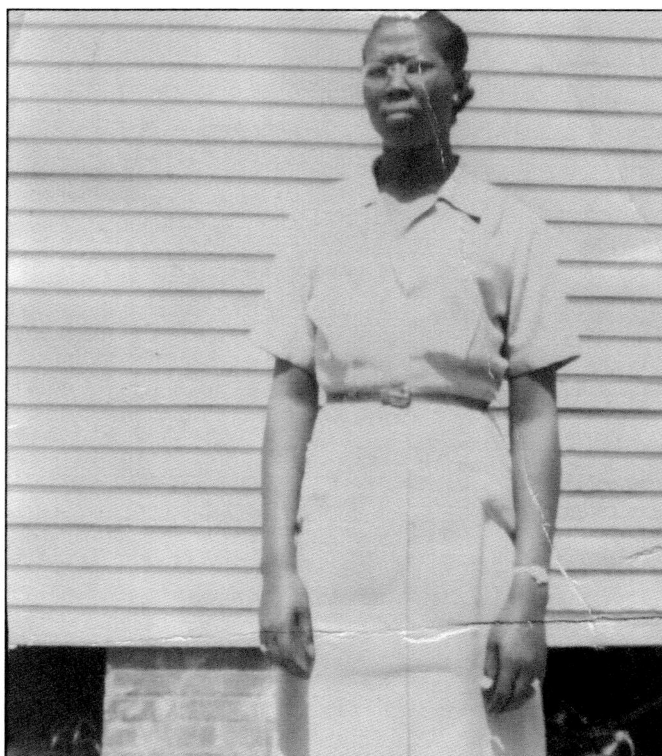

UNIDENTIFIED TEACHER, 1949–1950. A definable line stood between teacher and student. Helen Frick recalled that in 1934 she was physically "smaller than some of [her] third grade students," some of whom inquired of her age. Principal James Harrison's response was, "They don't need to know your age, just that you're the Boss in that room, and if they don't believe it, send them to me." (Courtesy of Matthew Wilson.)

UNIDENTIFIED TEACHER, 1949–1950. Male teachers, except the industrial arts teacher, routinely wore suits to school. Men were held to the same standards of professional dress as women. However, men could anticipate an administrative position, sometimes at the same school where they taught, while women remained in the classroom. (Courtesy of Matthew Wilson.)

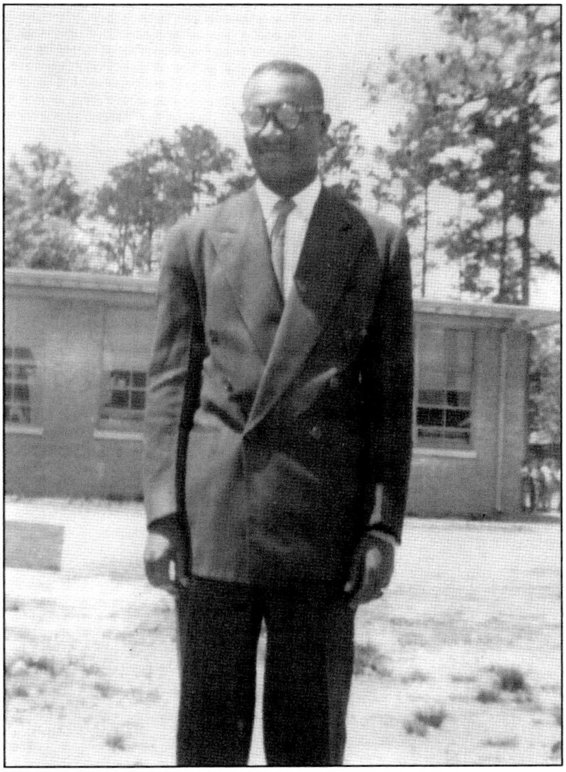

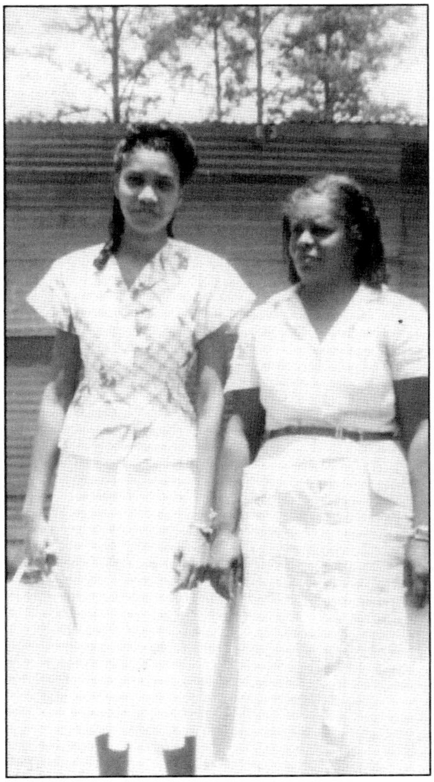

TEACHERS AT ROSENWALD, 1949–1950. Eula Mae Magee (left), home economics teacher, and Melba Cox, elementary teacher, native of Baton Rouge, shared living arrangements. Many teachers were not natives to Covington and therefore rented rooms or entire houses from local residents. This rental market provided additional income to many in the African American community. (Courtesy of Matthew Wilson.)

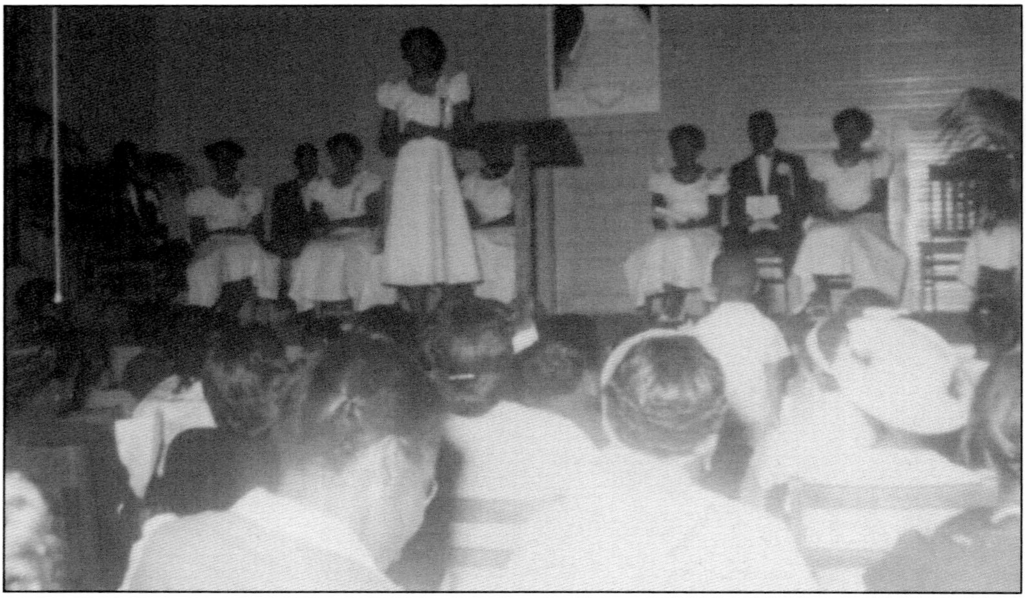

Class Night, May 22, 1950. The song "We Are Americans" opened the first Class Night program. Participants included Lester Dunn, invocation; the spiritual "Listen to the Lambs;" Joyce Henry, class history; Dorothy Laurent, class poem. Dave Diaz, class prophecy; Raymond Williams, class will; Ella Conerly, class grumbler; Almetta Route and Millie Williams, giftorians. Isabella Parker and Annie Clark, the song "The Bells of Avalon." The class song was "This Dear Old School of Ours." (Courtesy of Matthew Wilson.)

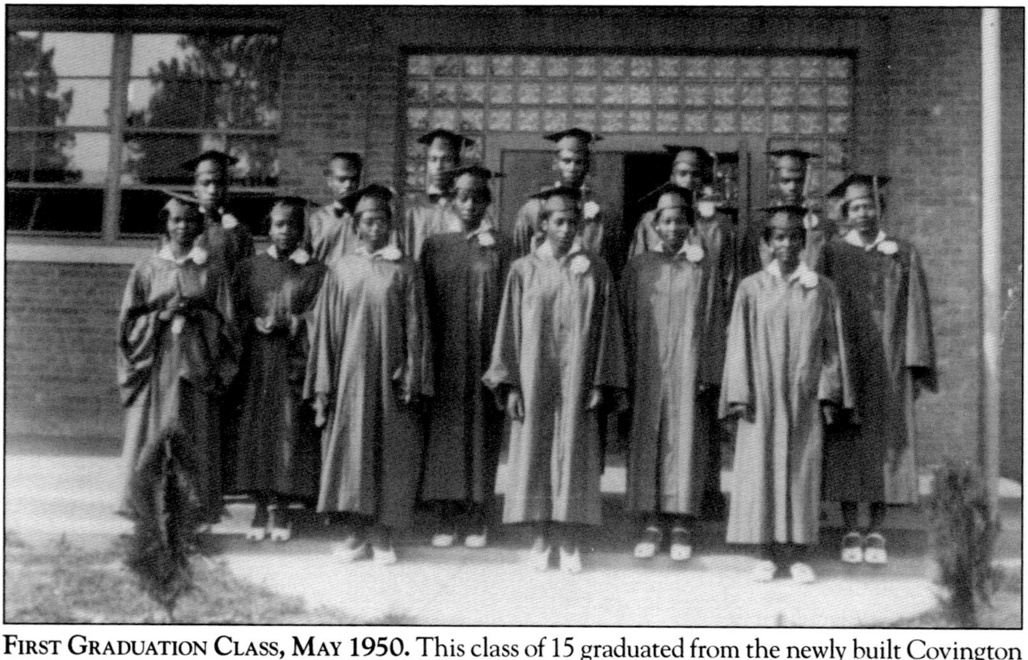

First Graduation Class, May 1950. This class of 15 graduated from the newly built Covington Rosenwald School. Lester Dunn and Delores Conerly received scholarships from Southern University. The remaining members were Dorothy Laurent, Almetta Route, Isabella Tyson, Clarize Bates, Anna Bula Clark, Millie Williams, Herman Williams, Raymond Williams, Wilfred Morgan, Dave Diaz, Theodore Kelly, Freddie Giddens, and Joyce Henry. (Courtesy of Matthew Wilson.)

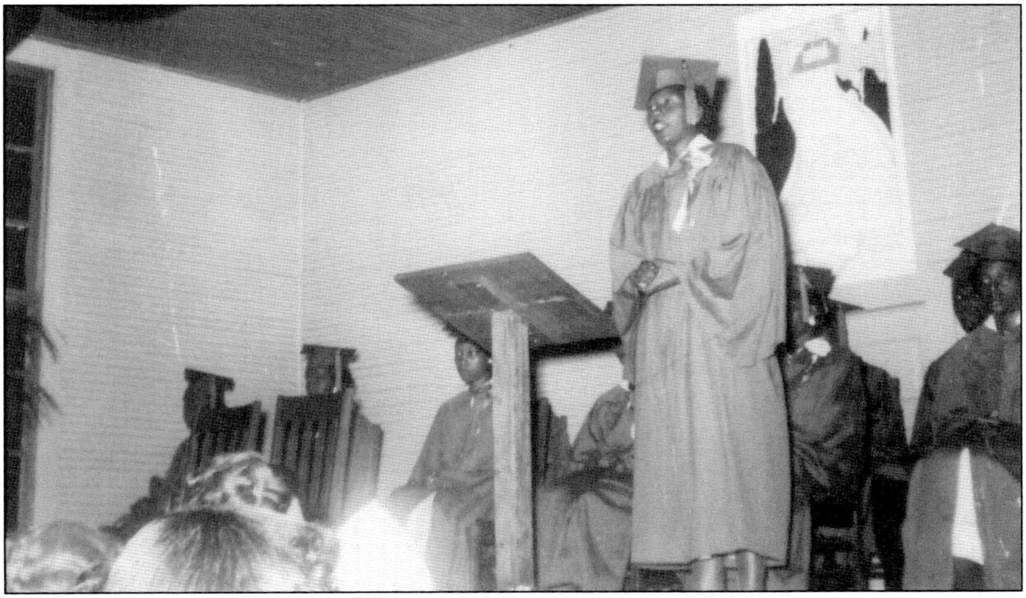

GRADUATION SOLOIST, 1950. The first high school graduation featured a student soloist. The seminal event marked a milestone for the education of Covington's African American children. A number of factors set the foundation for that first commencement: The 1880s classroom of Annie Dumas, the 1919 school of Mr. and Mrs. Thornton and Effie Williams, and the 1927 establishment of the Rosenwald School by Professor James and Lubertha Harrison. (Courtesy of Matthew Wilson.)

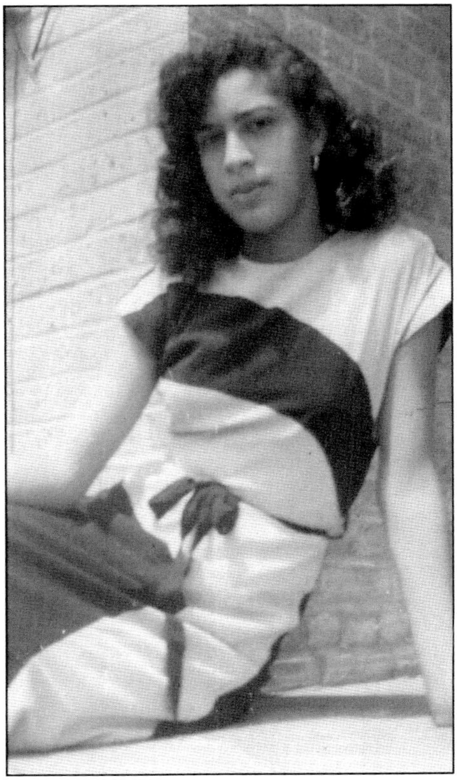

UNIDENTIFIED STUDENT, 1949–1950. Sitting on a low-level contour of the building, this student presents another example of life at Rosenwald High. Although this scene is posed, students relaxed between classes in a variety of ways. Some studied, read for pleasure, socialized with others, or just sat quietly. (Courtesy of Matthew Wilson.)

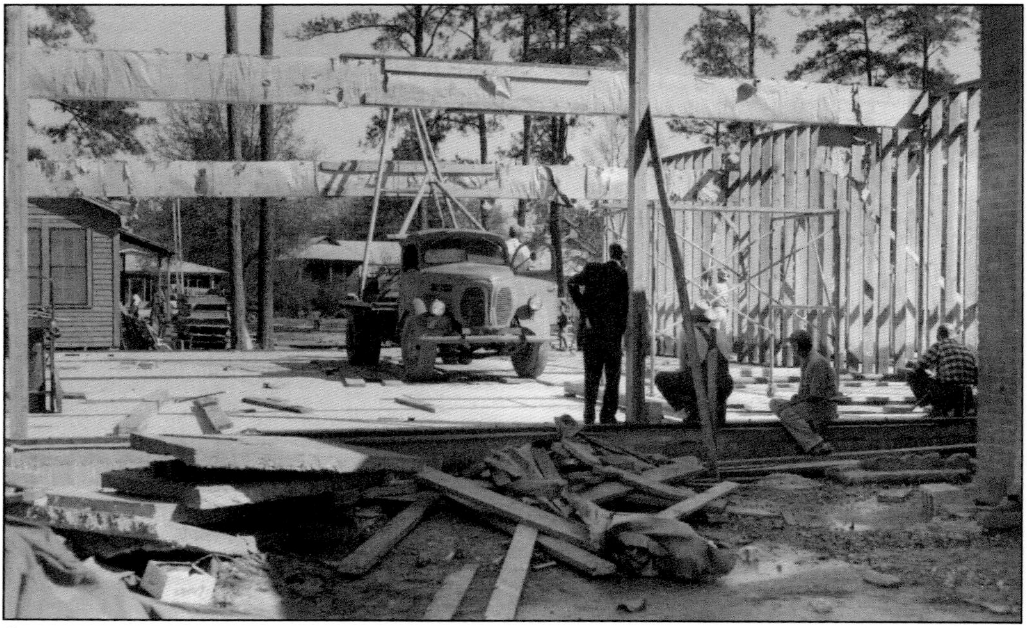

Construction of Covington Rosenwald Lunchroom, 1940s. "Bargain Basement Bill" was the sobriquet given to superintendent William Pitcher because of his success in securing surplus materials and equipment from the federal government following World War II. New schools, lunchrooms, gymnasiums, and other facilities were built. "The best is none too good and no price is too high for education," he wrote. Prof. James Harrison surveys the construction. (Courtesy of the STPSB.)

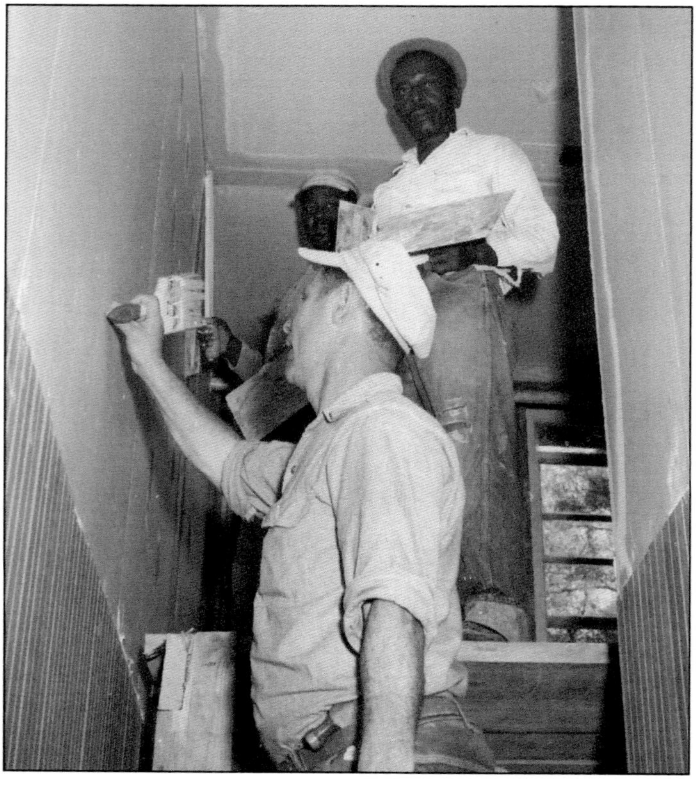

Drywall, Covington Rosenwald Lunchroom, 1940s. Work was finished on the building after a long, arduous practical campaign by superintendent William Pitcher to secure surplus building materials. The parish operated on a "midget budget" while faced with increasing student population. In a national journal, Pitcher advised, "Employ only experienced and capable construction men in your building crew. You will profit from their abilities and knowledge." (Courtesy of STPSB.)

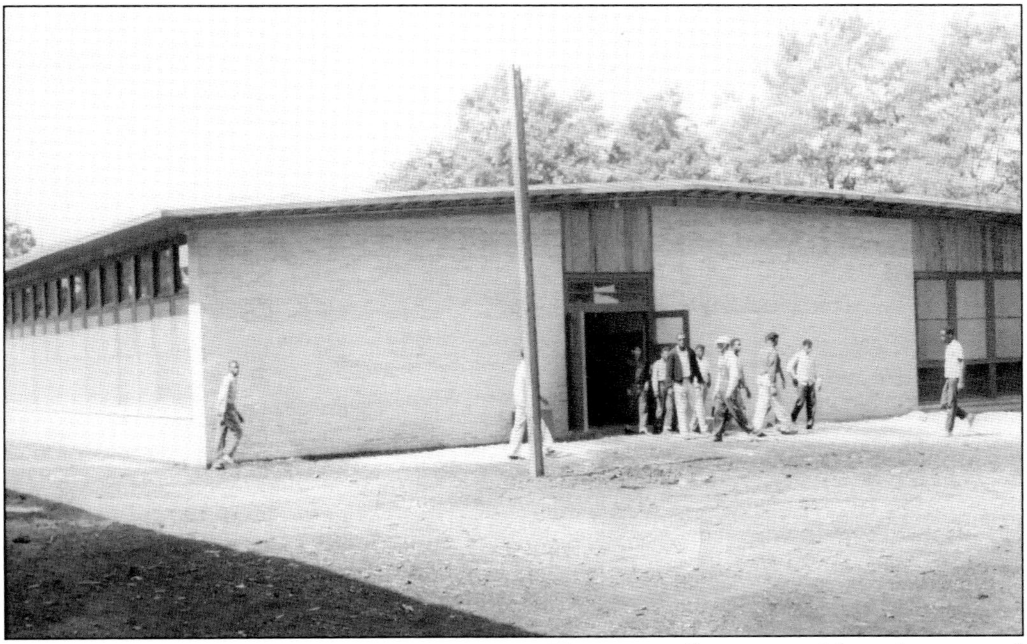

New Rosenwald Lunchroom Completed, 1949. This was an illustration of the utilization and benefits of surplus material. The lunchroom was built at $4.60/square foot at a cost of $5,854 with 95 percent surplus materials. Records show the good investment. Insurance replacement value equaled $26,500. (Courtesy of the STPSB.)

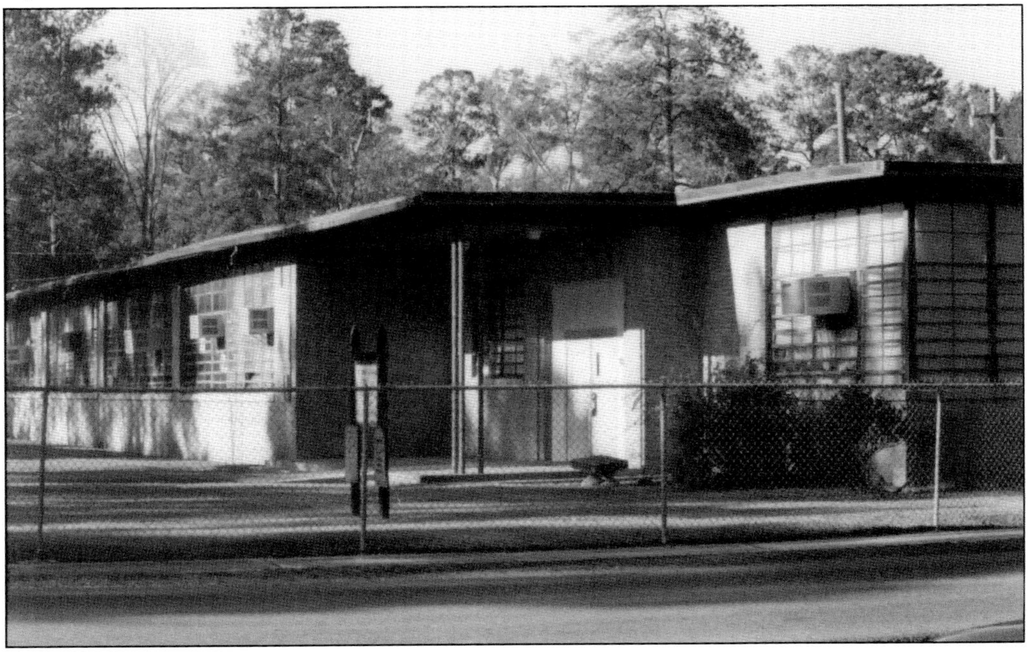

The New Covington Rosenwald, 1949. The new building, completed in November 1949, modernized facilities and eliminated both the lunchroom housed in an old train's dining car and the need for space in the Love & Charity Hall, which held first- and second-grade classes. It added classrooms for upper level grades. The four-room Rosenwald School with its potbelly stove remained as classrooms for third, fourth, fifth, and sixth grades. (Courtesy of the STPSB.)

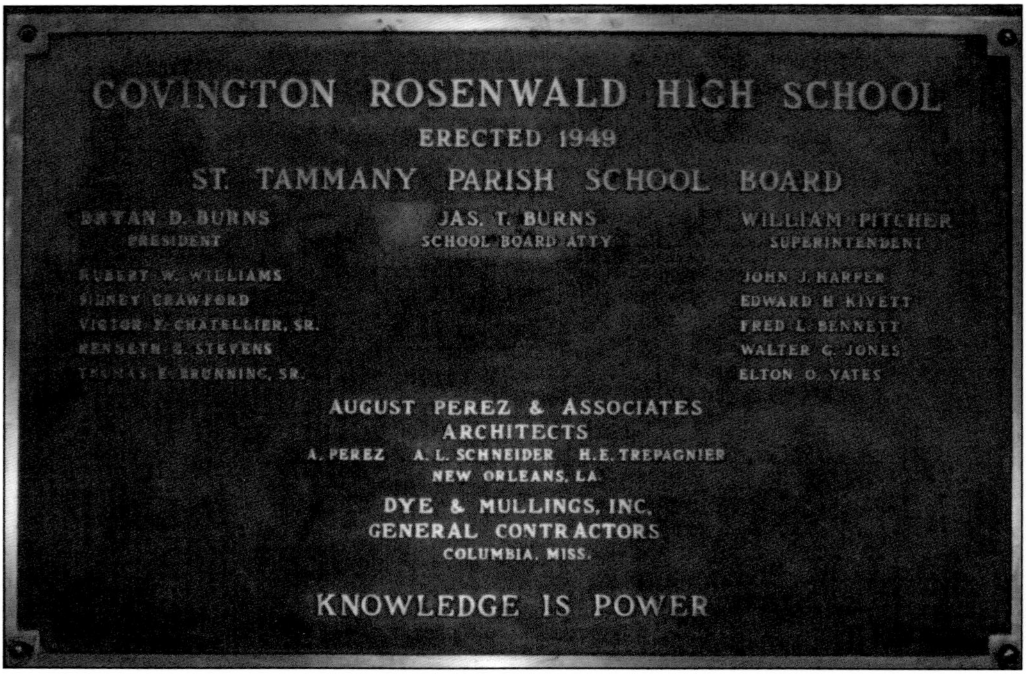

COVINGTON ROSENWALD SCHOOL, 1949. Nathaniel Johnson remembered lunchroom workers Laura and Ethel Webb, Artemese Briggs, Orelia Silvan, Nathalie Route, and Christine Harper; Alphonse Fabre's shop; the auditorium/gymnasium; Lubertha Harrison's music room; and "many enjoyable evenings of entertainment" including athletic events, plays, and musicals supported by the community. Helen Frick said, "Covington Rosenwald [is] the main contributing factor in the education of blacks of this area." (Courtesy of the STPSB.)

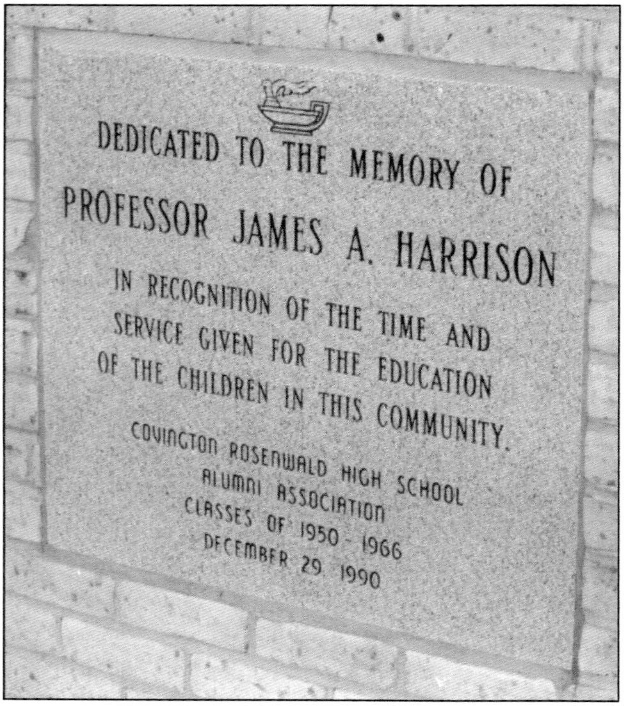

JAMES A. HARRISON MEMORIAL CORNERSTONE, 1990. An account notes that Harrison's first pay was in scrip, an IOU that was honored by some businesses. His authoritative leadership rested on reinforcing a sense of worth in students. "Punishment had to be redemptive; unruly children were . . . put to work to enforce the idea of the opportunity to gain an education as well as the value of self-reliance" and responsibility to others. (Courtesy of STPSB.)

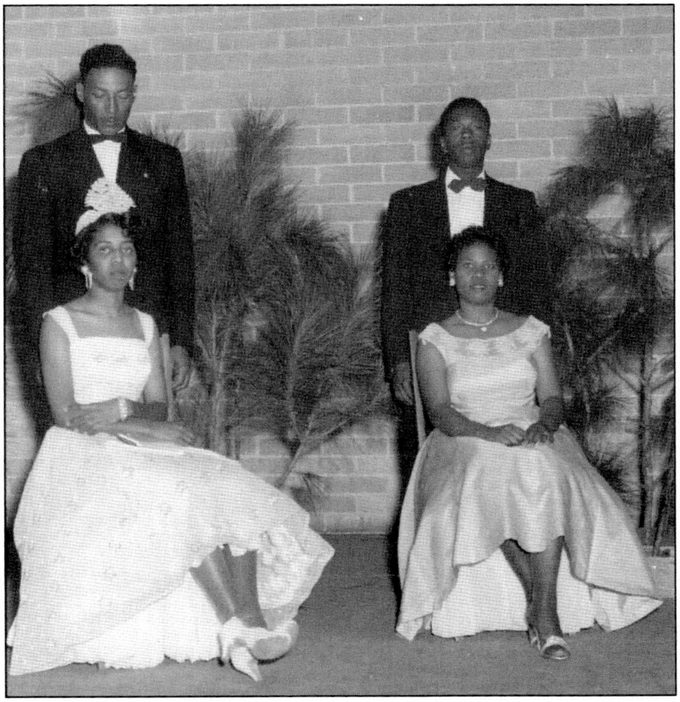

Queen and Runner-Up, c. 1950s. In a fundraiser to support Covington Rosenwald, Ms. Green (left), with an unidentified escort, placed first, and Marion Vaughn (right), escorted by Gilbert James, placed second. According to Vaughn, competitions among adults raised money for the PTA, band, school programs, and other school needs. The person raising the largest amount of money served as queen. (Courtesy of the Randle collection.)

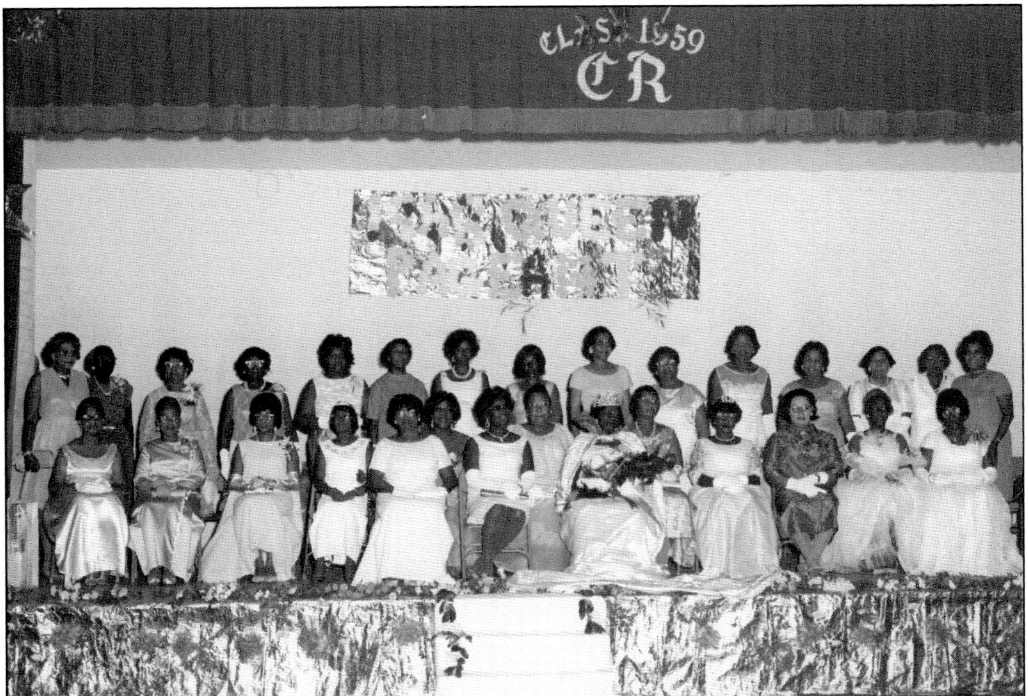

Women's Social Event, c. 1960s. The auditorium at Covington Rosenwald served as the venue for many community events. Several social and civic organizations held their annual formals at the school. According to former members, preparations were months in the planning, and decorations and catering were homemade collaborations. (Courtesy of Randle collection.)

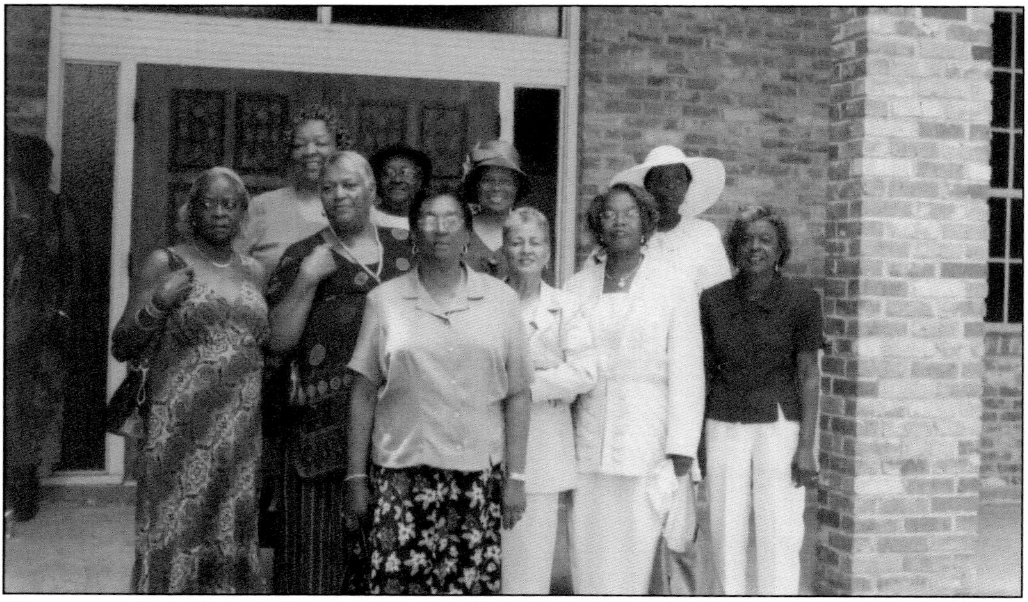

Covington Rosenwald Class of 1955. This reunion included, from left to right, (first row) Barbara Jean Strong, Margie Washington Williams, Rutha Mae Alexander, Eula Lange, Hattie Williams, and Shirley Weaver; (second row) Wanda Lee Frick, Inez Gray, Lucille Sheridan Moore, and Leola Brown Brumfield. Not pictured is Mack Williams. The valedictorian of the 27-member class was Alberta Delores Johnson. Doughty Chapel AME hosted the reunion for worship services. (Courtesy of Lucille Moore.)

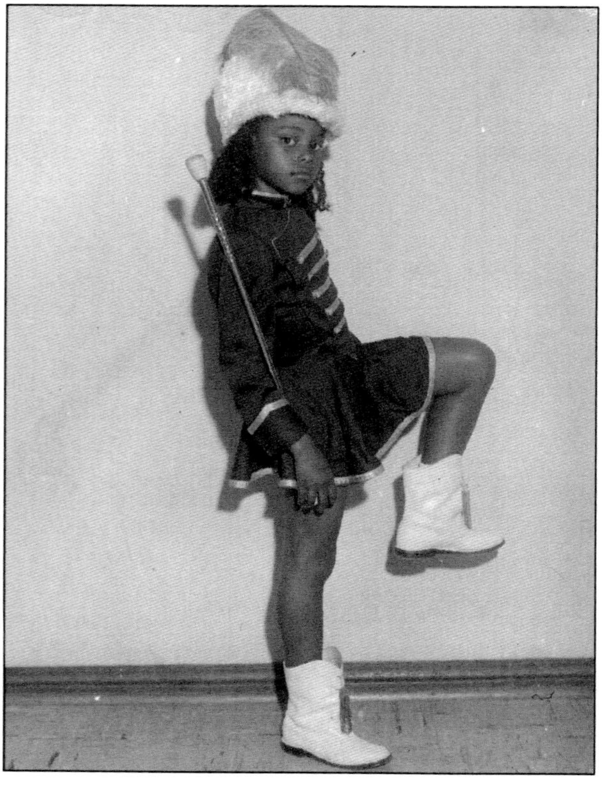

Barbara Randle, c. late 1950s. The elementary school majorette at Rosenwald became homecoming queen in ninth grade, 1962–1963. Her sister Nathelda was an outstanding basketball player, track participant, and band member. Her parents, Henry and Grace Randle, were actively involved in many facets of the community. (Courtesy of the Randle collection.)

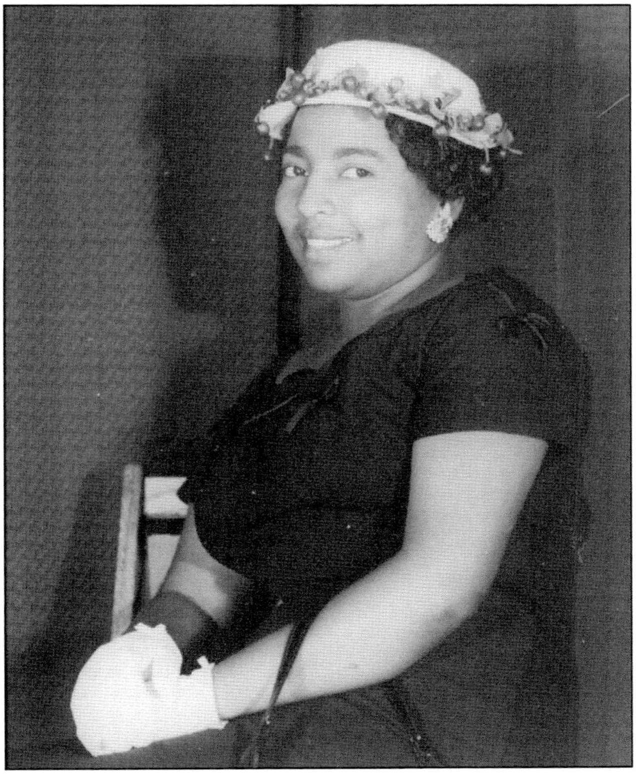

CARRIE OWENS, C. 1960S. A native of Baldwin, Louisiana, Carrie Grace Smith Owens taught from 1951 to 1988. She also served as assistant principal. The Carrie S. Owens Memorial Library stands as a tribute to her work in schools. Additionally, Owens was active with the Department of Housing and Urban Development. The Carrie Owens Village is named in honor of her work. (Courtesy of the Randle collection.)

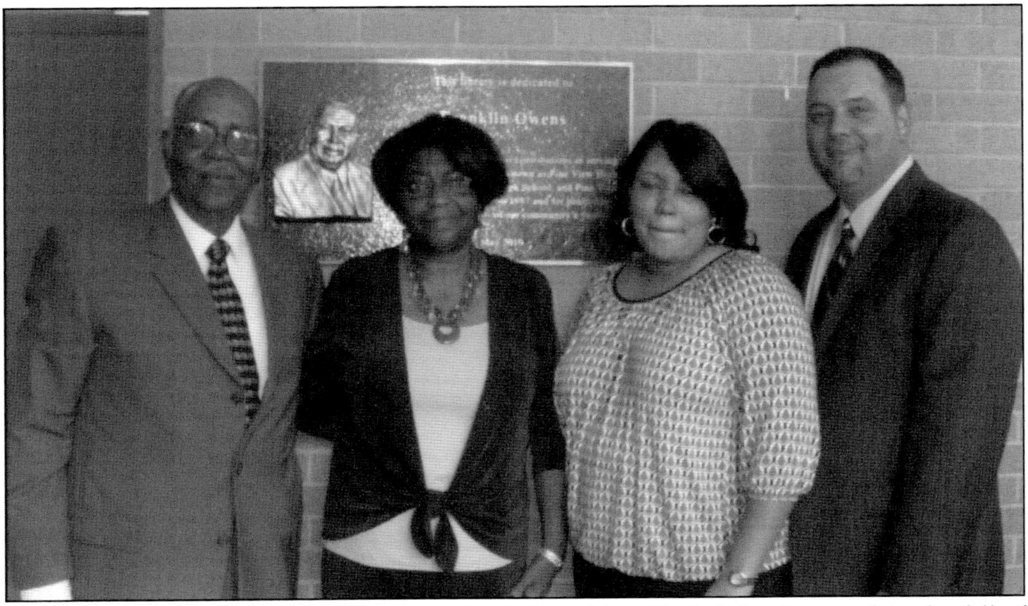

FRANKLIN OWENS LIBRARY DEDICATION, 2010. Pine View High School opened in the fall of 1966, following the closure of Rosenwald. Franklin Owens became principal. The school lasted two years; integration closed it as a high school. The school board addressed integration by segregating students in middle school by gender, and Owens was named principal of Pine View Middle. He was a graduate of Oberlin High School in Oberlin, Ohio, and Southern University in Baton Rouge. (Courtesy of the STPSB.)

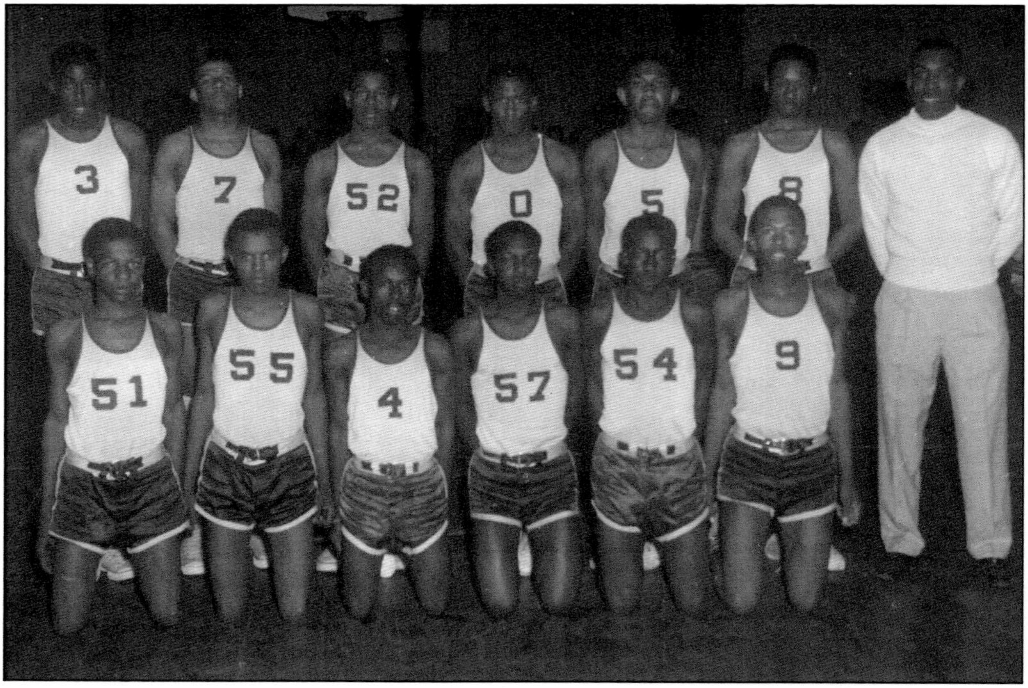

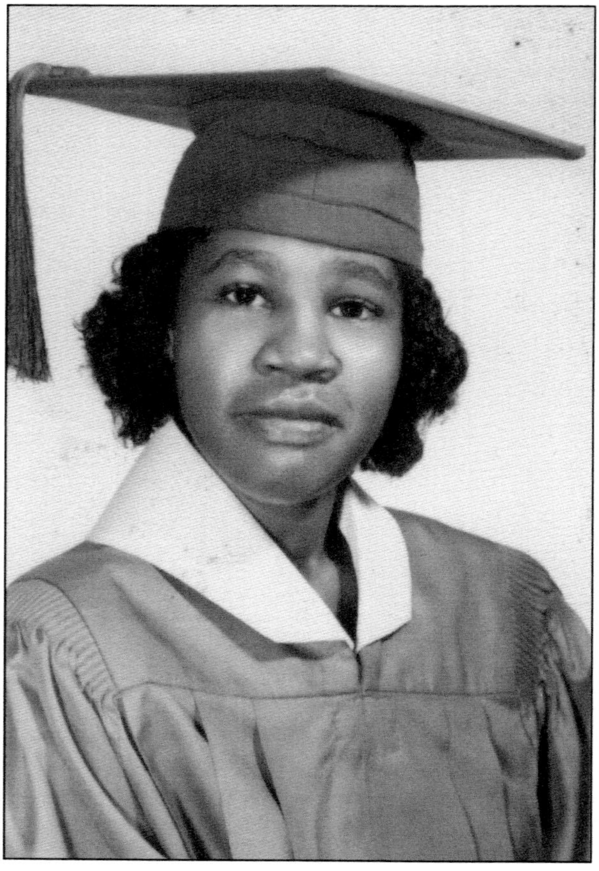

ROSENWALD BASKETBALL TEAM, c. 1950s–1960s. Coach Aaron Thompson stands with his winning basketball team at Covington Rosenwald. The coach's role as a firm teacher with a guiding hand made a mark on his athletes. Among those identified are Herman James (No. 9), Cass McCasskill (No. 7), and Lee Clark (No. 4). (Courtesy of the Randle collection.)

JUNE LEE PICHON, c. 1960s. Pichon graduated from Covington Rosenwald sometime between 1960 and 1966. She was a majorette and a basketball player. She is representative of many graduates who did not attend college or the military. She studied nursing, became a nurse's aide, and spent her career at St. Tammany Hospital in Covington. (Courtesy of Elizabeth Steele.)

Miss Covington Rosenwald High School, 1963–1964. Bonnie Lee James reigned over the homecoming events. The parade wound from the school, through downtown, and up Columbia Street to the Holy Family football field, where the court was presented. The formal homecoming ball was held the same evening. James is the youngest daughter of Ivery and Jessie R. James. (Courtesy of Jessie R. James.)

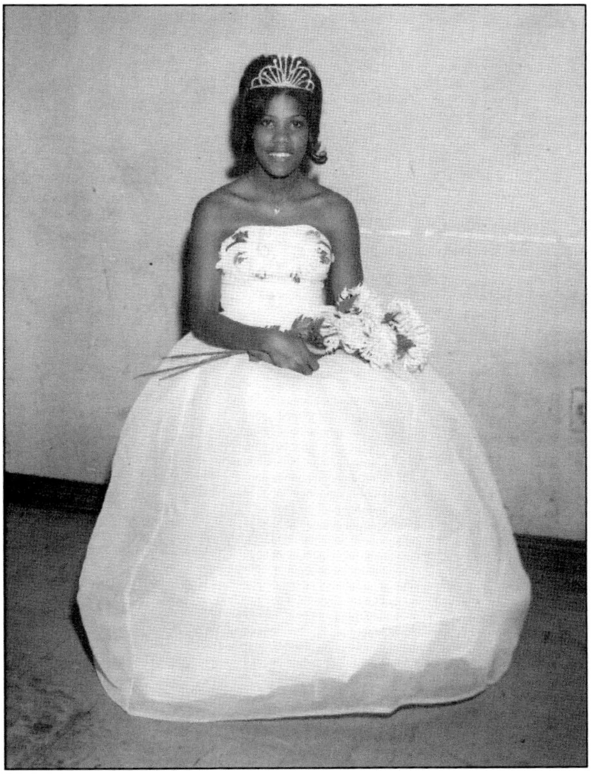

Grace Randle in the Middle. In all of her finery, the "queen of hearts" waits for direction from her sponsor. The school facilities turned out to be a community center, with both school and social groups holding their activities there. Grace Randle (center) played an important role in all of those functions. The other two women are unidentified. (Courtesy of the Randle collection.)

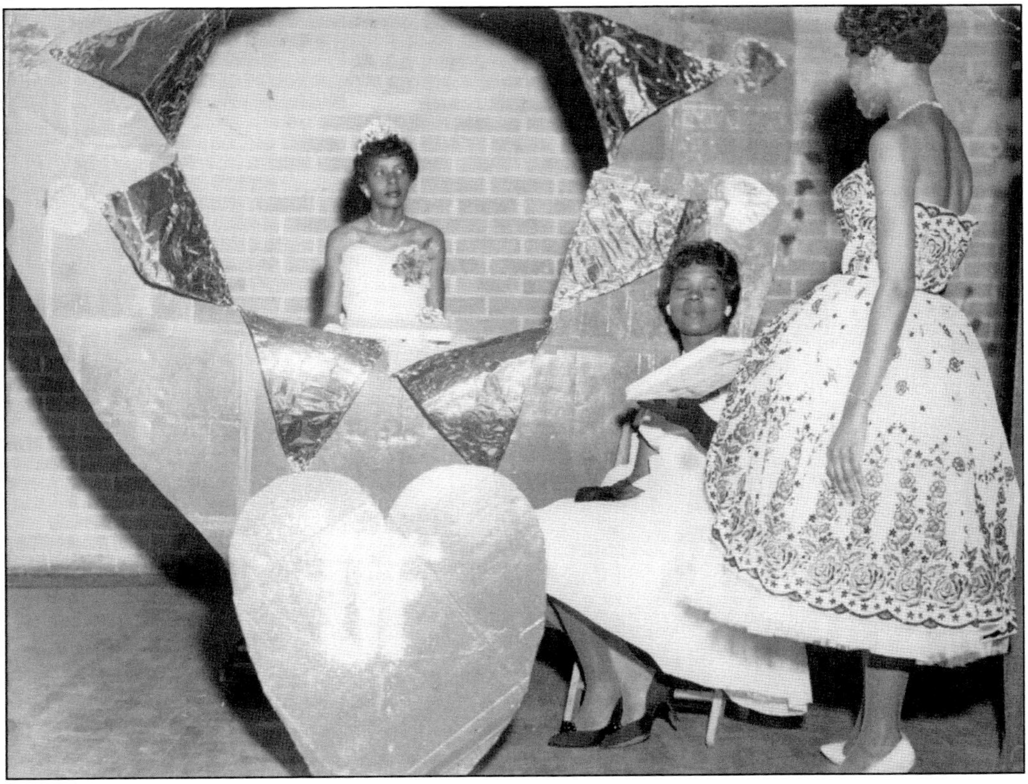

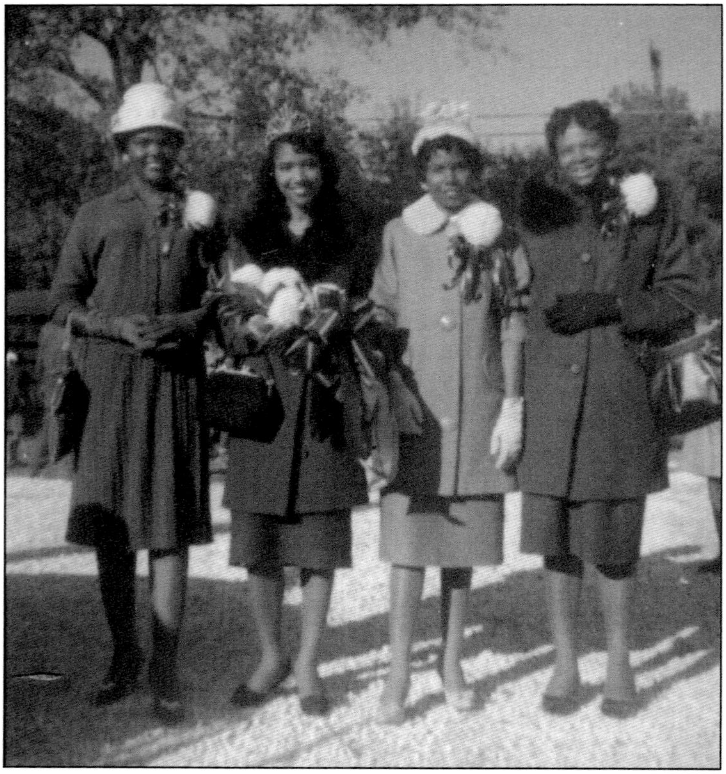

COVINGTON ROSENWALD HOMECOMING COURT, 1960. Members of the high school homecoming court were, from left to right, Joann Williams, queen Carolyn Frick, Lena Royal, and Diane Ducre. Students voted for the queen, who presided over a parade, the football game (where the presentation took place), and a formal ball in the evening. (Courtesy of Ida Thomas James.)

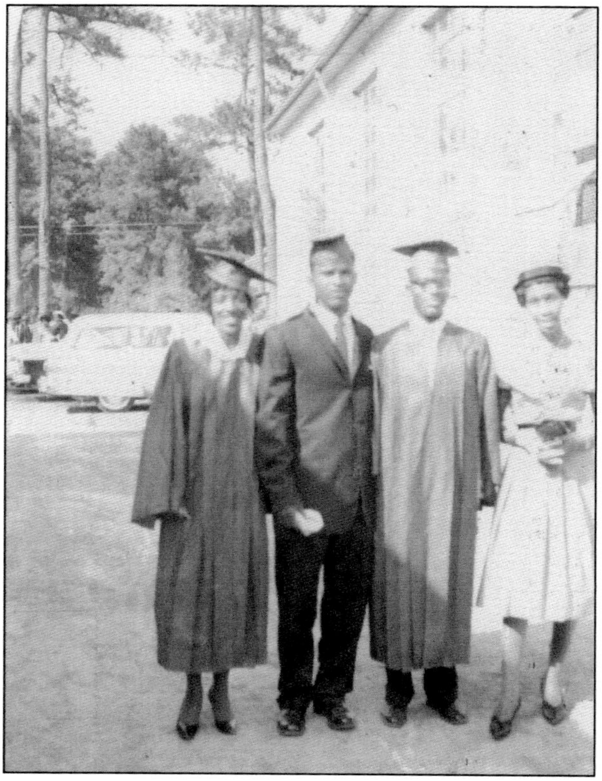

COVINGTON ROSENWALD GRADUATES, 1960. As the school entered its fifth decade and observed its tenth year as a high school, families gathered for commencement exercises. Posing for one last photograph near the gymnasium are, from left to right, Dorothy Weaver, Adrian Perkins, Jessie Garrett, and Ora Washington. (Courtesy of Ida Thomas James.)

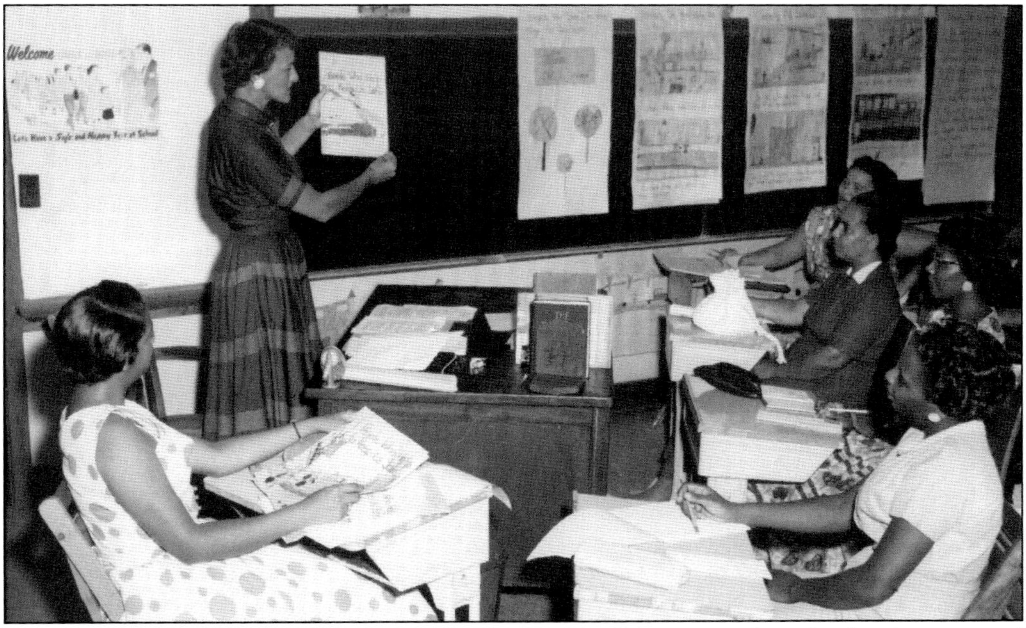

TEACHER IN-SERVICE, C. 1960S. Continuing education workshops contributed to development and implementation of current pedagogy and teaching methods. St. Tammany Parish School Board dedicated teacher in-service days for the workshops. A supervisor over curriculum conducted sessions separated by subject matter, including general sessions for all teachers. (Courtesy of the St. Tammany Parish School Board.)

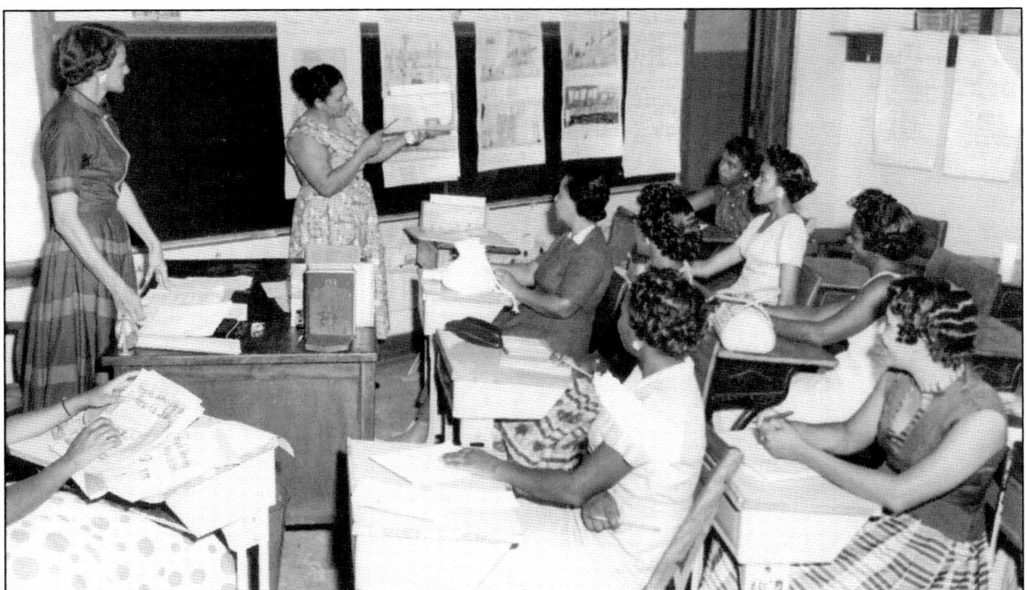

RAPT ATTENTION, C. 1960S. A second view of the continuing education workshops shows participation by teachers. Sharing and demonstrating their ideas and practices, teachers enhanced their classroom performance and sought progressive outcomes by their students. Prior to 1969, in-service days were segregated, although reportedly there were no African Americans in supervisory or administrative positions beyond local schools. (Courtesy of the St. Tammany Parish School Board.)

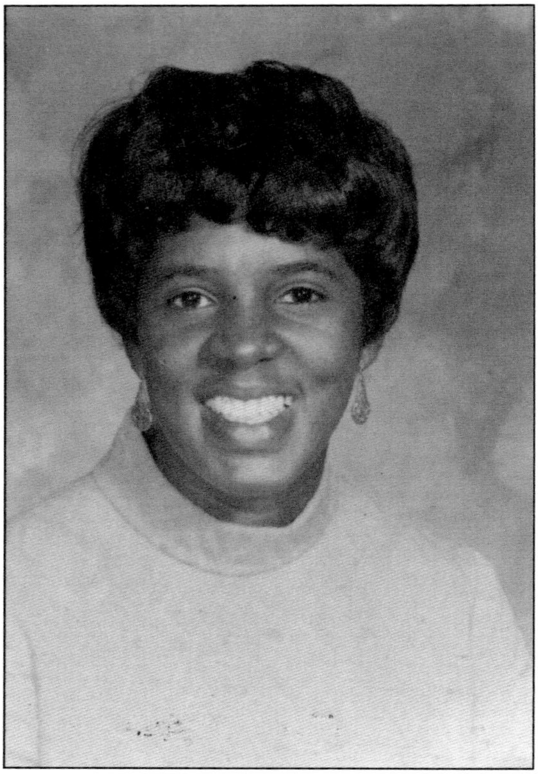

Elizabeth Steele, 1963. Covington Rosenwald graduate (1957) Elizabeth Steele earned her teaching degree in 1963 from Southern University. She landed her first job at St. Tammany High School in Slidell, returning to and spending her career in Covington. During the integration transition, she taught at the formerly all-white Lyon Elementary. According to her report, first through third grades progressed very well. (Courtesy of Elizabeth Steele.)

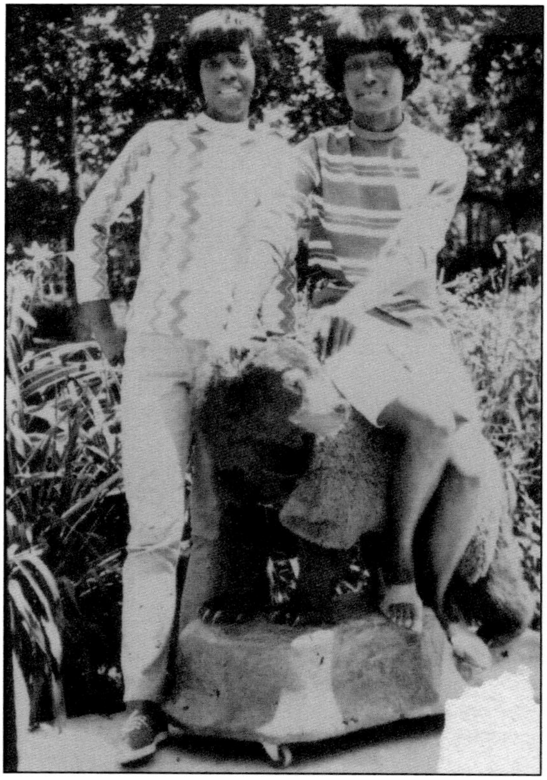

Ida Thomas James and Janice Smith, 1966. First-year teachers took their students on a field trip to the Audubon Zoo. Ida, a Covington native, and Janice, Slidell native, planned the trip as a learning experience and outing for the children, although field trips were allowed only on weekends. Most of their African American students had not gone beyond their communities. Parental support aided such adventures. (Courtesy of Ida Thomas James.)

Ruby Conerly, c. 1960s. Alphonse Fabre was principal of Rosenwald when Ruby Conerly began teaching second grade. Conerly spent 12 years at Rosenwald and recalls strong parental support and the many programs that kept the community involved. The May Day activity and fundraisers named a king and queen, and recognized community work to benefit the school. (Courtesy of Ruby Conerly.)

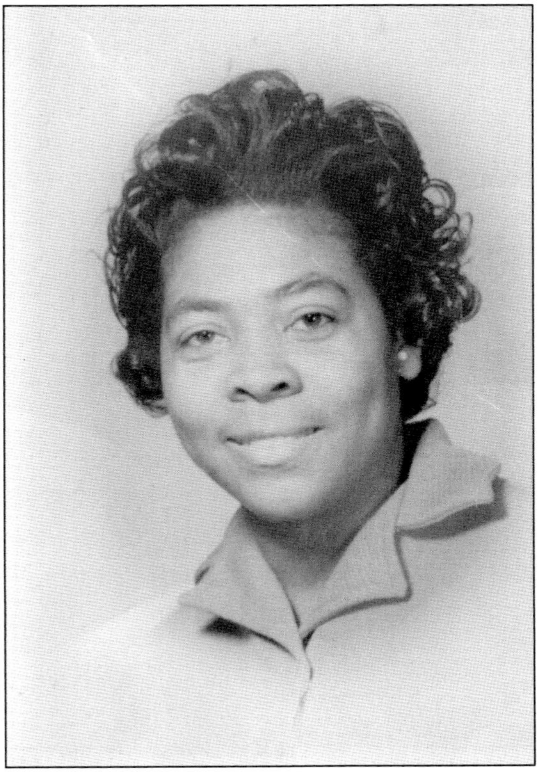

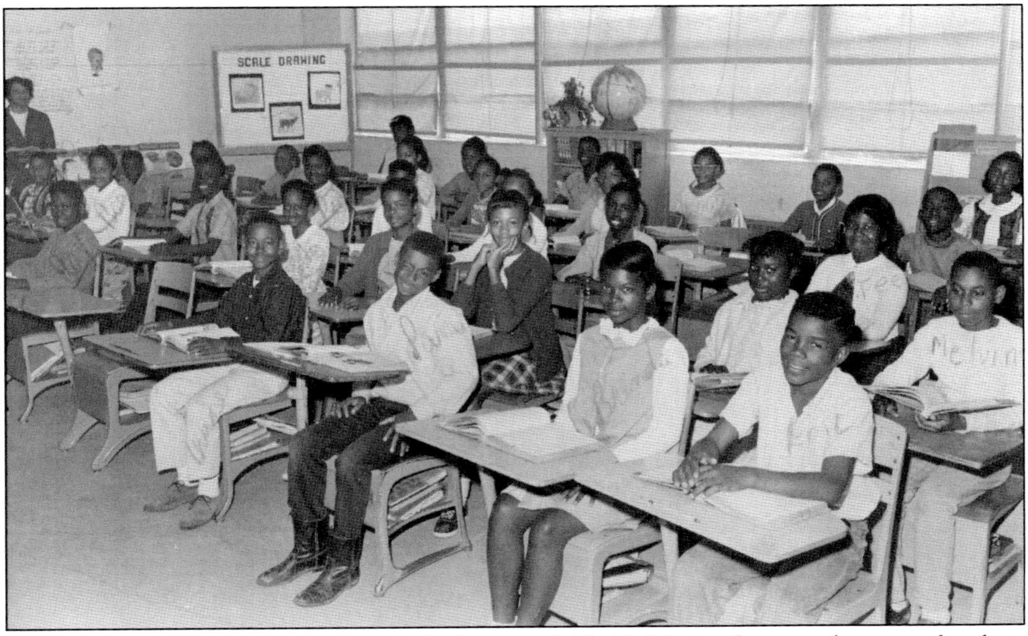

Bernice Anniston's Sixth-Grade A Class, 1965–1966. As these students sat for their annual portrait, Pine View High School neared completion just a few blocks away. The children would spend two additional years at Covington Rosenwald because it continued with grades one through eight. That status lasted only three years before integration eliminated separate schools. (Courtesy of Ruby Conerly.)

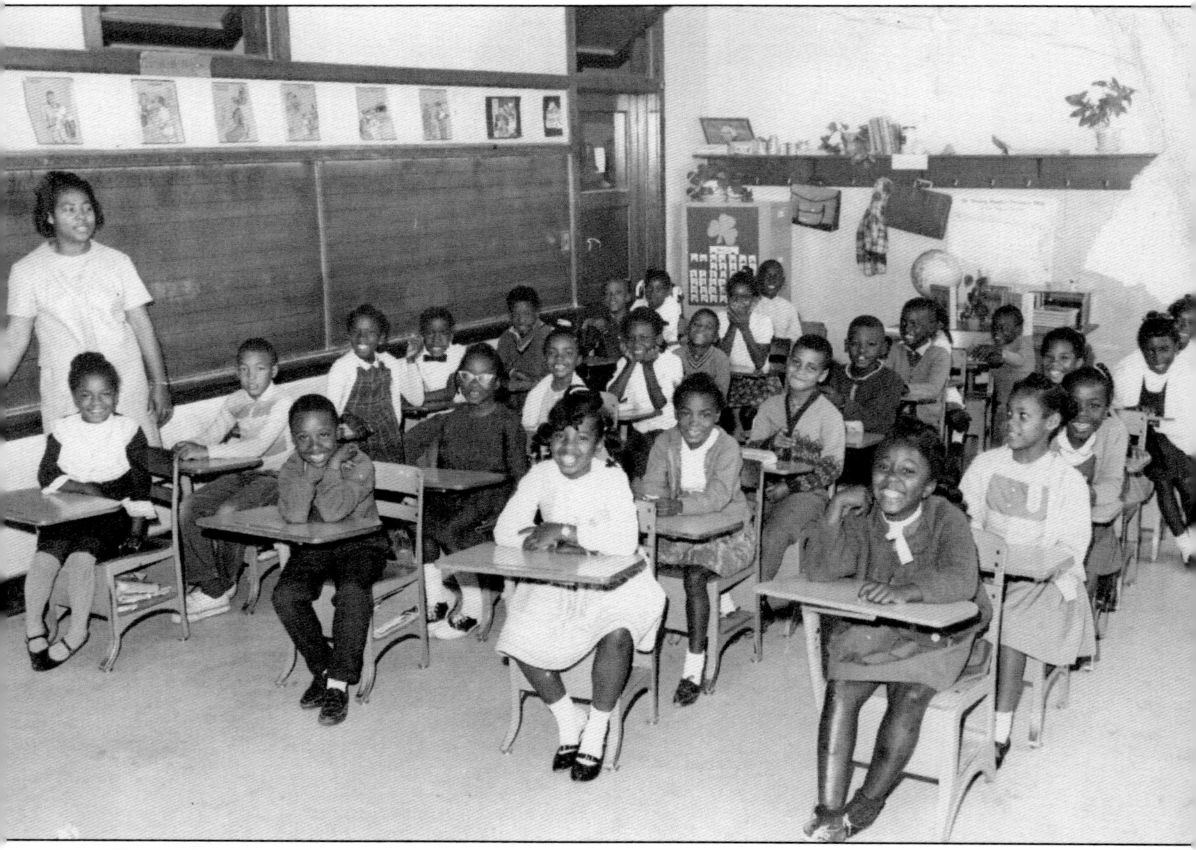

Ruby Conerly's Second-Grade Class, 1965–1966. A burgeoning student population and combination of smaller schools with Covington Rosenwald caused the school board to build a new high school, Pine View High School, just a few blocks away, separated from Covington Rosenwald's grades one through eight. (Courtesy of Ruby Conerly.)

Five

Holy Family Church and School

There were few African American Catholics in Covington between 1911 and 1939. Fr. Canisius Bluemel wrote in 1939 that he was "filled with the desire to keep and assist souls . . . souls for which Christ died on the Cross." Fr. Abbot Columban asked the Most Reverend Joseph F. Rummel, archbishop, to assign Father Canisius "to work up the nucleus of the colored at Covington." The archbishop agreed, and Holy Family Church and School were founded.

The first Mass was attended by 50 people and was held at the Love & Charity Hall, built by the African American benevolent society in 1938. Classes at an associated school began in September 1941 with two sisters from St. Scholastica (Covington) teaching Catholic and non-Catholic students. In 1943, Mother Elizabeth of the Sisters of the Holy Family (New Orleans) accepted an invitation to take over the school. Principal Emerentia and two sisters, Bonaventure and Theodosia, enrolled 58 children.

The school sat on low-lying property with poor drainage, which caused the sisters to become ill. Additionally, Mother Elizabeth reprimanded Father Canisius because the sisters performed all the janitorial work. "These sisters," she wrote, "have a full schedule of teaching and of their spiritual work at home, and I feel sure that your gift of management will save them that work." She threatened withdrawal of teachers if conditions did not improve. Help came with a new school built in 1947, aided by donations from both the abbot, the archbishop, and an anonymous donor. Two new arrivals joined the staff: Sisters Maris Stella and Joseph Angela.

At the 1948 dedication, the archdiocesan superintendent of schools, Msgr. Henry Bezou, observed, "It is the last word in school architecture, and one of which any parish would be proud." One high school student graduated in 1951, and high school enrollment increased. However, after the archdiocese ordered the end of segregation in 1964, the high school closed, leaving 110 children in the elementary grades. Holy Family could not sustain itself and closed entirely in May 1967. This ended a culture of school plays, an annual king and queen pageant, a basketball team, and, as sisters recalled, "very supportive parents." Catholics in Covington now had one church, St. Peter, and two historically white schools. African-American Catholics became an anomaly.

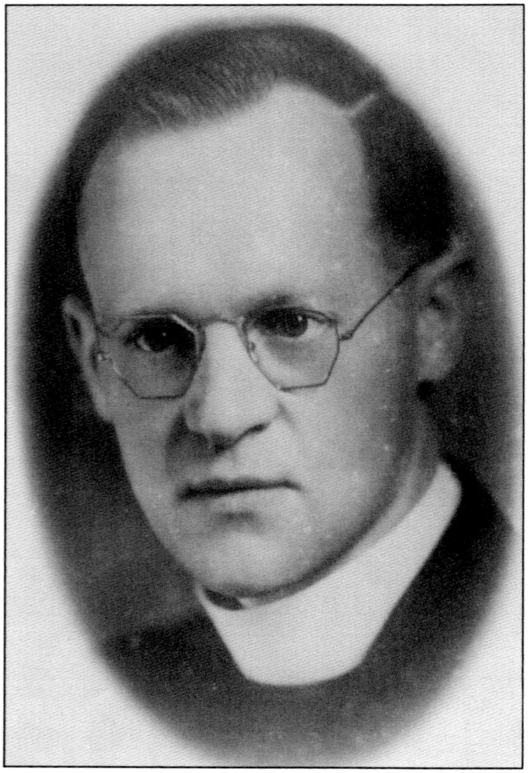

Fr. Canisius Bluemel, 1937. Holy Family budded in Father Canisius's spiritual desire to work among African Americans in Covington. He was born in Munich, Germany, in 1897, and immigrated to the United States in 1924. He arrived at St. Joseph's Abbey in 1926, made his solemn profession in Minnesota in 1929, returned to Louisiana in 1933, and founded Holy Family in 1939. He died on Christmas Eve 1976. The parish's namesake was the Sisters of the Holy Family. (Courtesy of St. Joseph's Abbey.)

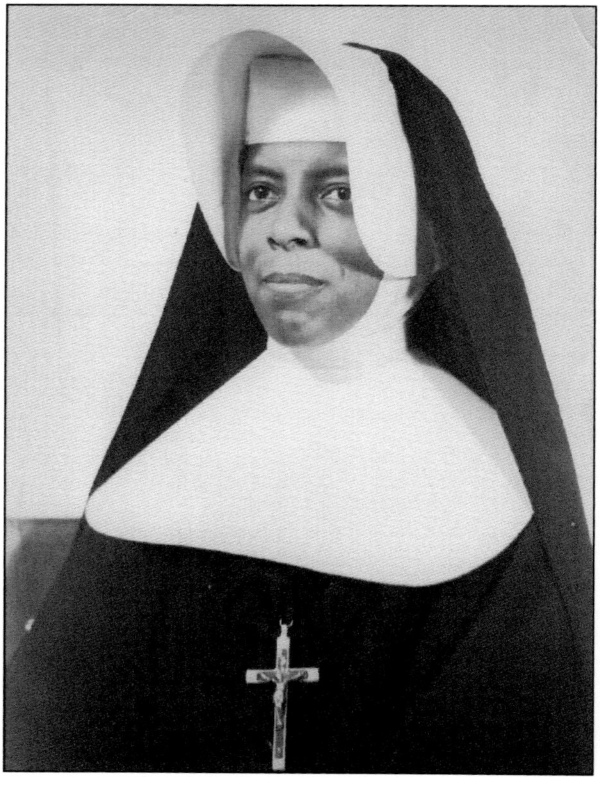

Sister Mary Joseph Angela (Parker), 1960. Beginning her tenure with the 1945 school session, Sister Mary Joseph Angela arrived in the early days. The school was small, but enrollment grew. She is a native of Washington, Louisiana, moved at three years old to New Orleans with her family, and graduated with a degree in education from Xavier University in New Orleans and Catholic University in Washington, DC. (Courtesy of Randle collection.)

Ida Ruth Thomas, Fifth Grade, 1955. Many non-Catholic students, including Ida and her brother Joseph, attended Holy Family. Surviving sisters recall Darryl Smothers, whose grandparents brought him daily. Marion Vaughn remembered her mother taking her and having breakfast with the sisters and watching them wash their clothes. "There was a lot of good teaching at Holy Family," Ida James recalled. (Courtesy of Ida Thomas James.)

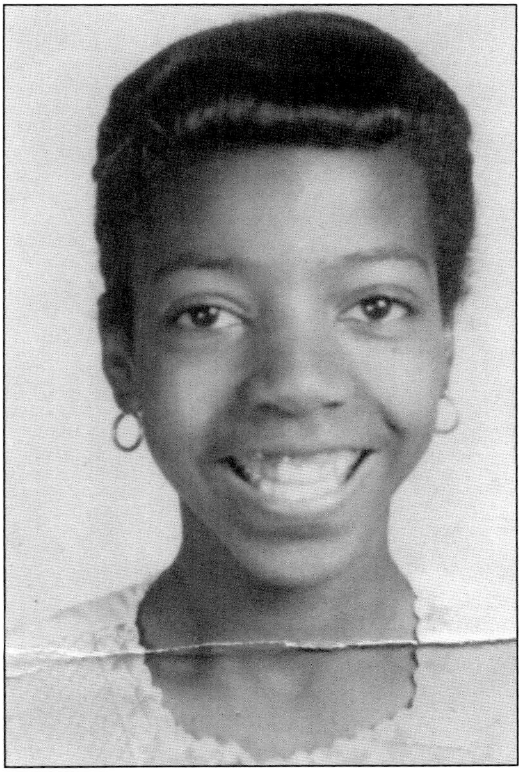

Holy Family Diploma, 1949. Joseph L. Thomas completed grammar school and transferred to Covington Rosenwald where he earned his high school diploma in 1953. At 17 years old, he joined the Navy with his parents' permission. Volunteers in the military needed to be 18 years old to enlist as adults. (Courtesy of Ida Thomas James.)

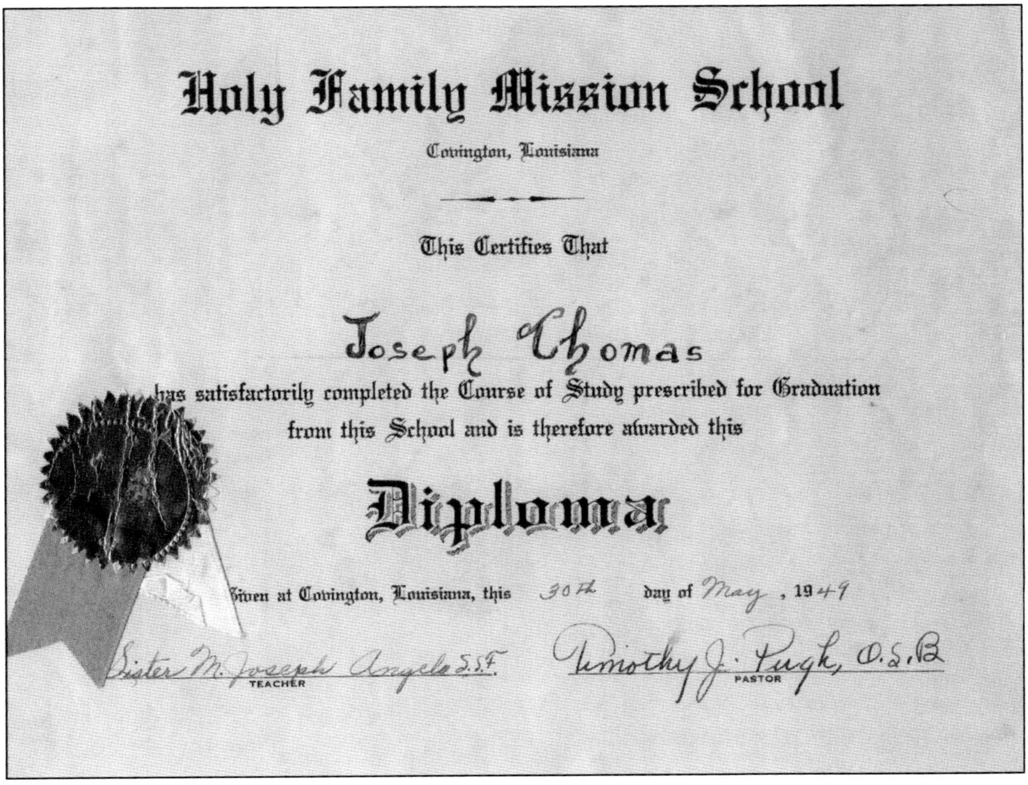

Holy Family Mission School

Covington, Louisiana

This Certifies That

Joseph Thomas

has satisfactorily completed the Course of Study prescribed for Graduation from this School and is therefore awarded this

Diploma

Given at Covington, Louisiana, this 30th day of May, 1949

Sister M. Joseph Angela S.S.F.
TEACHER

Timothy J. Pugh, O.S.B.
PASTOR

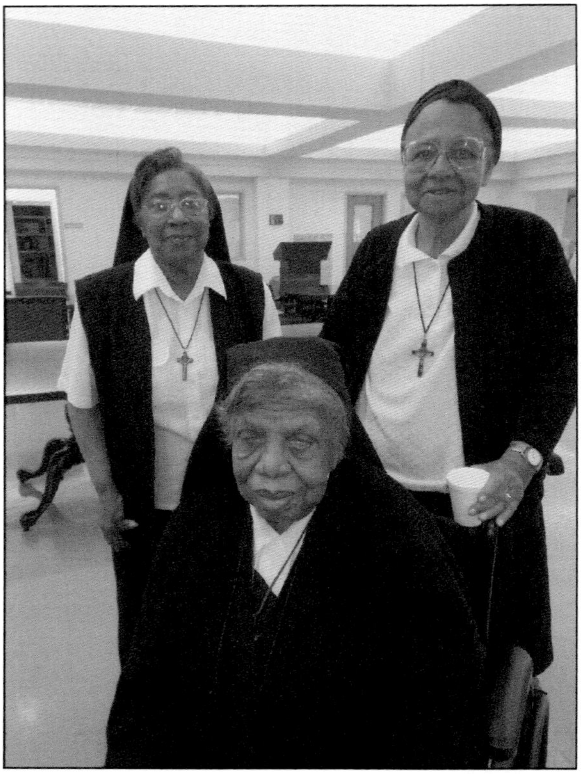

SISTERS OF THE HOLY FAMILY, 2013. Only Sister Joseph Angela (seated), 91 years old, taught during Father Canisius's pastorate. Fr. Maur Roberia served during the 1960s. Sister Josephine Francisco (left), 78, a native of Marksville, Louisiana, attended Xavier University. Sister Philomena Malveaux, 79, native of Plaisance, Louisiana, has a degree from Mount St. Joseph University in Ohio and a masters from Duquesne University of the Holy Spirit. (Photograph by Eva Baham.)

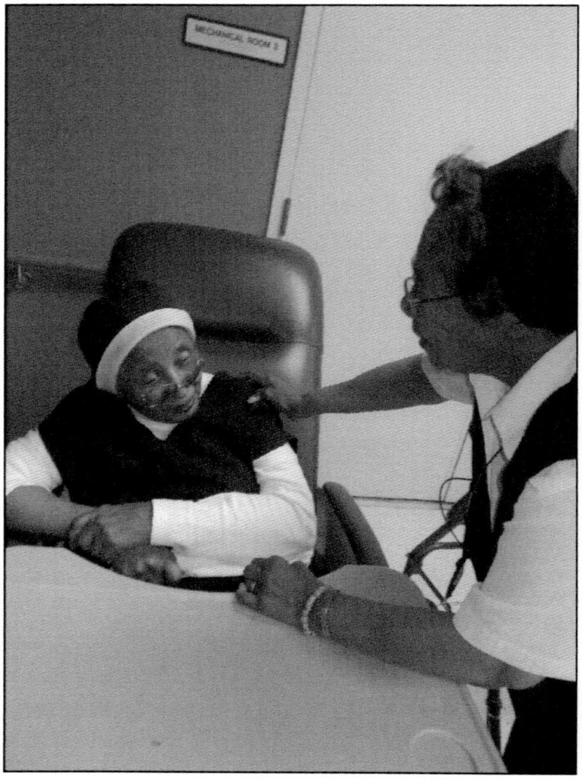

SISTERS OF THE HOLY FAMILY, NEW ORLEANS, 2013. Sister Josephine Francisco (right) greets Sister Bonaventure. Sister Bonaventure arrived with Sister Emerentia, principal and directress, and Sister Theodosia, in 1943. They combined academics with training children to sing the Mass, hosting plays, and fundraising activities. Sister Maris Stella arrived in 1944 and supervised cafeteria work. Families from Covington, nearby towns, and Mandeville and Madisonville enrolled their children. (Photograph by Eva Baham.)

Six

Pine View High School and Rosenwald Middle

A student committee chose the school mascot (Jaguars), colors (black and gold), and other symbolic elements. Hazel Johnson began her senior year at Pine View High School when it opened in the fall of 1966. It was all so new and thrilling. She was a cheerleader, played basketball, was named Miss Football 1966, and was a concert band soloist.

Hazel was the lead singer of the Magnificent 7, a teenage band. Backup singers Debra Crockett and Shirley Naylor joined Jerome "Bo" Elzy, trumpet; Isaiah Robertson Jr., saxophone; Donald Hamler, baritone sax; and Byron James, drums. "We were 'it' and we won the talent shows all the time, except once," Hazel recalled. "We lost to a quiet-spoken girl, Barbara Cooper, who sang, 'A Lover's Concerto.' The most beautiful voice ever; sang like a bird." Hazel graduated in May 1967, and headed to Southern University; so did Isaiah, on a football scholarship.

Young Southern graduates Roy and Alfreda Mouton arrived at Pine View in fall 1967. Principal Franklin Owens hired Alfreda to teach English and speech and Roy to teach music at Rosenwald Junior High. In the summer of 1969, the US Supreme Court ordered school integration. That was the end for Pine View High School.

The school hung on the cusp of being forgotten, although it left notable marks. When the school board announced Freedom of Choice, intended to diversify faculty and student body, two white teachers, Emily Diamond and Robert Zehr, volunteered to teach at the all-black school.

The spring 1969 issue of the *Jaguar Gazette* was, unknowingly, the swan song for Pine View. Assistant editor Mallery Callahan expressed regret for a delay in publication while urging readers to discover articles of interest. The booklet, a compilation of poems, club news, current events, tips, and sports, was intended to be followed by many more.

Pine View High does not evoke the romanticism of what came before it, the legendary Covington Rosenwald, or the challenges of what came after, trying times at newly integrated Covington High School. Memory of Pine View is obscured by its brief existence.

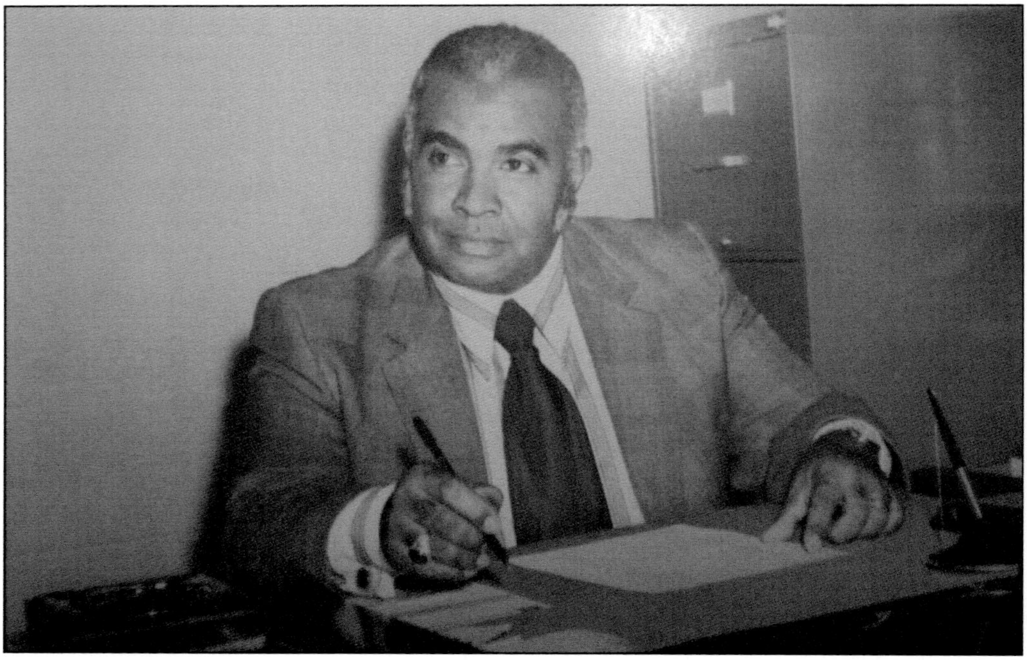

J. Franklin Owens, c. 1966. A native of Oberlin, Ohio, J. Franklin Owens studied at Southern University, Baton Rouge. He taught at Rosenwald, then became principal of Pine View High School. The school closed due to integration with Covington High, and Owens became principal of Pine View Middle School. (Courtesy of the STPSB.)

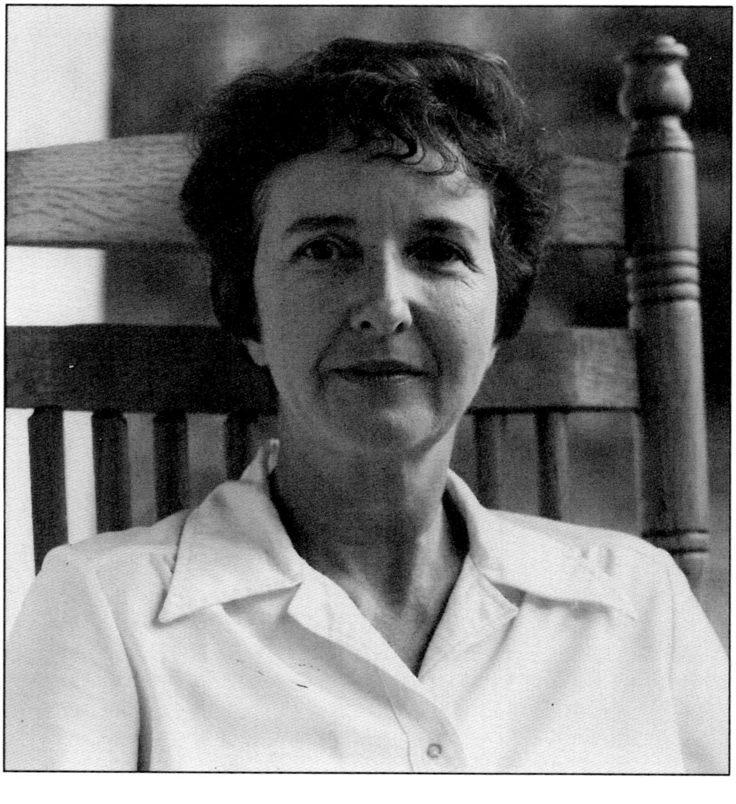

Emily Diamond, c. 1960s. Integration's response (1966) was Freedom of Choice, students' choice of white or black schools, or teachers assigned to any school. Two white teachers—Robert Zehr and Emily Diamond—chose Rosenwald Middle. Eulogizing his mother, Emily's son Dave Diamond said, "She was told that a white woman couldn't teach at a black school, but she persisted and she was hired. She sewed her heart into the lives of those kids." (Courtesy of Stanley S. Diamond.)

ALFREDA MOUTON, 2013. During her 40 years working in public and private schools, Alfreda Mouton held several positions. She taught English at Pine View High, Pine View Middle, and William Pitcher Junior High, and reading at St. Paul's Catholic School. She was supervisor of transportation and counselor in the Department of Child Welfare. (Courtesy of Eva Baham.)

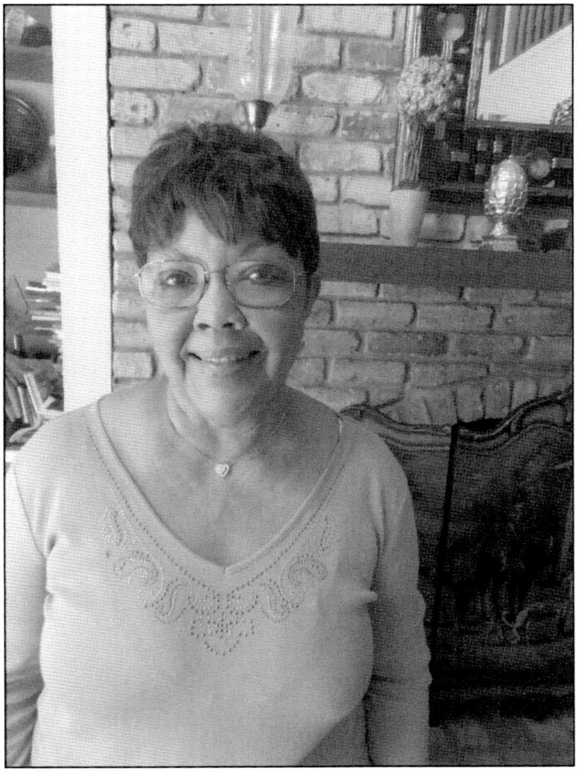

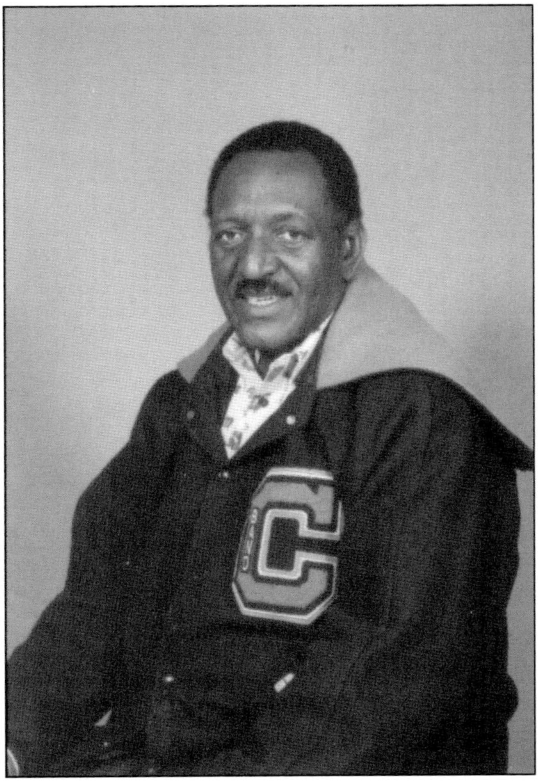

ROY MOUTON, C. 2000. Roy Mouton was the music teacher for two years at Pine View High before integration removed him. Emily Diamond urged him to apply to all-white St. Paul's High. He became its first African American teacher, staying 13 years. He integrated its student body with Dwight Robertson, Johnny Parker, Gordon Johnson, and Clyde Baham. From 1986 to 2004, he taught at Covington High. (Courtesy of Alfreda Mouton.)

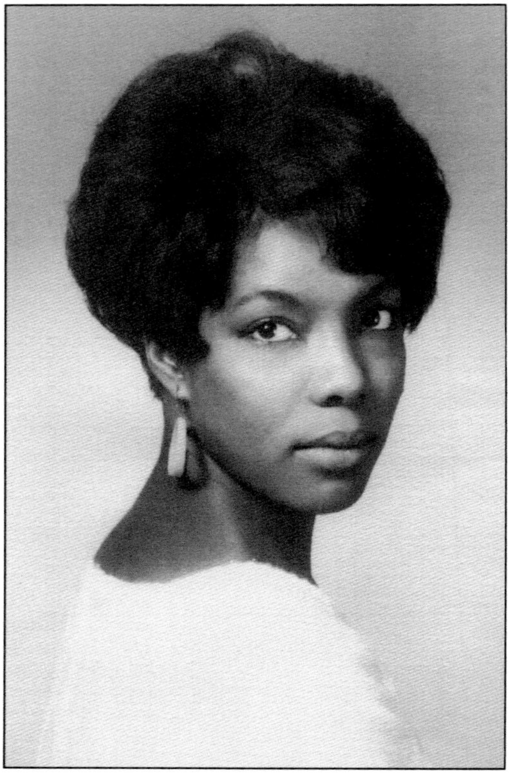

Hazel Johnson, 1967. Hazel epitomized the typical high school student, especially in a new school, Pine View. Another chapter began in African American education. Compromise on the mascot and school colors followed loyalties to either Southern University or Grambling College, where most faculty were alumni and most students anticipated attending. They chose the Jaguar and colors black and gold. Integration closed Pine View in 1969. (Courtesy of Hazel Johnson Reed.)

Covington Rosenwald Middle, Sixth Grade, 1969. Sixth-grade students wait for May graduation ceremonies to begin. Among those pictured are Victoria Johnson (far left), Lolita Perkins, Sidney Ray (far right), and Theard Robertson (seated). The African American school's short three-year existence ended with the Supreme Court's decision during the summer to end segregation. Rosenwald Middle became a public girls' school to satisfy that order. (Courtesy of Victoria Johnson Trevigne.)

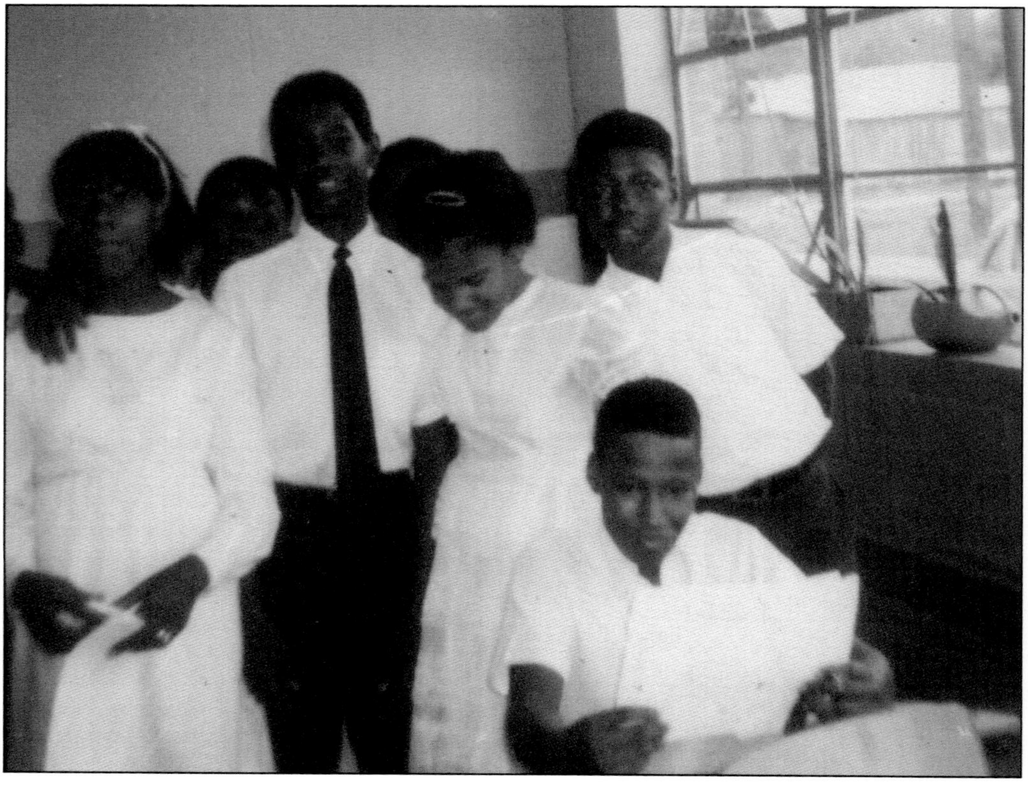

Seven

Good People, Good Citizens

Twins Jacob and Joseph Kelly remembered roaming freely through Tin Can Alley in the 1930s and 1940s and recalled families growing vegetables and raising animals. No one went hungry, and homelessness did not exist. Although some pointed to blurred realities of the Great Depression during the Kellys' idyllic youth, systemic poverty made bartering and sharing necessary among African Americans.

The cottage industry within the African American community from the late 1800s through the 1960s sustained individuals. Many people respected Willie Walter Lewis Davis Sr. for his keen medicinal sense; locals called him "the medicine man." As a cement finisher, Davis constructed headstones. The area's midwife was Katie White, serving between White Settlement and Covington.

Moses Davenport and his wife, Pauline, were independent workers in the 1930s. He drove a truck hauling materials, and she worked at home as a seamstress and washerwoman. Her daughter, Gilda Davenport Alexander, was well known as a seamstress into the 21st century.

Generational families lived together, as documented in the 1940 census. Priscilla, widowed mother to the Kelly twins, supported seven children and a niece. Alma Wilson, a dishwasher at a school cafeteria, boarded with Willis Davis, a painter; and his wife, Clothilde, a cook, on Twenty-ninth Avenue. Ernest and Luvenia Route, a laborer and a cook, shared their home with her parents, the Russells: Dan, 71, and Charlotte, 69. Dixie Shears headed a household that included her niece Emma Ordone, Emma's husband, and their four children.

During the 1960s, John and Letha Wright reared their grandson Darryl, emphasizing that education was second only to the Bible. When Letha attended night school, young Darryl was her tutor. He graduated from college and served in the military, a route of opportunity for many African Americans. Rare was the family without a history of a relative in the military. March Davis served in World War I. Henry Randle was the first aid man in Gen. George Patton's Third Army during World War II. Willie Laurent and Joseph Vaughn joined the military together in the 1950s. James "Gus" Davis joined the Marine Corps and served in Vietnam, where he received three Purple Hearts.

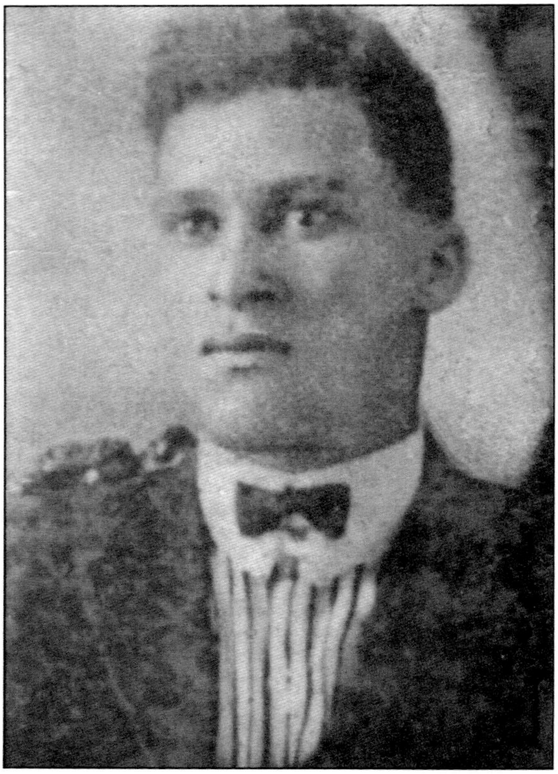

Moses Davenport, c. 1920s. Young and newly married, Moses Davenport left Covington for New Orleans. In 1920, he "lived on the premises"—a local reference for domestics and laborers who lived on the property of their employers—of Walter Poynot. He was the yardman, and wife Pauline, the cook. A decade later, the couple were back in Covington, working independently to support their four children. (Courtesy of Wanda Frick Fabre.)

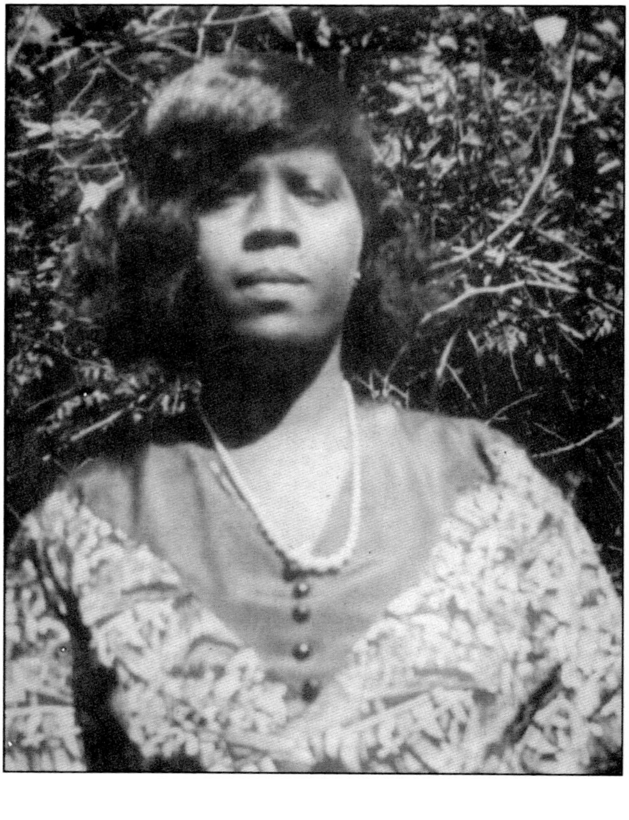

Pauline Booker Davenport, c. 1920s. Mrs. Davenport in 1930 used her skills as a seamstress and a washer in her home to help support the family. Her children, Arthur, Gilda R., Ernest and Pauline, attended school. By 1940, Mrs. Davenport, a widow, lived alone in the home she and her husband built. Her children were either married or just living elsewhere. (Courtesy of Wanda Frick Fabre.)

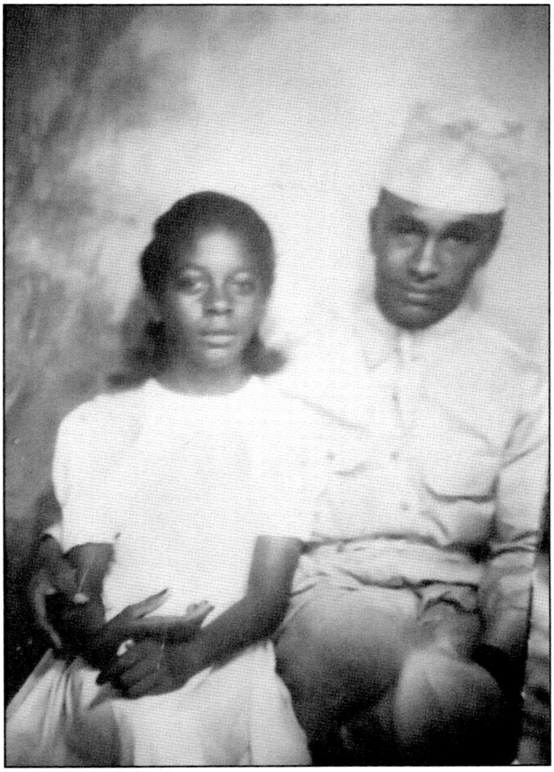

Dorothy Laurant and Clarence Laurant, 1941. Here, 10-year old Dorothy is pictured with her father at Fort Benning, Georgia, when she and her grandmother Hannah Oliver visited. Dorothy, an only child, was always curious. She observed Covington's poverty, where African Americans worked an entire week for $3, and buying large items meant justifying the purchase to the storeowner. She noted, "I've never found an answer to my 'why.' " (Courtesy of the Williams family.)

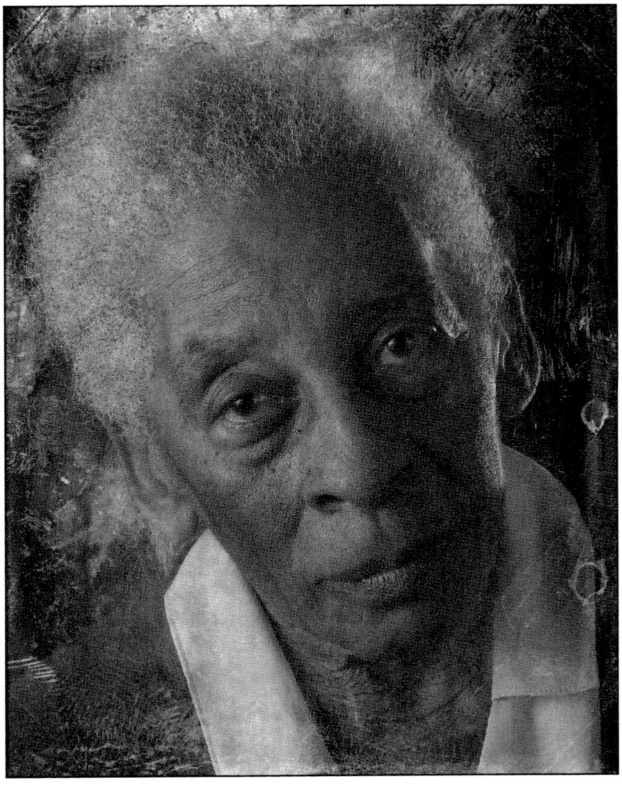

Dorothy Laurant Williams, 2013. Williams became "the Book Mobile Lady," a moniker for her goodwill. She began in the early 1960s as the librarian at the J.S. Clark Library, one—later, two—rooms of the old Rosenwald building; integration closed it. She then ran the Book Mobile, where she faced racial epithets. "I've always loved books," she said, and it was this passion that won others over. She retired in 1972. (Courtesy of Robert and Lisa Dutruch, Lost Hills Studio.)

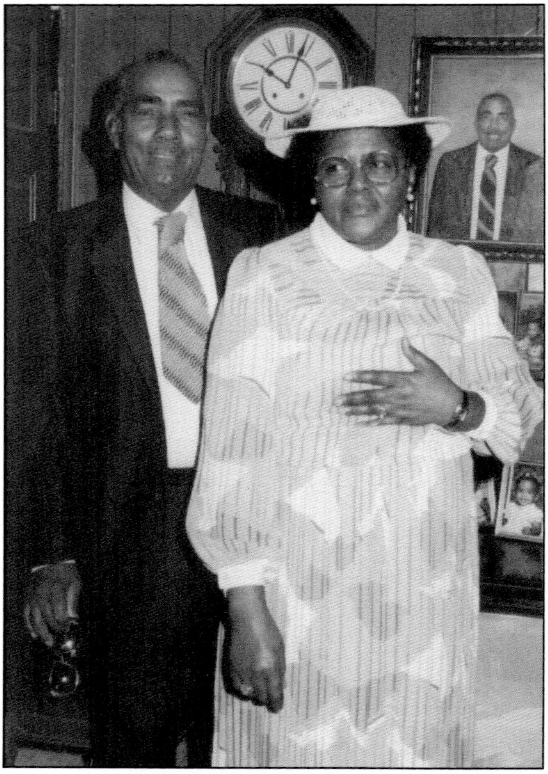

Clarence and Juanita Penn. The Penns raised meats and vegetables, and their farm supported 15 children. Clarence was famous for his barbecue, and Juanita was known as "the greatest bread pudding maker." He drove a school bus and received school board recognition as the "No. 1 Bus Driver." His familiar saying, "Step light, hurry, hurry," motivated groggy morning riders. Retiring in 1979, he purchased the Penn Shell station at the corner of Columbia and Tyler Streets. (Courtesy of Irma Penn.)

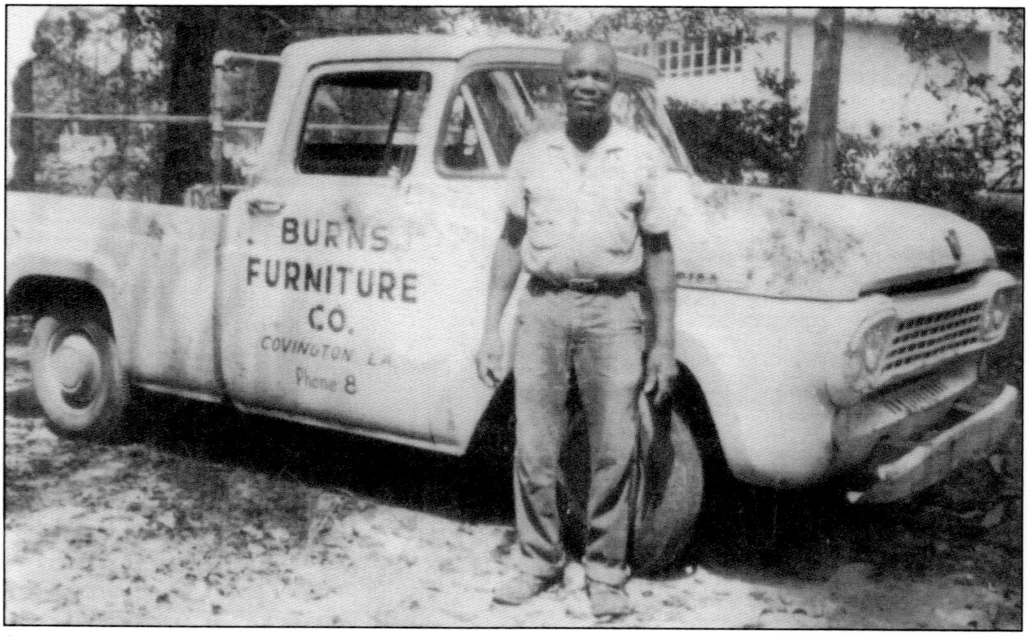

Samuel Wright. Samuel and Helen E. Wright, married 40 years, supported their 14 children with his work at Burns Furniture Store. He performed a variety of duties, from receiving and repairing furniture to delivery and installing. The Wrights are indicative of the many large families in the African American community, sustaining themselves on the wages of low-paid laborers. (Courtesy of Mary E. Wright.)

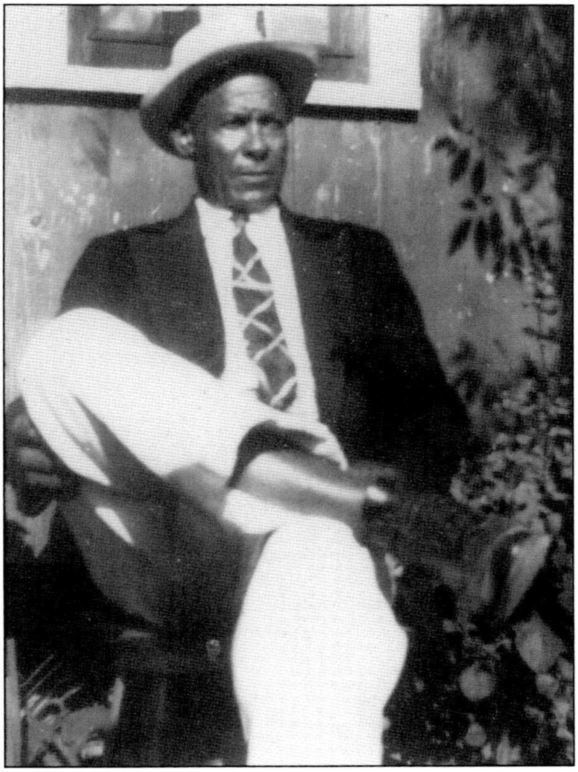

Arthur White, c. 1960s. Arthur White, a native of White Settlement and a 35-year Covington resident, had seven children with wife Bertha: Arthur Jr., Leroy, Edna Mae, Betty Jean, Sherry, Brenda, and Betsy Mae. Upon Arthur's death in 1975, Thelma Hendry, supervisor of the St. Tammany Humane Society, commended him for his dedication and for being one of the earliest persons associated with the shelter. (Courtesy of Melanie Garrett Allen.)

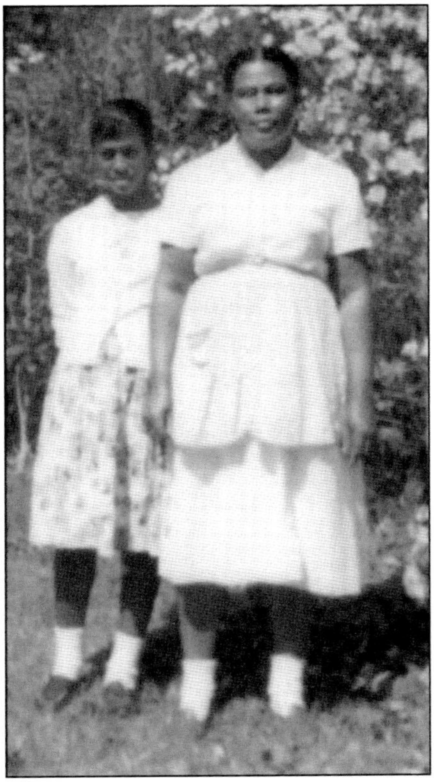

Gertrude and Zena White, c. 1950s. Domestics sometimes took their daughters with them to work. Zena lived on the premises at her employer's residence in New Orleans, about 60 miles away. She sometimes took her 12-year old daughter, Gertrude, with her as a helper. Gertrude later worked for the same family. Breaking the cycle of domestics, Gertrude's daughter finished college and became a teacher. (Courtesy of Melanie Garrett Allen.)

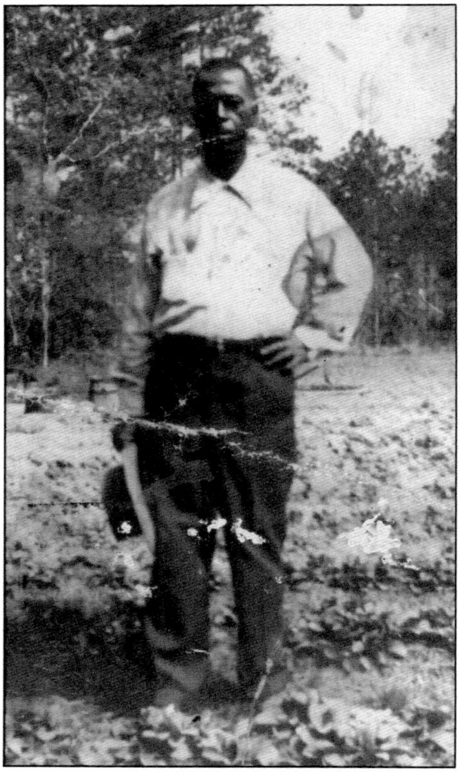

CONLEY WHITE. The White family traces its lineage and property ownership in White Settlement to the 19th century. They worked and lived off the land. Conley White raised a garden, which was shared with other families. He grew strawberries as a cash crop and drove a pulpwood truck to support their family. Conley and Zena lived in the area all their lives. (Courtesy of Melanie Garrett Allen.)

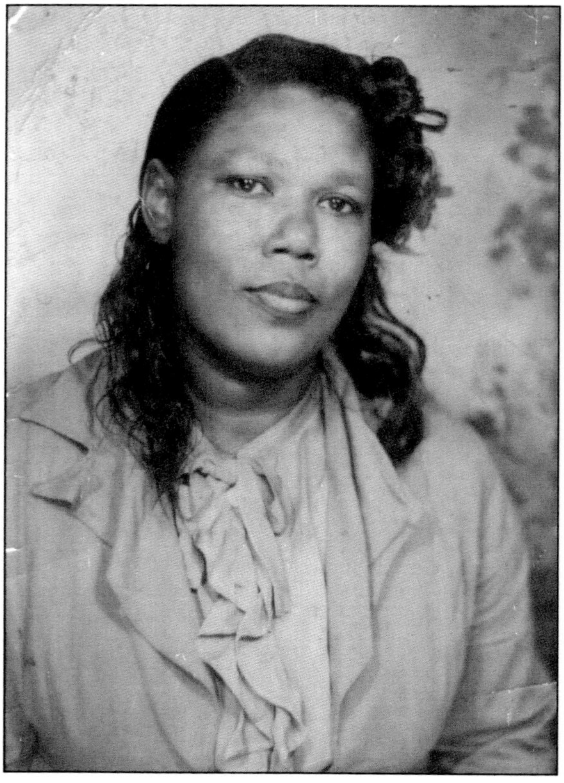

ZENA WHITE, C. 1950S. Zena's life as a domestic presents a paradox for some black/white relationships. She lived on site Sunday to Friday, receiving $3 a week. Zena's daughter and granddaughter were namesakes of her employer, who at times supplemented the granddaughter's tuition. Zena returned to Covington and worked as a domestic until she was 83 years old. Her granddaughter became a teacher. (Courtesy of Melanie Garrett Allen.)

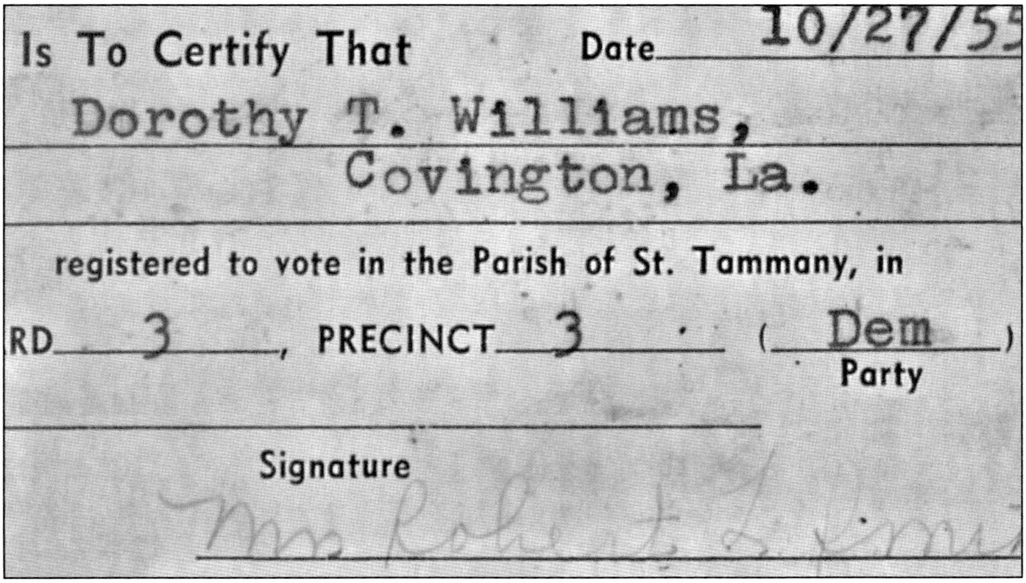

Is To Certify That Date 10/27/55

Dorothy T. Williams,

Covington, La.

registered to vote in the Parish of St. Tammany, in

RD 3, PRECINCT 3 (Dem)

Party

Signature

VOTER REGISTRATION, 1955. Dorothy Williams's family has kept her voter registration card as a reminder of both the responsibilities of citizenship and their mother's pride in being able to vote. Prohibitions such as poll taxes and other artificial obstacles hindered African American voting for almost a century. The right to vote symbolized another step toward full participation in American life. (Courtesy of Gwendolyn Williams.)

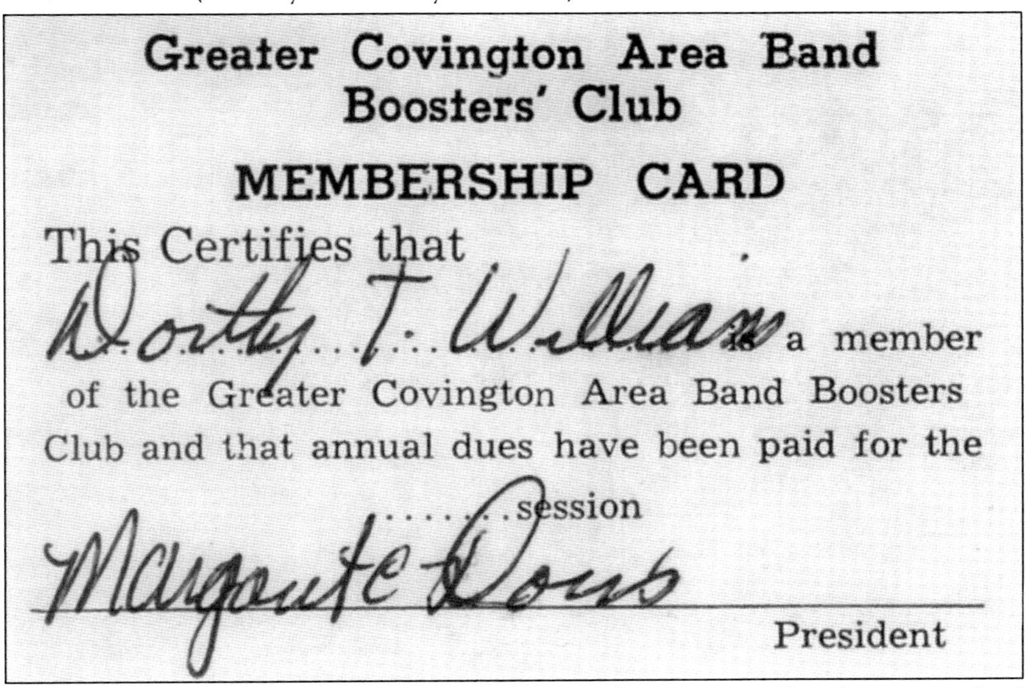

Greater Covington Area Band Boosters' Club

MEMBERSHIP CARD

This Certifies that .... is a member of the Greater Covington Area Band Boosters Club and that annual dues have been paid for the .... session

President

BAND BOOSTERS CLUB MEMBERSHIP, 1976. Seven years after integration forced a unitary school district, African American children involved themselves in various activities. Dorothy Williams's son was a band member, hence her booster club membership. She worked as a domestic and her husband, Albert, a World War II veteran, lived on the premises as a caretaker for a family. (Courtesy of Gwendolyn Williams.)

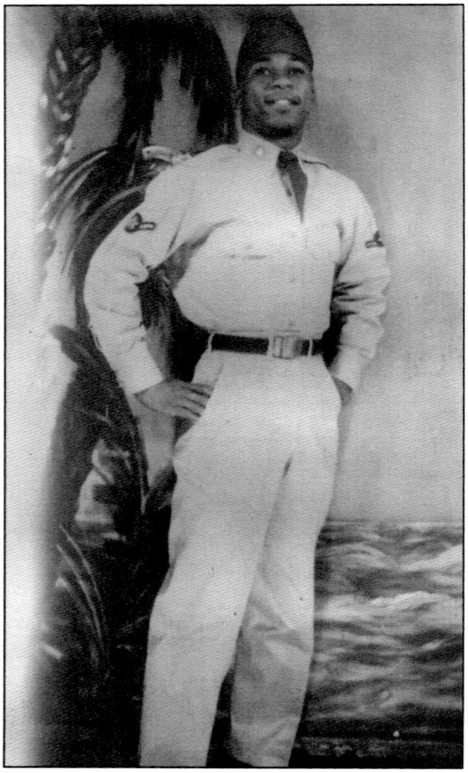

Joseph Randolph Vaughn, 1952. Pursuing opportunities open to African Americans in the military, Joseph left high school before graduating. He received his diploma while in the Air Force and pursued boxing. After serving in the military, he lived in Detroit, worked in the automobile industry, and reared a family. (Courtesy of Marion Vaughn.)

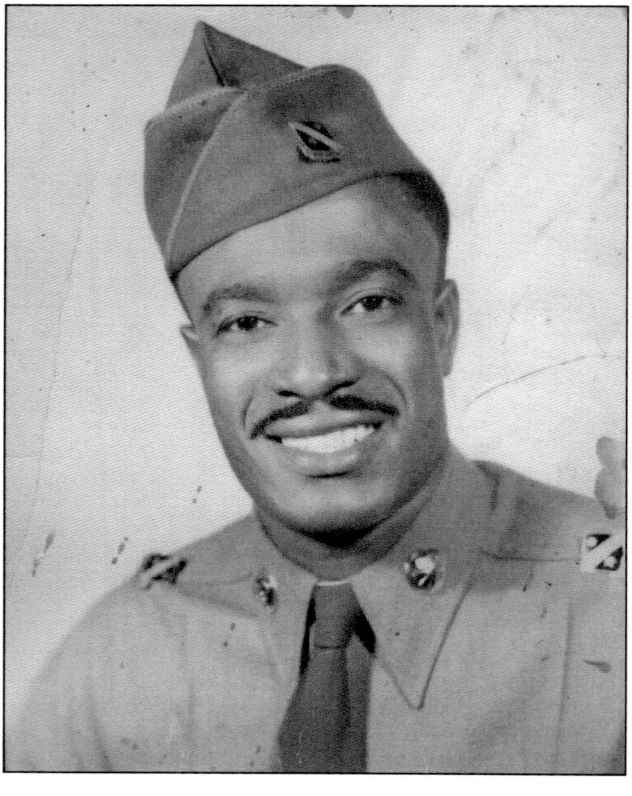

Roosevelt Polk. African Americans in Covington either volunteered or were drafted into the military from World War I through the Vietnam War. In November 1940, the *St. Tammany Farmer* announced Robert Edward Green, a "Negro," as the first number pulled for the draft. Many, like Polk, took advantage of the GI Bill to further their education. (Courtesy of the Randle collection.)

Charles Harry, 1960s. Opportunities to improve oneself could be found in military service. Many young men received skilled training and traveled across the United States and abroad. As a result, veterans like Charles Harry found work outside of Louisiana, where they settled, married, and reared families. (Courtesy of the Randle collection.)

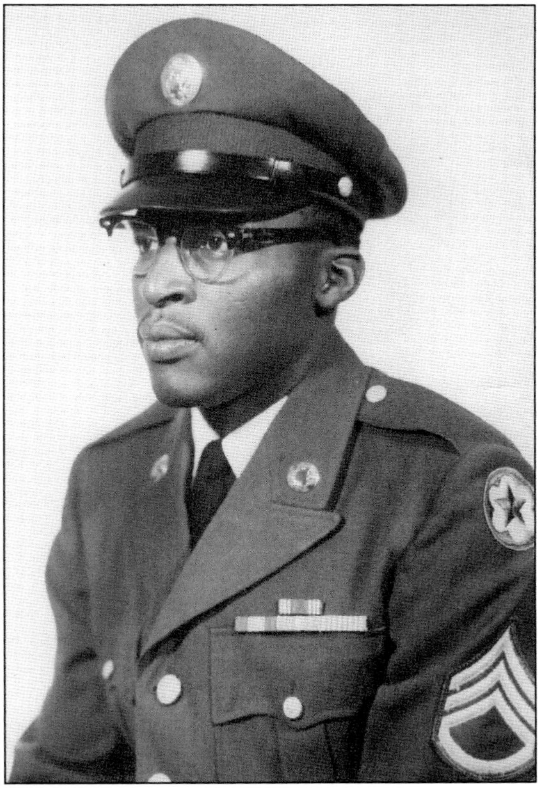

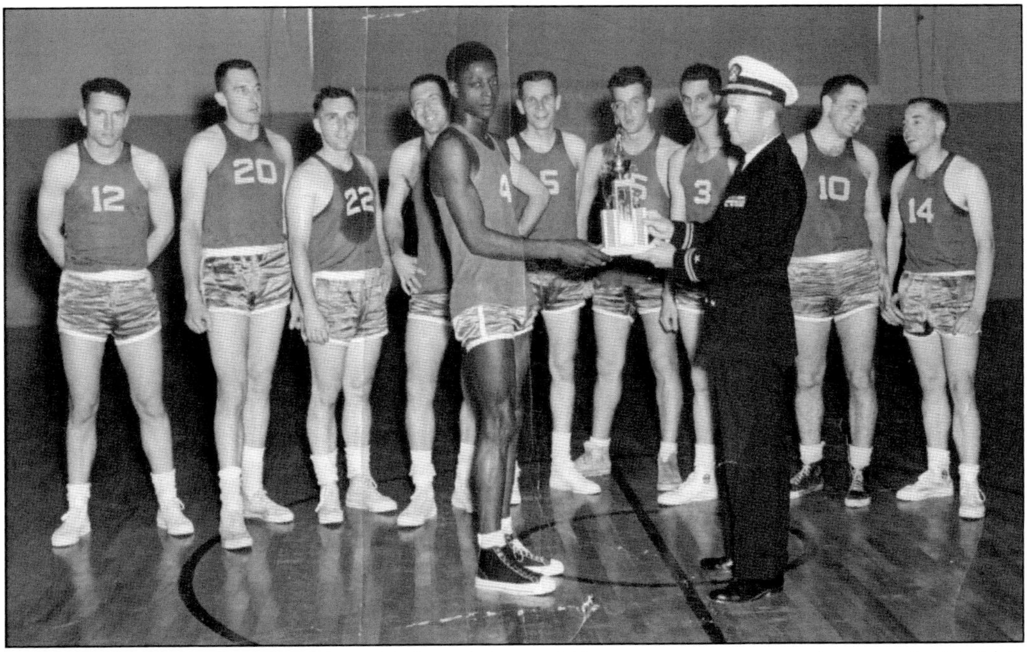

US Navy Basketball Team, 1956. Joseph Lewis Thomas receives a trophy on behalf of his team. He achieved the rank of master chief petty officer, a senior enlisted person who serves as an advisor in matters dealing with enlisted personnel and their families. (Courtesy of Ida Thomas James.)

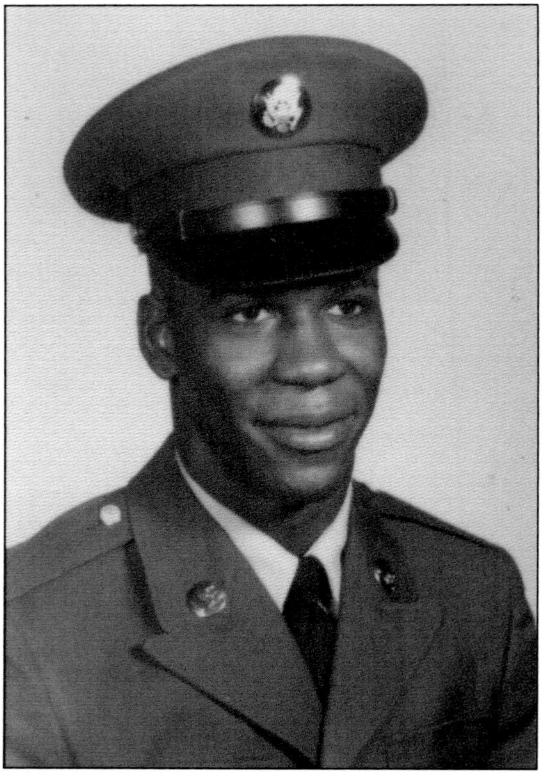

EVERETT "DUCK" STEELE, C. 1966. Since he was 14 years old, Steele wanted to join the military. He graduated from Covington Rosenwald in 1964 and later enlisted in the US Army. He married Mae Evelyn Dixon, and they had two sons, Vince and Eric. He died on Christmas Day 1990. (Courtesy of Elizabeth Steele.)

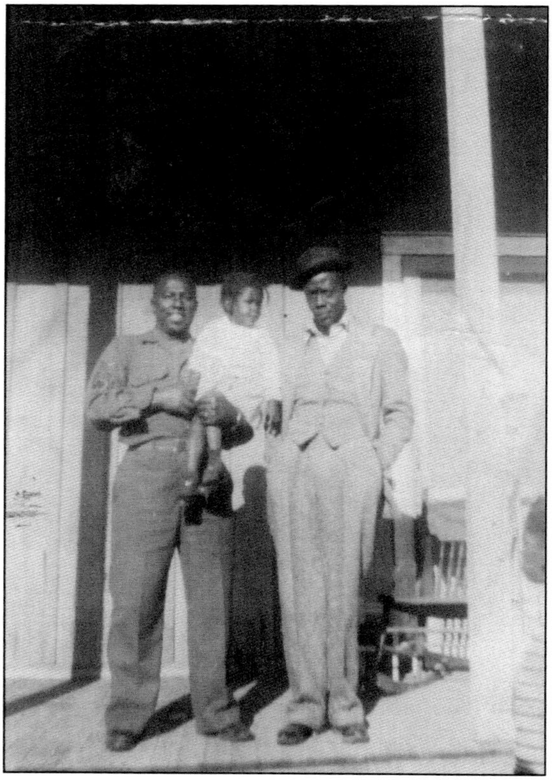

SOLDIER'S HOMECOMING, C. 1940S. Henry Steele holds his three-year-old daughter, Barbara, and visits with Lionel Sorrell. After his return to Covington, Steele and his wife, Evelyn, supported their children, Lionel, Betty Lou, Leonard, Catherine, Elizabeth, Joseph, and Everett, through his long-term employment with the St. Tammany School Board. (Courtesy of Elizabeth Steele.)

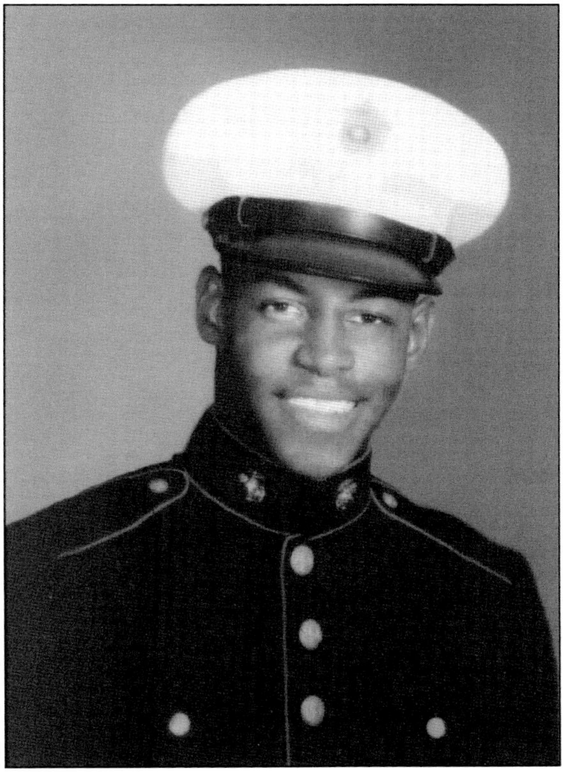

JAMES "GUS" DAVIS, 1962. Davis volunteered for opportunity. He was stationed at Parris Island, South Carolina, and was one of five outstanding Marine Corps recruits. He was sent to Morocco and then to Camp LeJeune. His tours took him to Spain, Puerto Rico, Gibraltar, London, and Cuba. He served in Vietnam from 1964 to 1965 and from 1966 to 1967. (Courtesy of James Davis.)

JAMES "GUS" DAVIS, JANUARY 1967. Lt. Gen. Lewis W. Walt awarded Davis the first of three Purple Heart medals when his tank killer ran over a land mine. In June 1967, shrapnel shattered in his head; in September 1967, he was injured when a land mine exploded. This time, he returned stateside to the US Naval Hospital in Charleston and was placed in charge of Marines waiting for medical discharge. He received an honorable medical discharge in December 1968. (Courtesy of James Davis.)

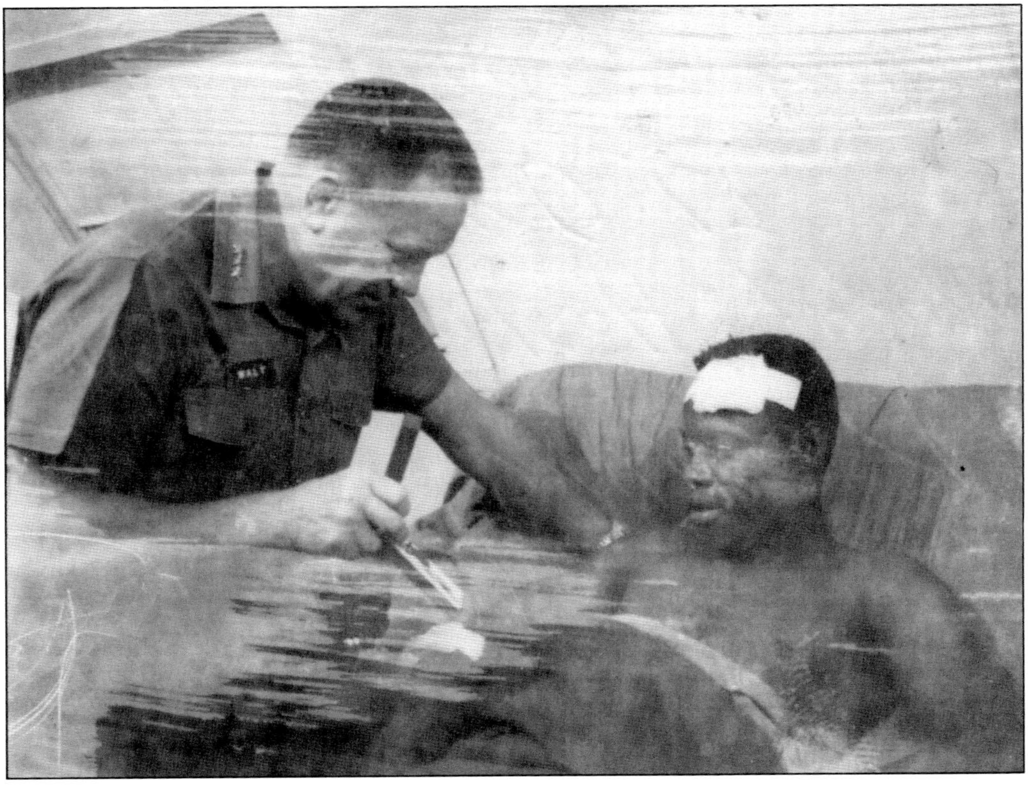

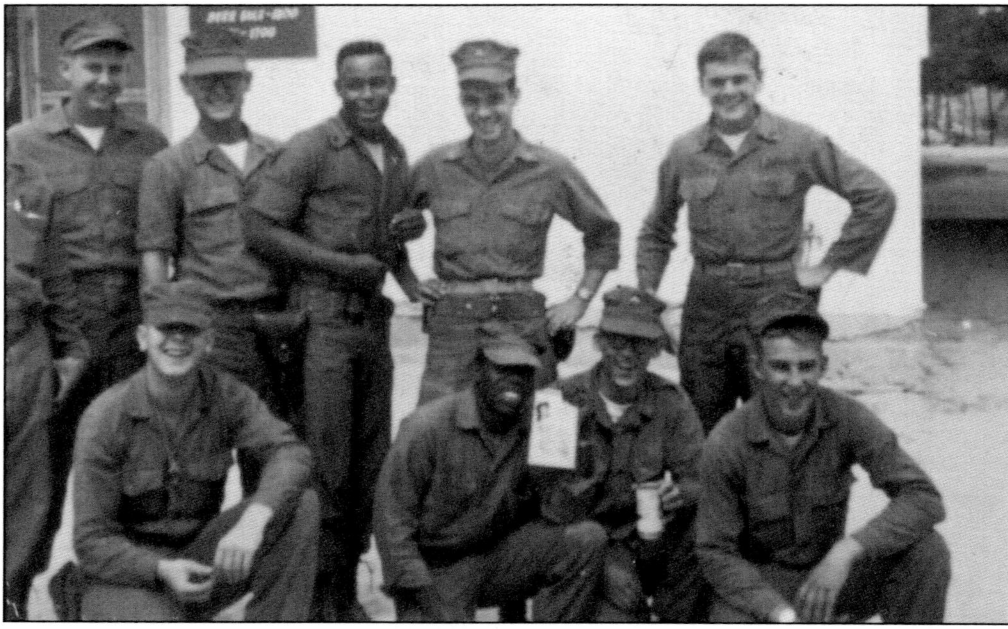

VIETNAM SOLDIERS, 1964–1967. James "Gus" Davis, standing center, says that he "had a ball" during his enlistment in the military. Since his return, his leadership in Covington has been stellar. He has served as president of the NAACP branch, Prince Hall Mason, senior commander of Military Order of the Purple Heart Chapter 741, trustee/treasurer of Bethel Reform, president of his homeowners' association, and school board ambassador. (Courtesy of James Davis.)

DAVIS MILITARY MEN, 2012. James "Gus" Davis (with hat) encouraged his sons to join the military. Also pictured are, from left to right, Eric Davis, former sergeant first class, who works with the St. Tammany Parish School Board Maintenance Department; Gus's grandson Dylan; Derrick James, sergeant first class and 23-year veteran, who works with malpractice insurance; grandson Demille; and Edward, E6 staff sergeant, who is a supervisor with Bridgestone in South Carolina. (Courtesy of James Davis.)

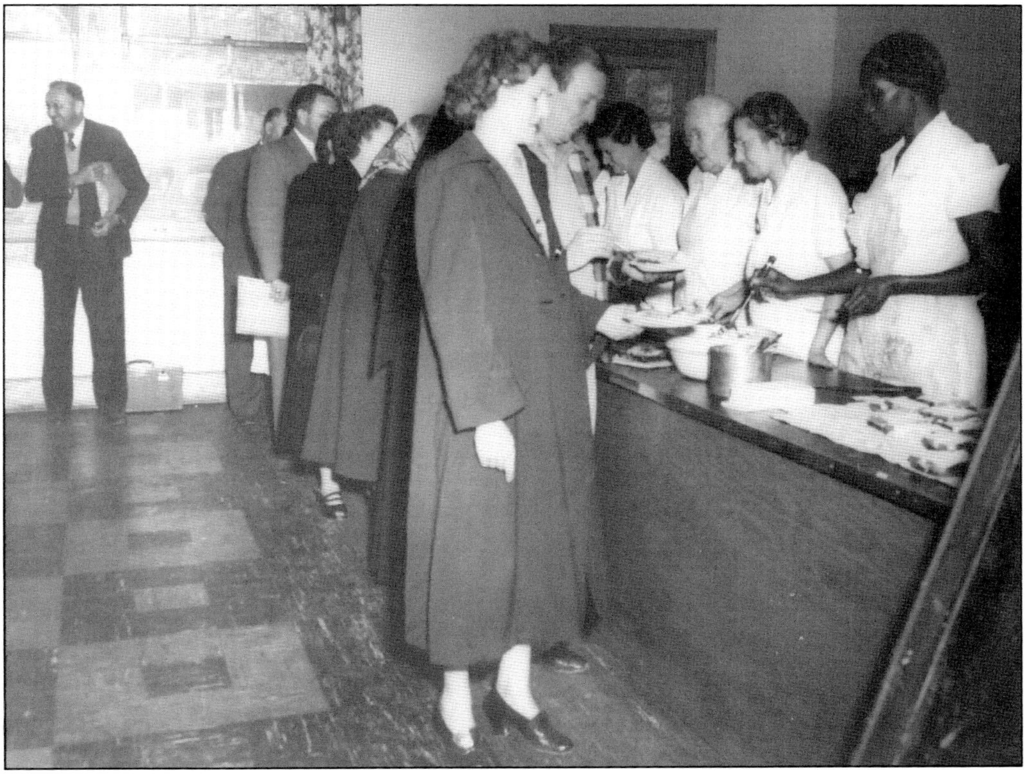

COVINGTON ELEMENTARY SCHOOL, 1940s. Lunchroom workers serve visitors attending a meeting at the elementary school. Schools and their workplaces were segregated, although an African American woman is one of the servers in this photograph. This is possibly Alma Wilson, who boarded with the Davis family and listed her occupation as lunchroom worker at the elementary school. (Courtesy of the STPSB.)

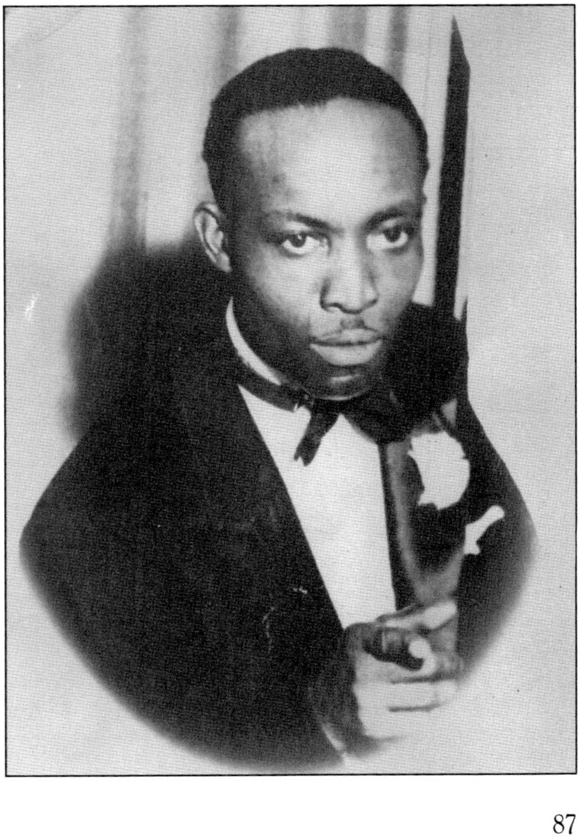

EUGENE ELZY. The response to the sudden death of Eugene Elzy demonstrates the cohesiveness of the African American community. Elzy worked for Delta Pine Oil, and his death was caused by an accident at the workplace in 1951. There was no insurance money, leaving his wife, Arie, to rear their eight children. The family received support from local organizations, churches, and individuals. (Courtesy of Jerome Elzy.)

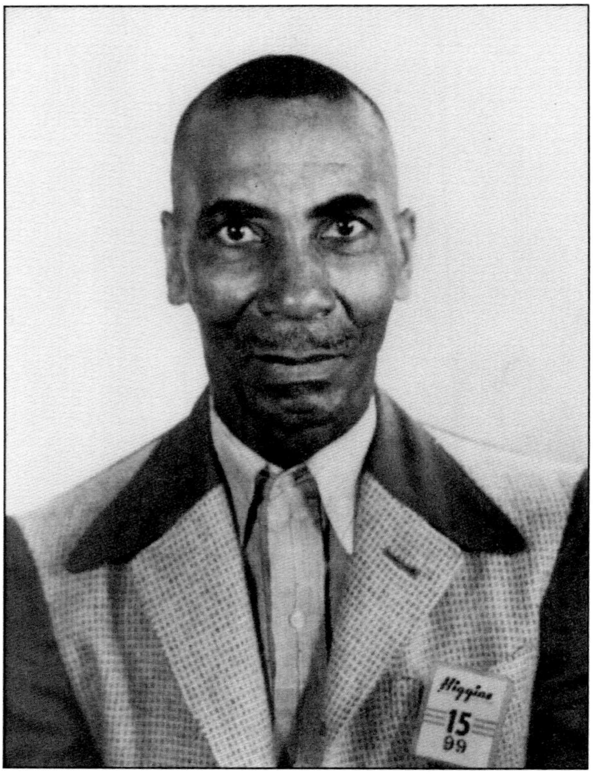

Earnest Antoine Richardson. Richardson, born in 1892, was the "Ice Man," delivering ice only in the African American community in Covington. Later, he delivered to other sections as white deliverymen abandoned that work for better jobs. He also supported his family by hauling logs for the Strain & Quave Company. The family attended Bethel Reform, where he was a trustee. (Courtesy of Jessie R. James.)

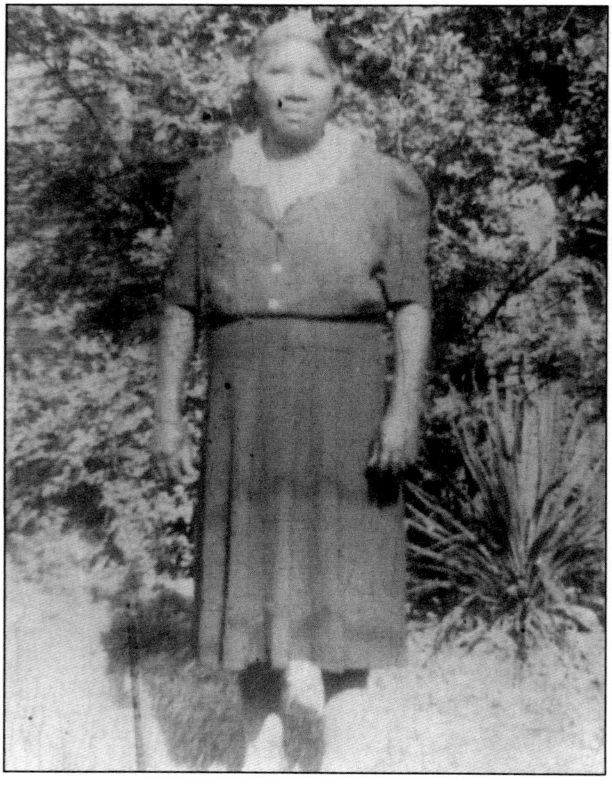

Lutie Williams Richardson. While visiting her aunt Cindy Williams in Goodbee, Louisiana, Lutie, a native of Clinton, met Earnest Richardson. They were married in 1919. Earnest and Lutie began their family in Covington, where they reared Charlie, Jessie Irene, Frankie, and Percy. She worked inside the home. (Courtesy of Jessie R. James.)

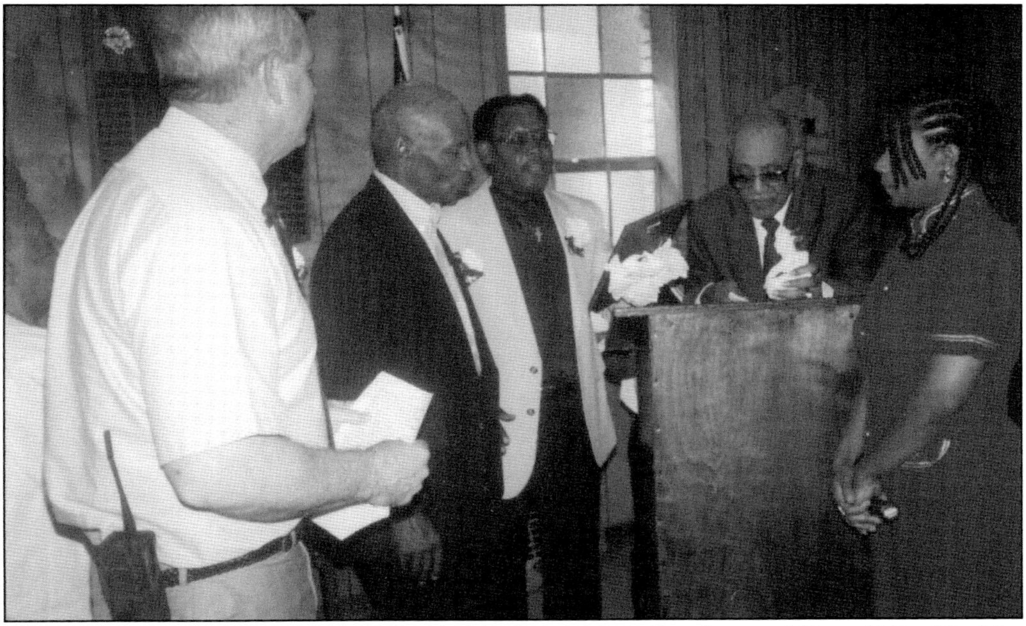

Burnell Bradford Sr. Honored. Bethel Reform's Men's Day honored Burnell Bradford for his volunteer beautification program in Covington. It was noted that "he could plant a seed on concrete and it would grow." He began planting flowers, trees, and bushes on street corners around Covington as his personal service to the city in 1976. Several organizations and the city government honored him. (Courtesy of Shirley W. Bradford.)

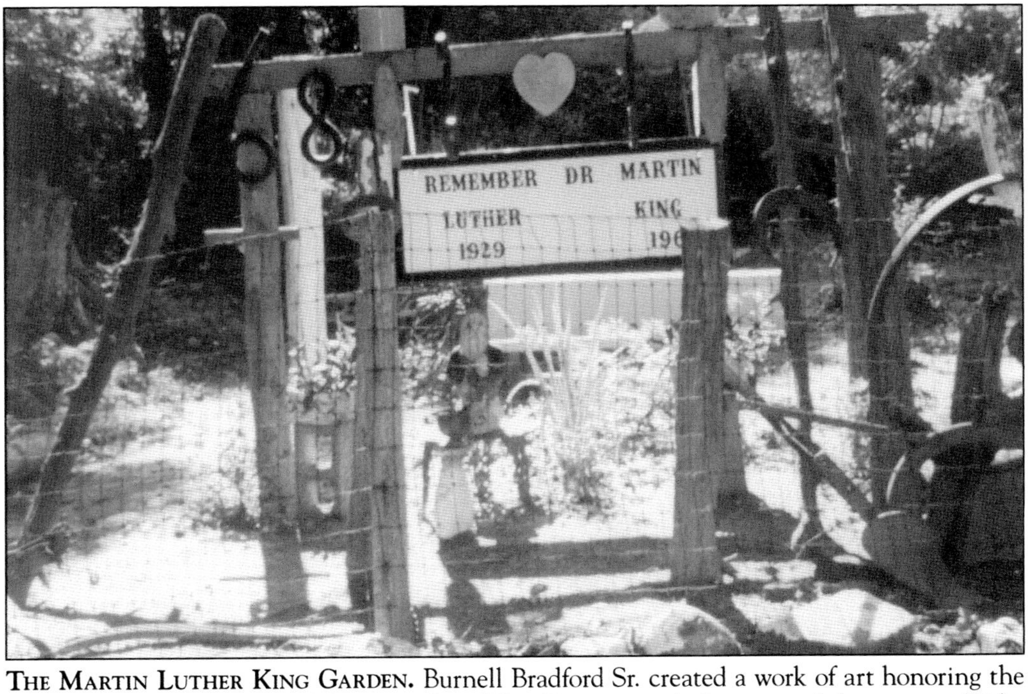

The Martin Luther King Garden. Burnell Bradford Sr. created a work of art honoring the civil rights leader. He located the artwork on West Twenty-ninth Avenue and the corner of Tyler Street. It reflected his special talent for mixing natural and artificial elements to express his theme. (Courtesy of Shirley W. Bradford.)

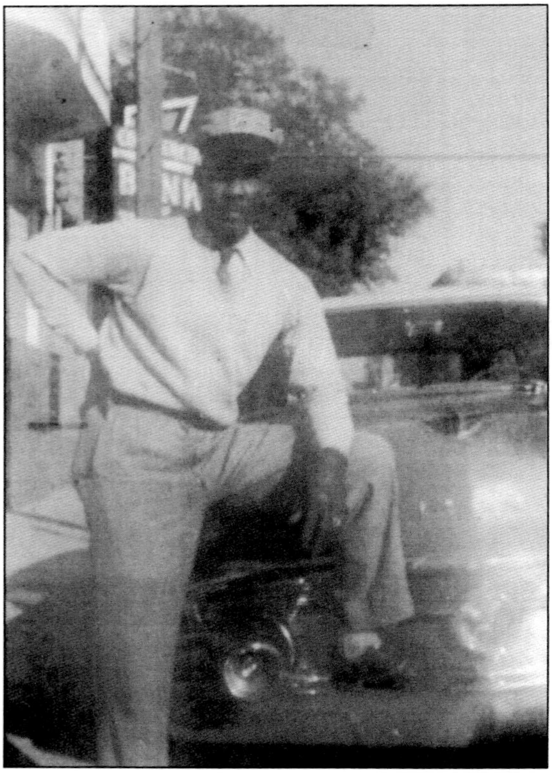

Alphonse Thomas Sr. As the Southern Hotel porter during the 1950s, Alphonse Thomas unloaded luggage from both the guests' cars and from the Greyhound buses, from 7:00 a.m. to 7:00 p.m. He alternated weeks working from 7:00 p.m. to 7:00 a.m. on the Causeway Bridge and doing landscaping jobs on Jahncke Avenue. He died from a heart attack in 1959 and is remembered as a hard worker and a caring father and husband. (Courtesy of Ida Thomas James.)

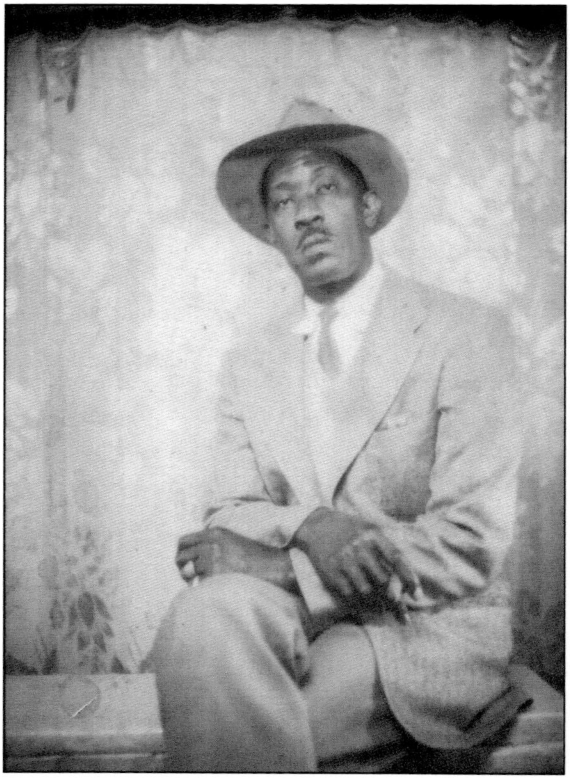

Alphonse Thomas Sr., 1951. Locals described him as "a sharp dresser" and a cigar smoker. Active church members, he and his wife Eula Mae "Ms. Honey" reared five children: Linda, Bettye Jean, Alphonse Jr., Joseph, and Ida Ruth. When he died at 49 years of age, his oldest son was in the Navy, and one daughter was a freshman at Grambling College. (Courtesy of Ida Thomas James.)

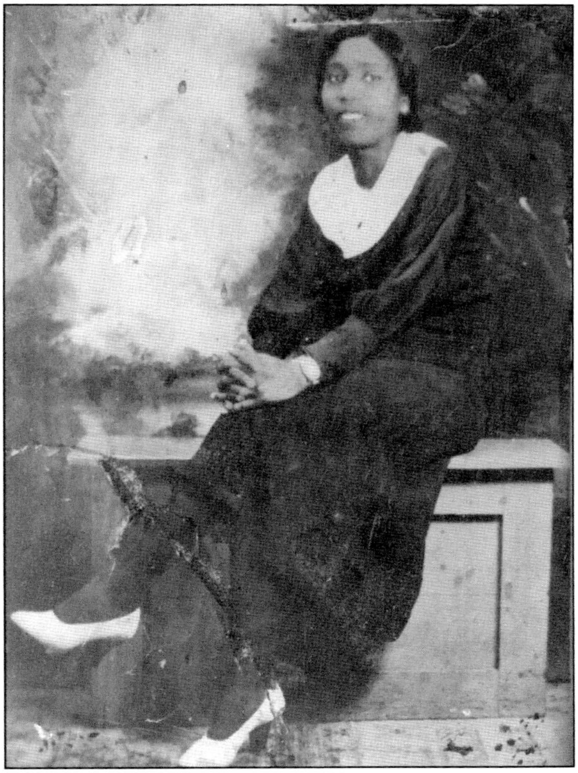

"Ms. Honey," 1934. Few people knew her as Eula Mae Thomas. Ms. Honey moved from Beaumont, Texas, to Covington when she married Alphonse Thomas in 1935. Active in her church, Bethel Reform, she reared her children after Alphonse died in 1959. She worked several jobs to educate her three daughters; all became teachers. Both sons joined the Navy and earned college degrees. (Courtesy of Ida Thomas James.)

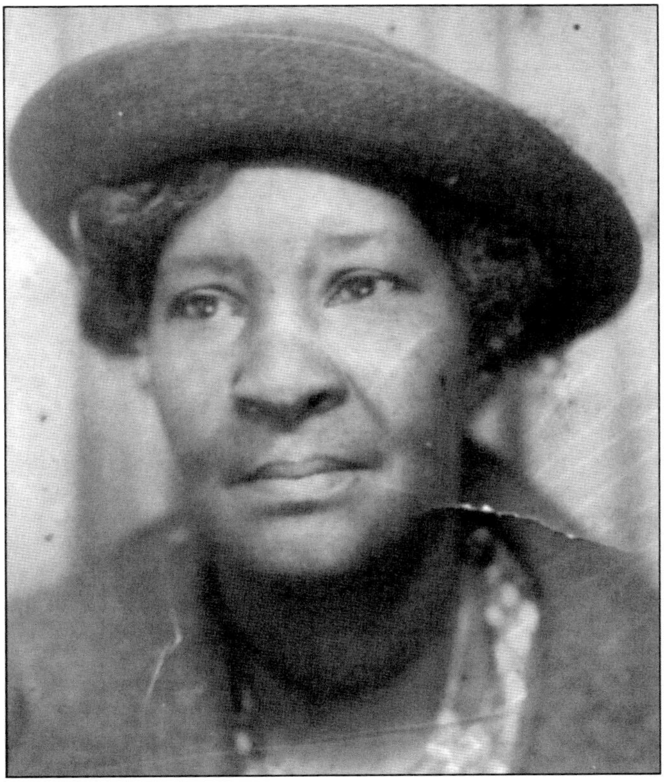

Ida Harvey Bell Thomas, 1920. A traveling photographer framed this close-up of Ida Thomas. She and her husband, Will E. Thomas, lived on Guillot Street (renamed Claiborne) in Covington. She was a homemaker and a domestic. He was a laborer and baseball player. Their children were (Miss) Willie Luteal and Alphonse. (Courtesy of Ida Thomas James.)

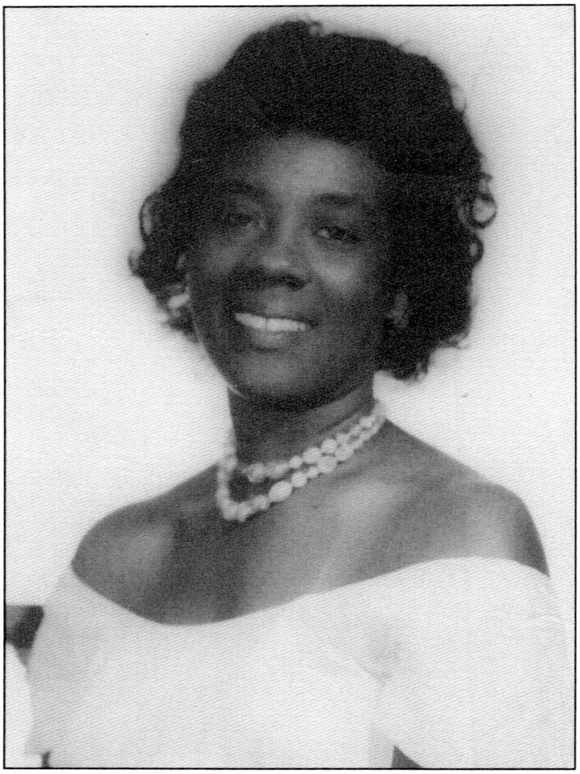

Grace Polk Randle, c. 1950s. Grace Randle's husband, Henry Sr., chronicled her involvement in several organizations. She coordinated events for Covington Rosenwald, where she watched her children excel in sports and music. Additionally, she provided leadership for formals, such as the Sangaria Ball. She worked at the South East Hospital in Mandeville and as a private-duty nurse. (Courtesy of the Randle collection.)

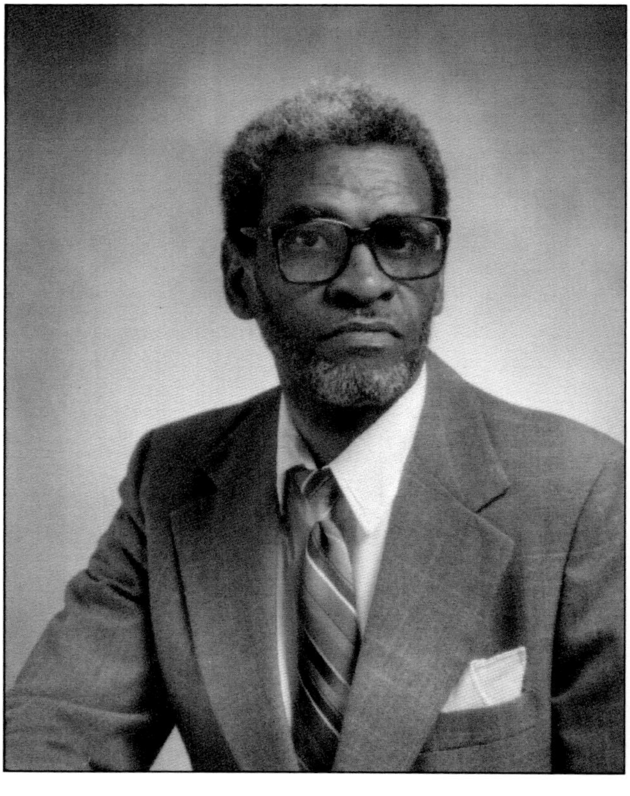

Henry Randle Jr. Weddings, school and social events, and personal portraits of African Americans were photographed by Henry Randle. Along with his job as a Veterans Affairs inspector, he owned Henry I. Randle Builder and Cabinet Millwork, held an electrician's license, and co-owned BrCaRA Production Systems. His charitable and community activities involved Head Start, civil rights, recreation for children, and serving as a deacon in his church. (Courtesy of the Randle collection.)

Eight

Love and Charity

Organizations had serious reasons for social, recreational, and civic engagement. Efforts on behalf of children looked forward both to their future and the community's. Adult leadership was infused with respectability, with menial laborers sharing the same respect as teachers.

Examples include a 1920 committee, the Colored Division of the St. Tammany Parish Fair Association, which planned an exhibit at the Negro Building on the fairgrounds. Prof. T.F. Dickerson, chair, met with Josephine Moore, Delphine Heisser, F.P. Jackson, V.C. Thornton, A.W. Jones, and Willie Murray to organize agriculture, culinary, textile, livestock, entertainment, and fundraising subcommittees to develop exhibits.

Additionally, the Love and Charity Benevolent Association built a community hall in 1939. It housed community events, church services, and classrooms for Rosenwald's third and fourth grades. Rev. Henry Randle, Clarence Rout, Granville Moore, J.W. Badon, Robert Richardson, and Eugene Henry were founders.

The Covington Athletic Association of the early 1960s had one premise: "We need to take care of our children." Members included Edward Conerly, Henry Randle, Holly Clark, Alvin "Buck" Frederick, Albert Smith, Joseph Elliott, Riley Callahan, Leroy Frick, and Herman Williams. They used personal resources and raised money within the community. Additionally, the sheriff had lumber hauled; the Great Southern Paper Mill Company provided poles for lights, and an anonymous white donor gave financial support. Also, Rev. Peter Atkins organized a playground and founded the first Boy Scout troop in the neighborhood. Additionally, Prince Hall Masons, Crescent Lodge No. 236, and Eastern Stars, Naomi No. 161 included highly respected men and women; among them was Helena Sheridan.

Adult baseball teams practiced against white teams, though they were not allowed to play against them in an official game. Isaiah "Sonny" Robertson was remembered by one former player as a baseball pioneer and the best. A Negro League team, the original Covington Eagles, organized by Percy Smith and James "Cud" Barney, played one year in 1950 before merging into a second Little Eagles team, coached by Robertson. Original players were Harold "PeeWee" Heisser, Herman James, Charles Moore, Eugene "Skull" Elzy, Lee Spencer, Arthur "Tarzan James" Davenport, Henry Kelly, Albert "Smitty" Smith, Calvin Badon (also known as "Angeletti"), Raymond Weaver, William McCaskill, Rudolph Batiste, and Louis Johnson. Its chief sponsor was HJ Smith's Sons hardware store.

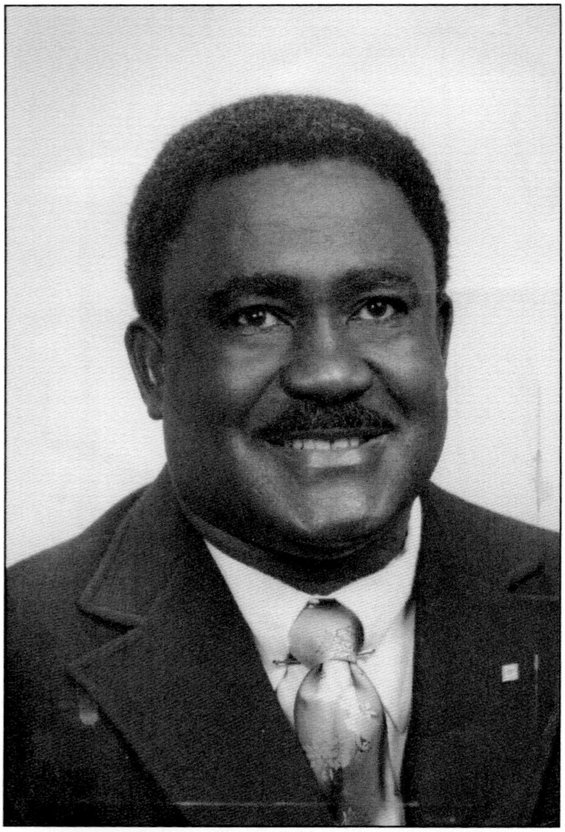

Edward Conerly. Conerly (1929–2014) and wife Ruby had one son, Bruce, although Edward Conerly's involvement in children's activities made it appear that he had several. He was a founder of the Covington Athletic Association, which organized recreation for African American children during segregation. He worked at Sears for 30 years, then as a food stamp manager, and was active in his church. (Courtesy of Ruby Conerly.)

The Mighty 15, 1978. This initial group had 15 men. They awarded scholarships and helped needy families. Pictured are, from left to right, (first row) Oscar "Dusty" Elzy, Nolan Anderson, president Harold Heisser, and Charlie Richardson Jr.; (second row) Freddie Simms, Sonny Robertson, Freddie Primus, Joseph "Sippy" Elliott, Willie Coleman, Roy Mouton, and Robert Winston. Not pictured are Guy Williams, J.D. Brown, Edward Lee Brown, "Brother" Thedo Brown, LeRoy Garrett, Melvin Washington, and Ellis Andrews. (Courtesy of Harold Heisser.)

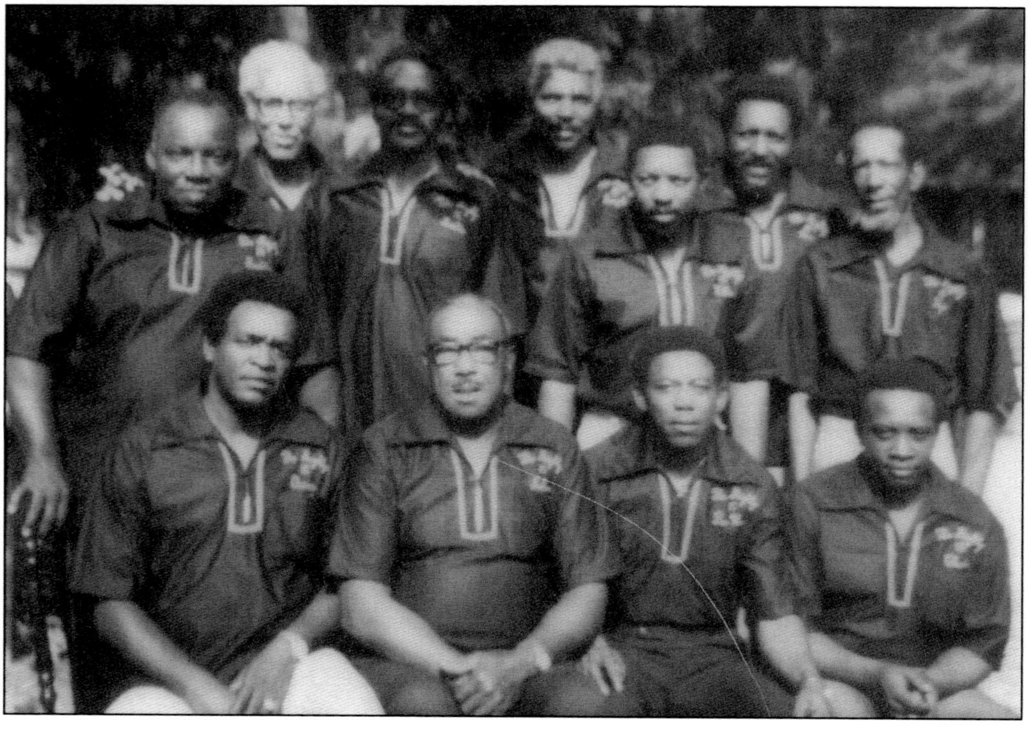

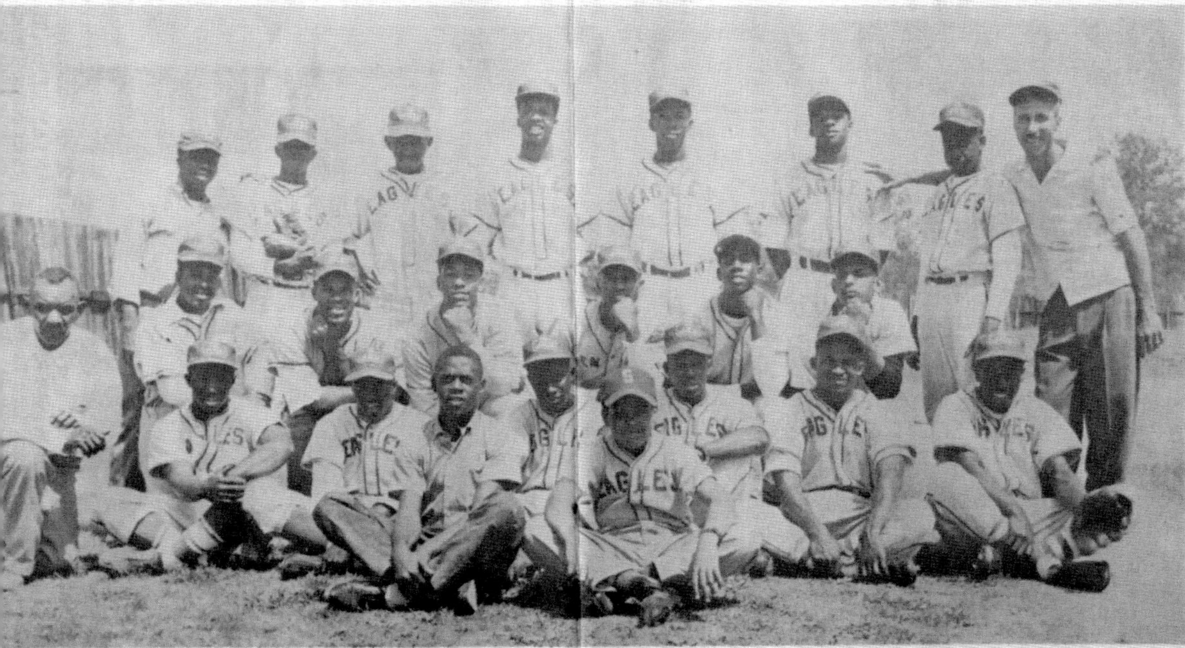

THIS LOCAL TEAM, THE COVINGTON EAGLES, SUPPORTED BY H. J. SMITH'S SON, PLAYED IN THE 1950'S. Said to be one of the best teams Covington has ever produced. Seated in front row, Joe Steel, Batboy (unknown). Second row, seated, Charles Moore, Skull Elzy, Lee Spencer, Tazan James, Adrian Perkins, and Henry Jones. Middle row, kneeling, Frank Mitchell (Assistant Coach), Meyers, Grover Perkins, Butchie Simmons, Ben White, Jones, Floyd Baham. Back row, standing, Alvin Frederick, Unknown, Henry Kelly, Albert "Smitty" Smith, Herman James, William McAllister, Jones, Isiah "Sonny" Robertson, Sr. (Head Coach).

THE COVINGTON EAGLES, C. 1950S. The Big Eagles gave way to the Little Eagles (pictured). Percy Smith and James "Cud" Barney created the original one-year team. Members were Harold "Pee Wee" Heisser; Herman James, "The Closer;" Charles Moore; Eugene "Skull" Elzy; Lee Spencer; Arthur "Tarzan James" Davenport; Henry Kelly; Albert "Smitty" Smith; Calvin Badon, also known as "Angeletti;" Raymond Weaver; William McCaskill; Rudolph Batiste; and Louis Johnson. (Courtesy of HJ Smith's Sons.)

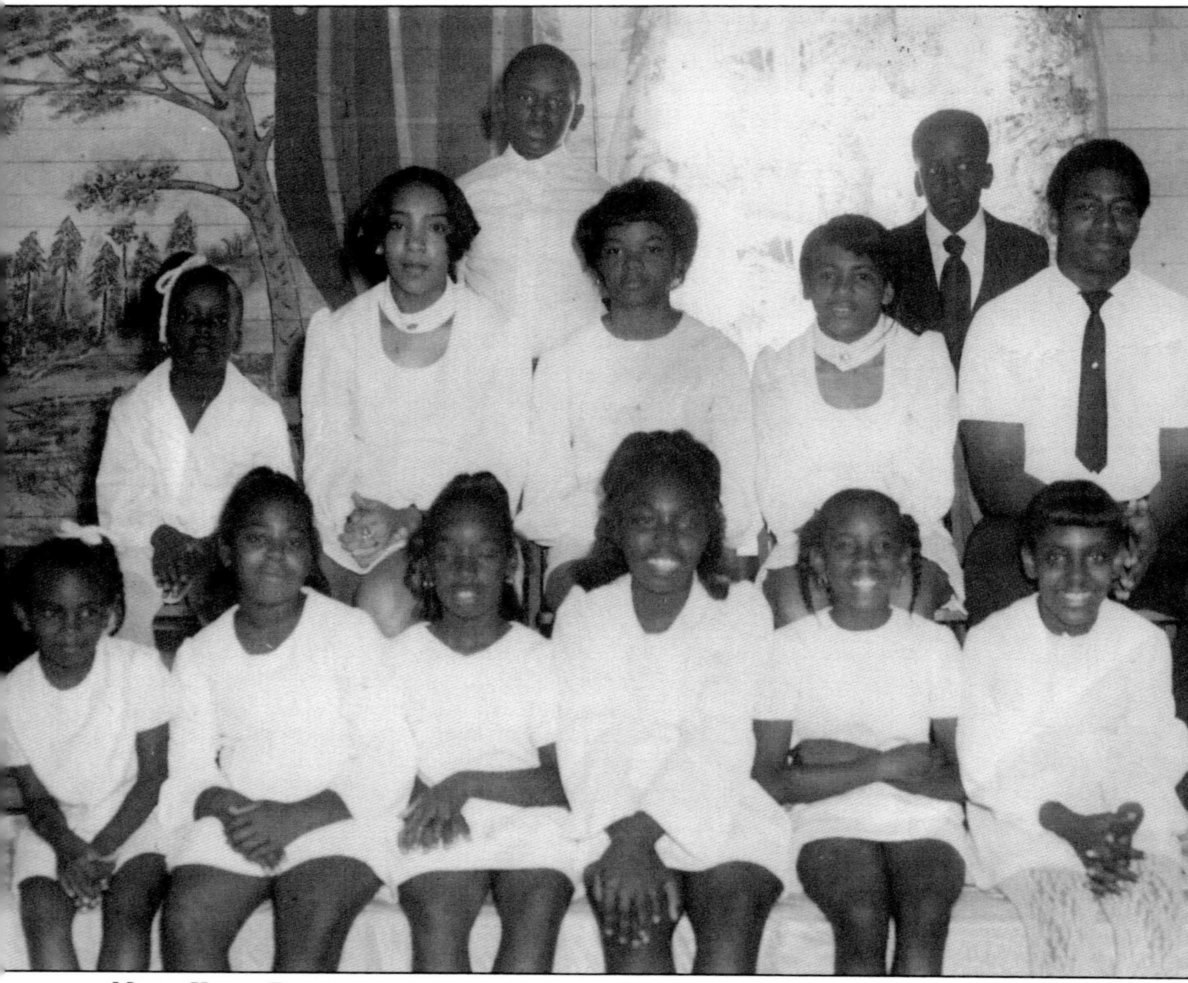

Naomi Youth Fraternity No. 104. The Order of the Eastern Stars (OES) nurtured and mentored youth through activities, programs, and camps. Pictured from left to right are (first row) Carolyn Peters, Darlene Brumfield, Tina Mitchell, Viola Brumfield, JoAnn Marigny, and Arleen Sheridan; (second row) Rhonda Austin, Sharon Sheridan, unidentified, Marilyn Sheridan, and Papa Marigny; (third row) Billy Marigny and unidentified. (Courtesy of Sharon Sheridan Wilcox.)

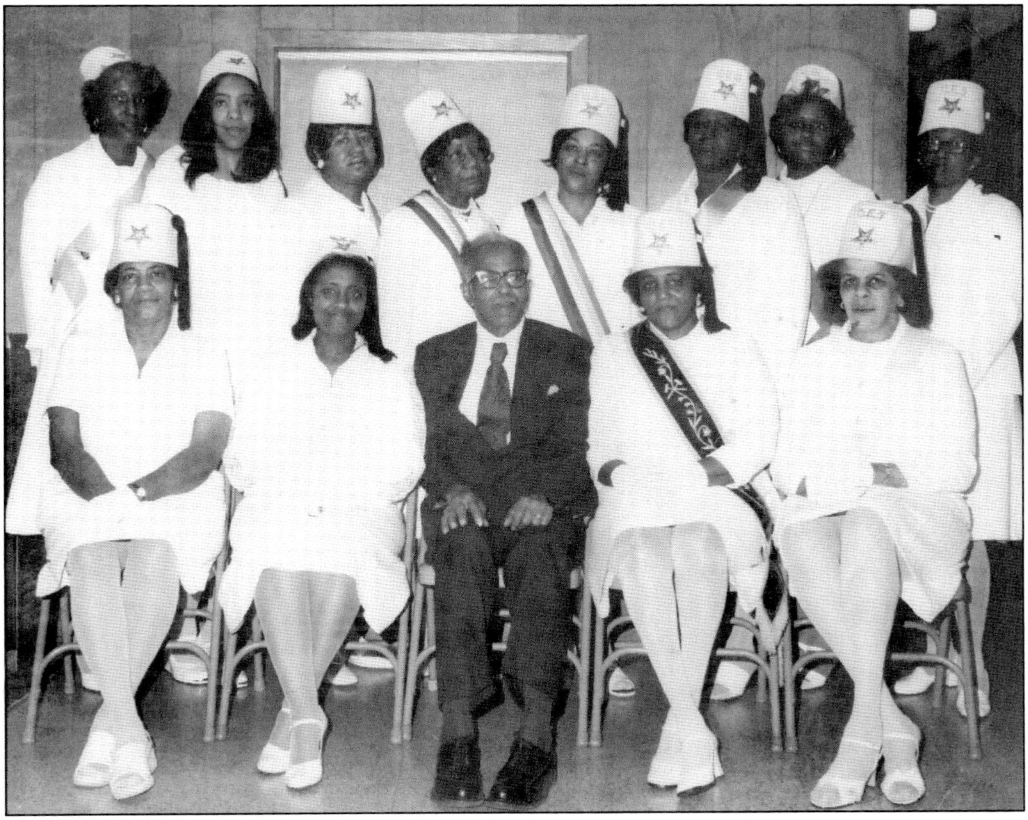

Order of the Eastern Stars. African Americans valued fraternal organizations for their leadership and moral standing. Shown from left to right are (first row) Helen Demley, Lillie Mae Gordon, Alex Sheridan, Helena Sheridan, and Corretta Anderson; (second row) Charlene Gordon, Sharon S. Wilcox, Bobbie Harper, Magglie Reed, Velma Anderson, Sister Harper, Patricia G. Strong, and Mable Thomas. (Courtesy of Sharon S. Wilcox.)

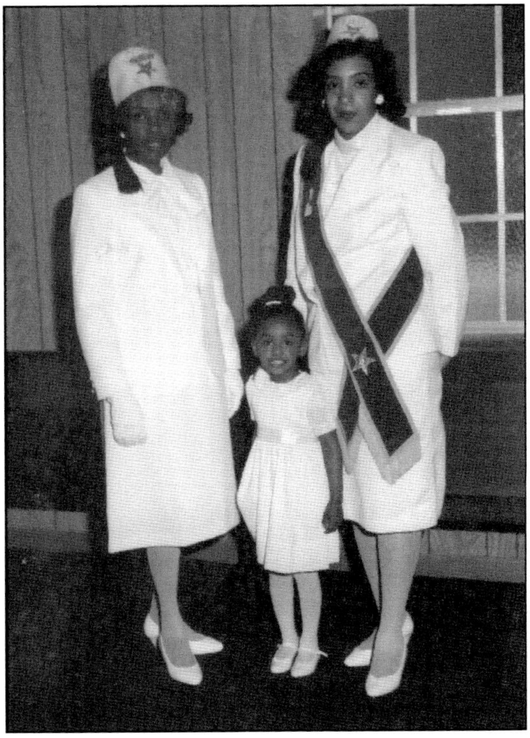

Three Generations of OES. From left to right, Katie Wilcox, little Serena A. Wilcox, and Sharon S. Wilcox continue in the Sheridan tradition of leadership in the OES. Sister Helena Sheridan was the first worthy matron with Naomi No. 161. Brother Alex Sheridan was one of the founding members of the Masons. (Courtesy of Sharon Sheridan Wilcox.)

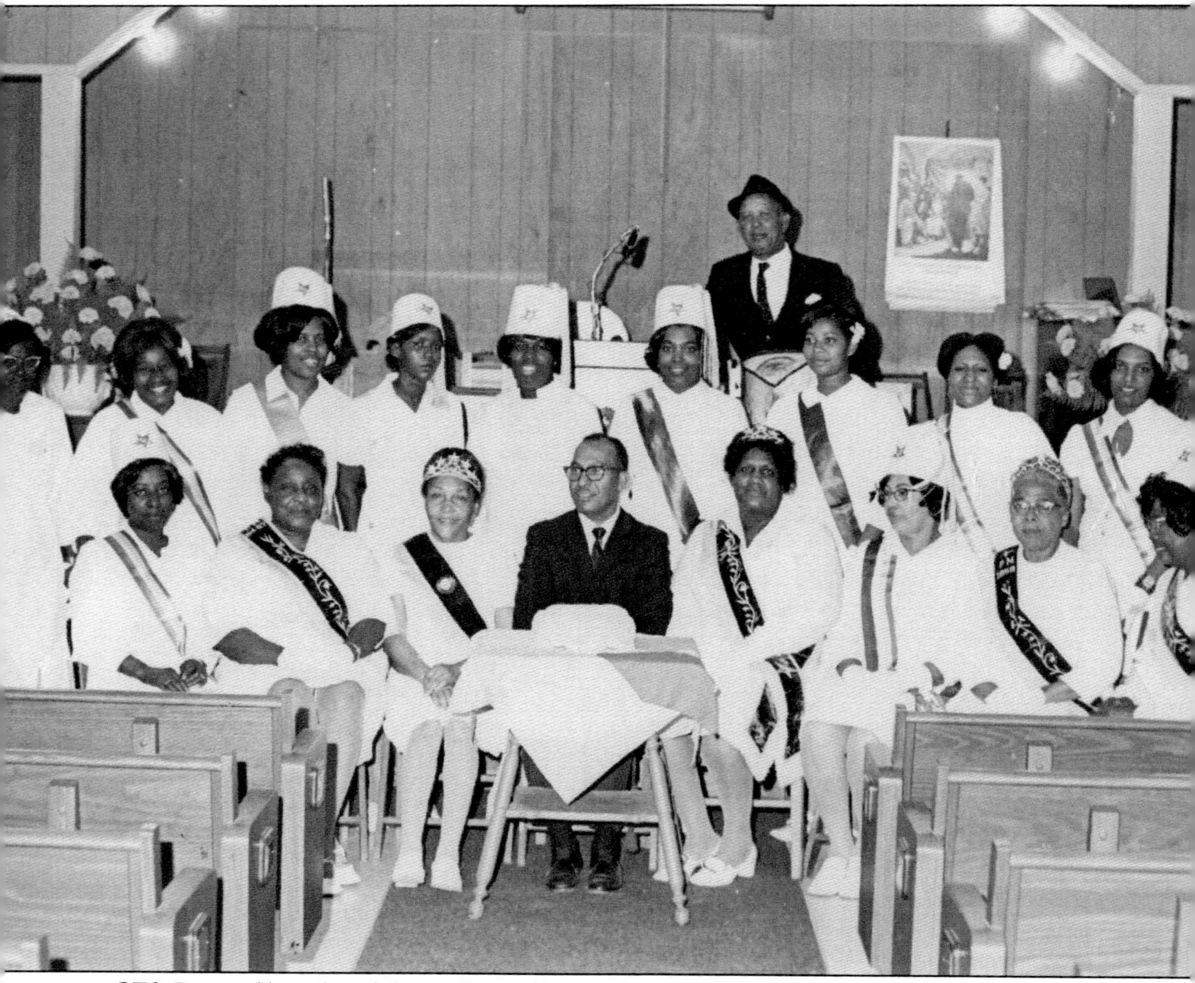

OES. Pictured here from left to right are (first row) Ella Selmon, Lula Jones, Virginia Prophet, Lester Dunn (worthy patron), Jennette Dunn (worthy matron), Mammie Barge, Neomi Joseph, and Ida Prioleau; (second row) two unidentified ladies, Louise Williams, Carol Dunkins, Johnnie Golden, Elma Brazil, unidentified, Idell Jones, and Beatrice Dunn Penn; (third row) Eddie Joseph (worthy patron). Some unidentified members are not Covington residents. (Courtesy of Ella Selmon.)

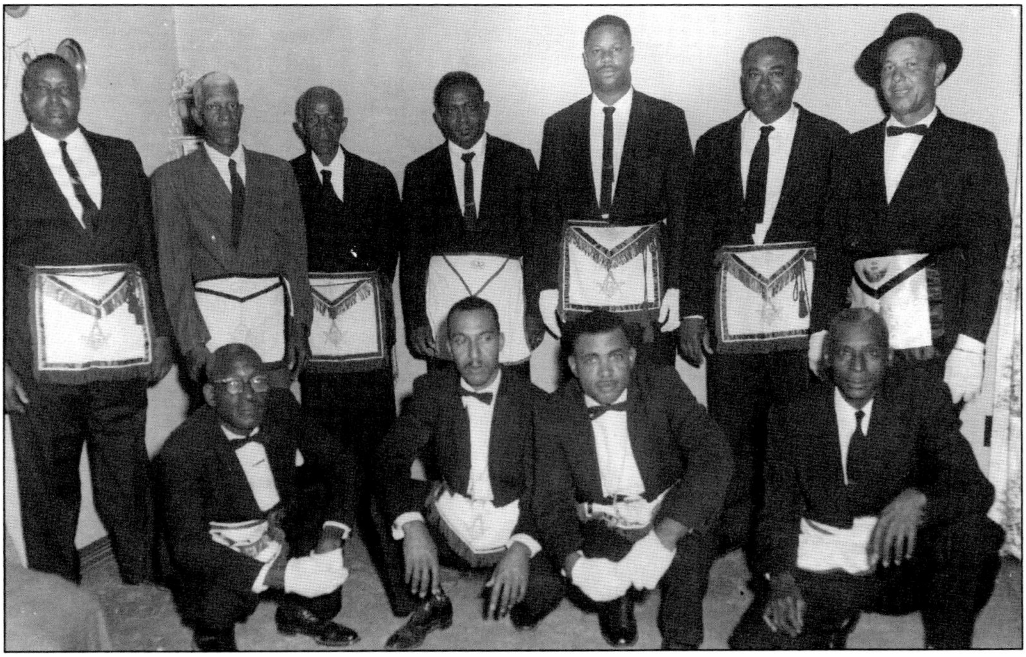

PRINCE HALL MASONS. The local chapters of Prince Hall Masons consisted of members from several towns. Although a local meeting place is in Covington, towns in Washington Parish supplied brothers. The national organization formed when Prince Hall separated from the British Order during the American Revolution, forming African Lodge No. 1. Louisiana traces its first chapter to 1863. (Courtesy of the Randle collection.)

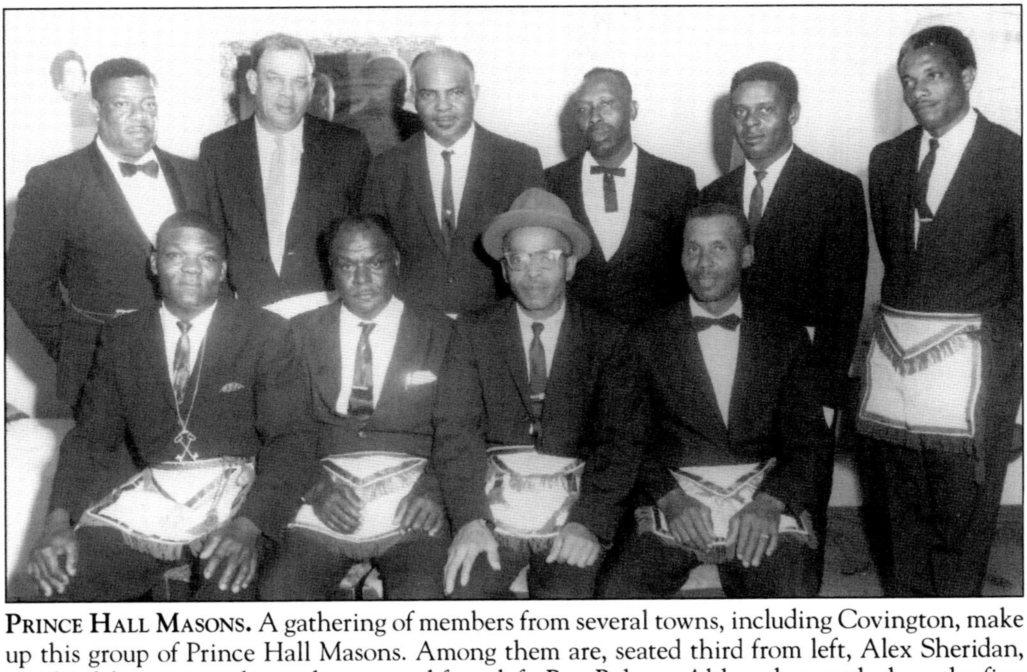

PRINCE HALL MASONS. A gathering of members from several towns, including Covington, make up this group of Prince Hall Masons. Among them are, seated third from left, Alex Sheridan, worshipful master, and, standing second from left, Roy Baham. Although records show the first chapter organized in 1863, there were free blacks in New Orleans who claimed to be Masons as early as the late 1830s. (Courtesy of Randle collection.)

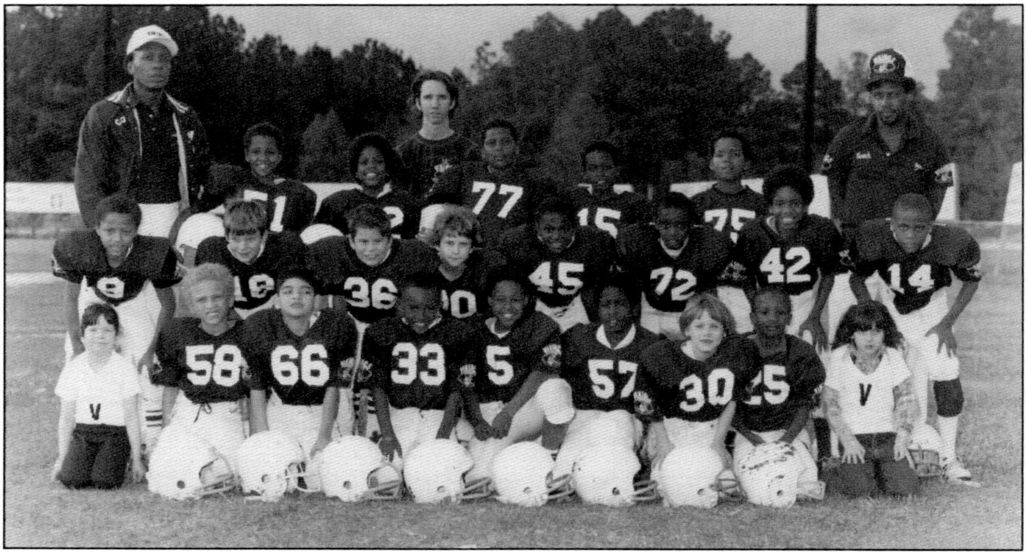

The Vikings, 1979. To remedy the lack of African American coaches in little-league play, James "Gus" Davis and Lonnie Boykin organized this team. The team won the league championship during this first year. Coaches include, from left to right, Lonnie Boykin, head coach; Mitchell Davis, assistant coach; and, James "Gus" Davis, defensive coach. (Courtesy of James Davis.)

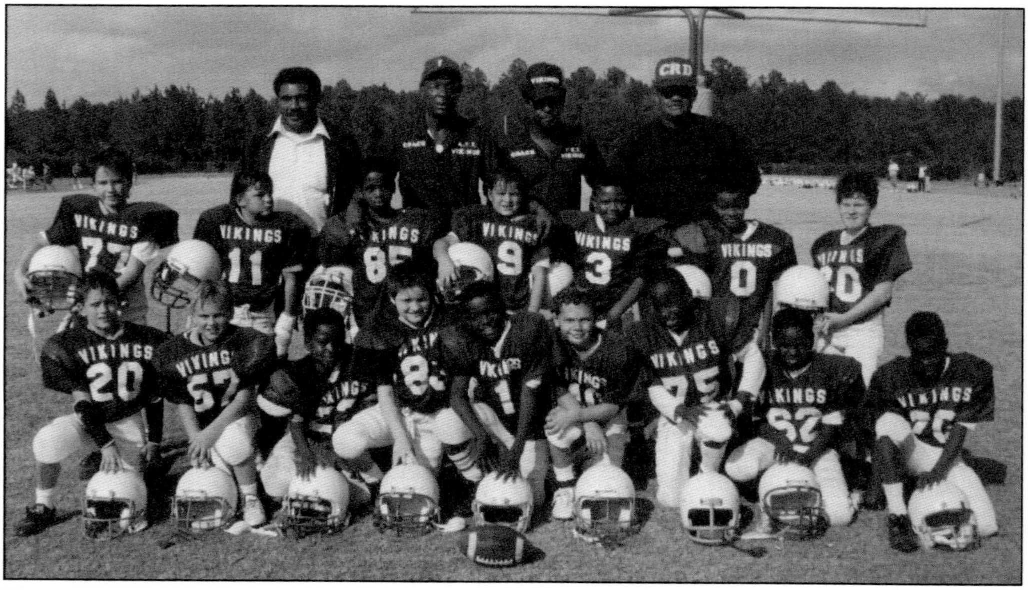

The Vikings, 1991. After several years of winning championships, the Vikings became the team to beat, according to James "Gus" Davis. Guiding the champions to success were, from left to right, Johnny Keller, assistant coach; councilman Lonnie Boykins, head coach; James Davis, defensive coach; and Ellison Gordon Jr., assistant coach. (Courtesy of James Davis.)

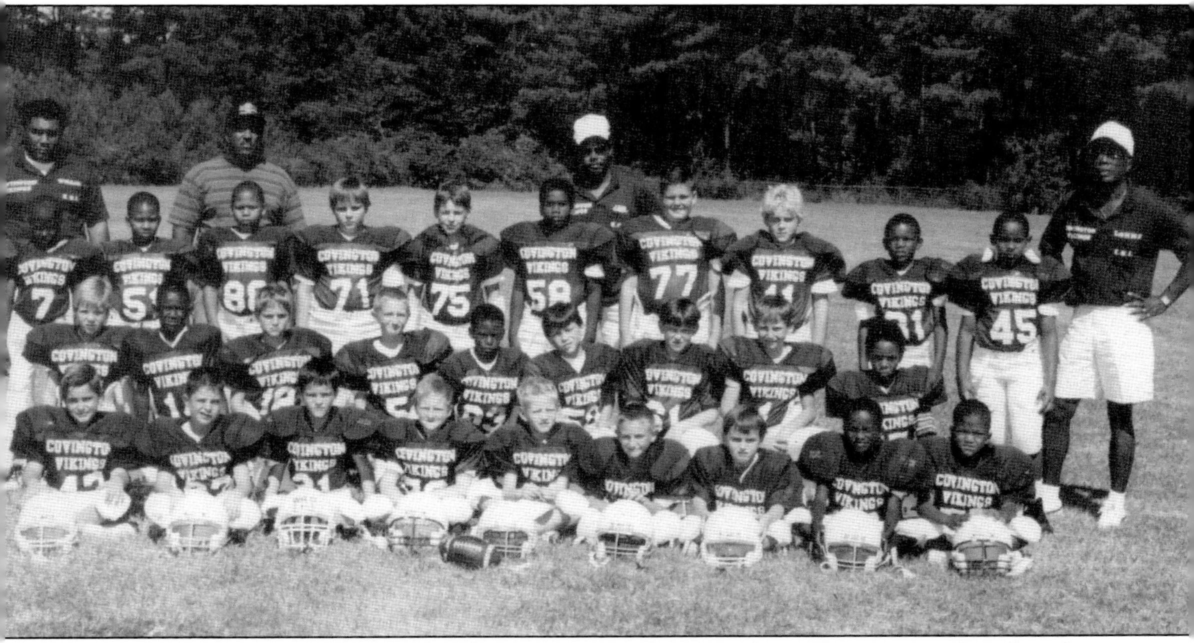

The Vikings, 1995. In 17 years of play, the team won 12 championships. They set records and made African American coaching of integrated teams commonplace. Here, the coaches are, from left to right, Johnny Keller, assistant coach; Aaron Fabre, assistant coach; James "Gus" Davis, defensive coach; and councilman Lonnie Boykins, head coach. (Courtesy of James "Gus" Davis.)

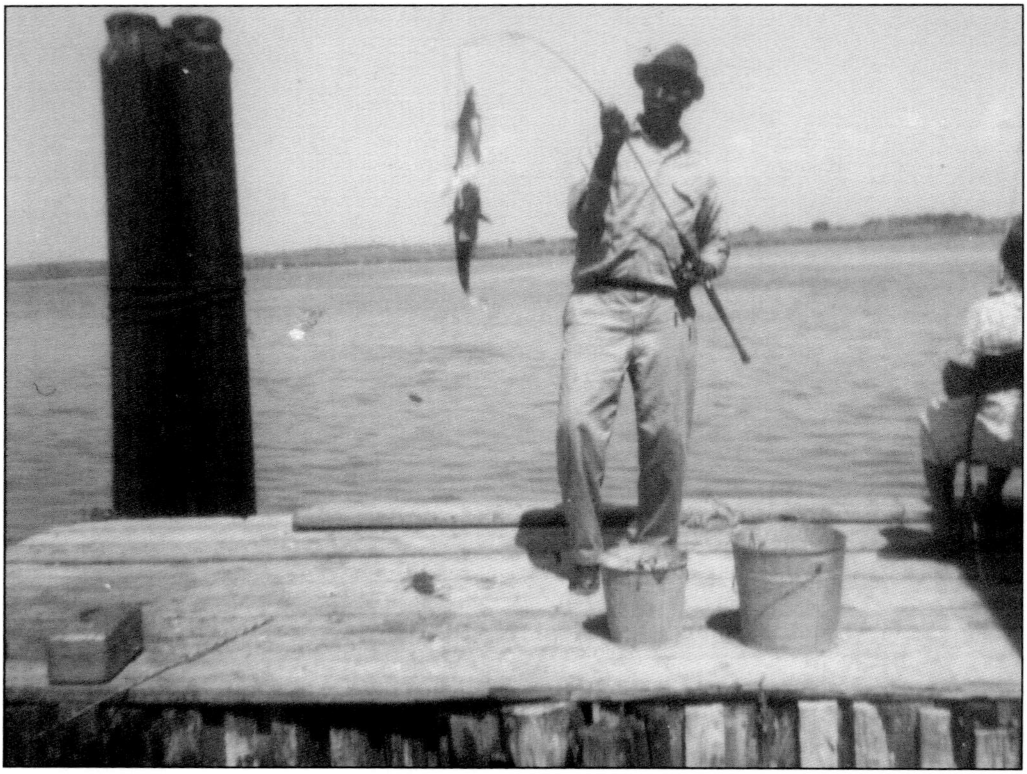

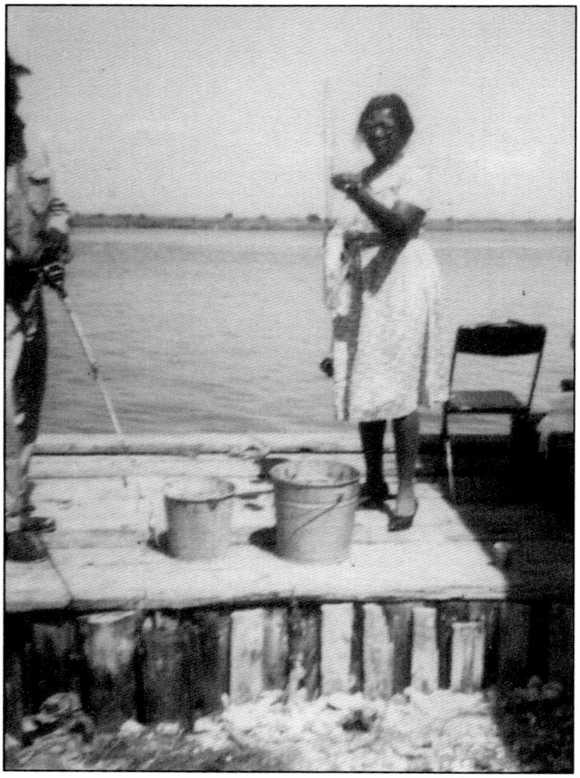

Fishing for Funds. African American churches, particularly until the 1980s, did not have access to financial resources to build and support their churches. Members often worked menial labor, and their earnings reflected it. Rev. Peter Atkins and his family drove 135 miles to Grand Isle, Louisiana, on the extreme southern tip of the state, to catch fish for fundraisers. (Both, courtesy of Ida Thomas James.)

Nine

TAKING CARE OF BUSINESS

African Americans were largely employed by the agriculture and lumber industries and by facilities like Mackie Pine Oil, later Delta Pine. Lumber companies exploited workers as much as their processes destroyed virgin forests, although exploitation was not exclusive to them. In addition, many women worked as domestics and teachers. Both men and women, however, found ways to work independently, often as second jobs.

Isaiah "Sonny" Robertson cleaned offices and delivered beer. Having learned the process of buying and selling liquor, Robertson opened the Dew Drop Inn with a business partner. He and his wife, Doris, also owned Dot's Ponderosa, a club that she managed and that conducted nightly bingo games benefiting various charitable groups. The Robertsons reared seven children—daughter Beverly and sons Charles, Isaiah Jr., Kenneth, Theard, Dwight, and Andre—all of whom attended college on athletic scholarships. One newspaper account on Doris Robertson noted that she worked "long and hard hours while rearing children, entertaining grandchildren, and keeping up with her hobby of making ceramics."

Women owned beauty shops, often while holding full-time jobs elsewhere. Among them were Marie Hamler on Florida Street, Willena Bennett on Lee Road, and Jeannette Dunn, whose husband owned a barbershop. Some women did grueling work, laundering clothes in their homes and providing childcare. As teachers relocated to Covington, local families, especially older, sometimes widowed, women, provided housing. One of the very few apartment buildings available to blacks was Roosevelt Landor's rooming house. Other African American–owned businesses included Teal Lott's, the "working people's café;" Silas Down's Café; and the Rock Palace, also known as "Little Vietnam."

The best job for both men and women was teaching. So few career opportunities existed for African Americans that the majority of college graduates were teachers. Although principals were men, women dominated the classrooms. Rosenwald principal James Harrison's 1944 faculty consisted of Quida Fabre, Lubertha Harrison, Mary Porter, Thelma Washington, Henri Ella Clayton, and Helen Frick. In 1960, of 29 faculty under principal Alphonse Fabre, 18 were women; of 54 listed in a reunion memory book, 34 were women. All the lunchroom workers were women; janitors were men.

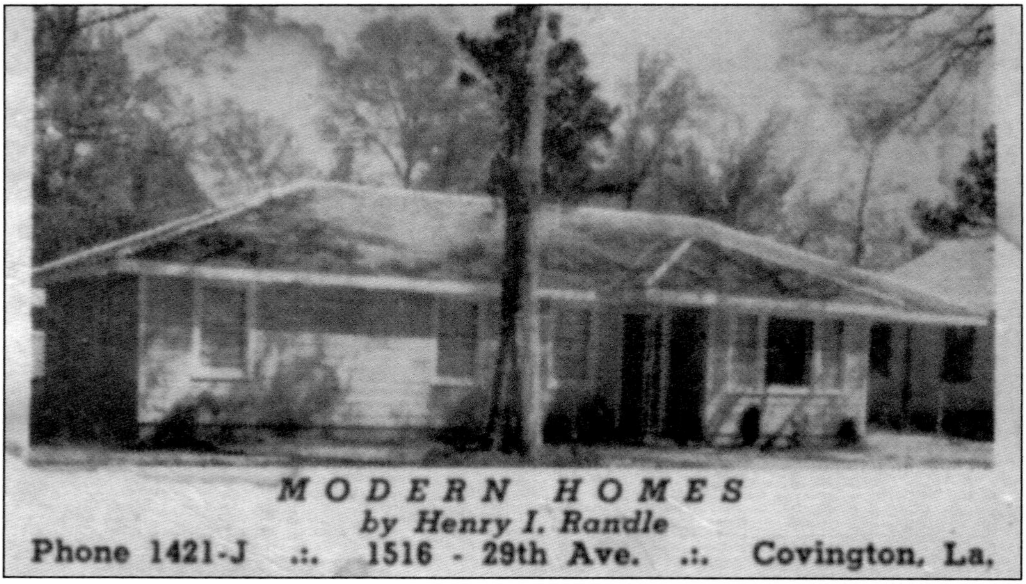

MODERN HOMES POSTCARD, c. 1960s. Henry Randle Sr. owned a construction company, among several businesses. He trained in carpentry at Southern Technical College in Baton Rouge, Louisiana. He built homes in the African American community, including one for his family, illustrated here. One daughter continues to live in the home. (Courtesy of the Randle collection.)

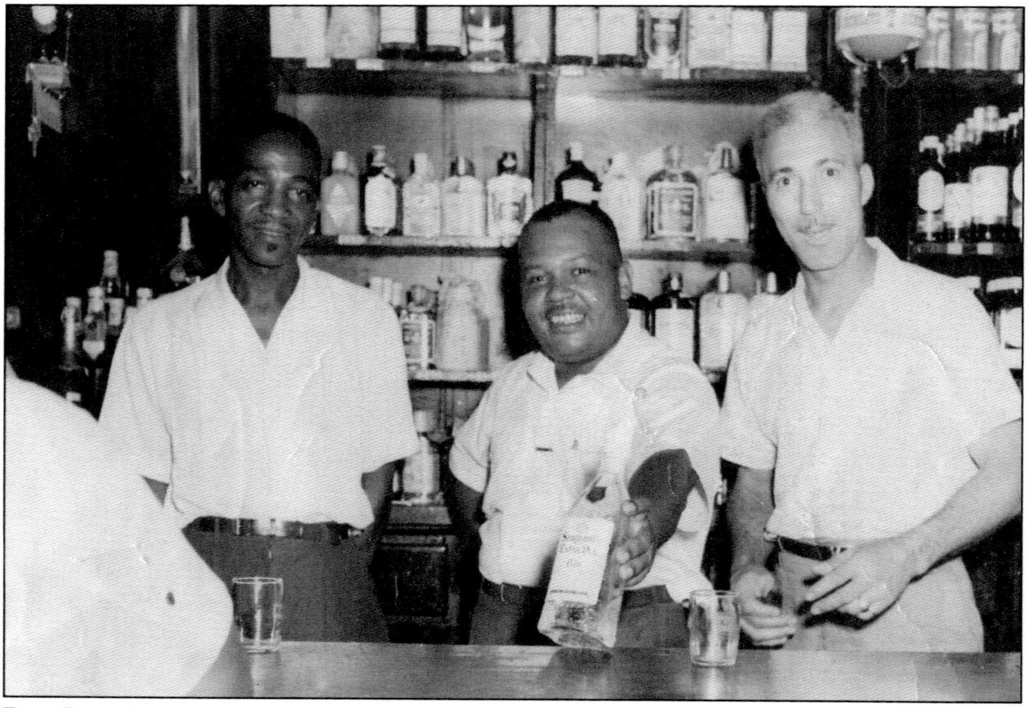

DEW DROP INN, 1961. Isaiah "Sonny" Robertson (far right) was unmatched as an athlete. His business acumen was exceptional as well. He built the Dew Drop Inn and later opened Dot's Ponderosa with his wife. The Dew Drop Inn was one of the top outlets for Seagram in south Louisiana. With him are associates Albert "Dempsey" Jones, sales representative (center); and Percy "Johnny" Smith. (Courtesy of the Robertson family.)

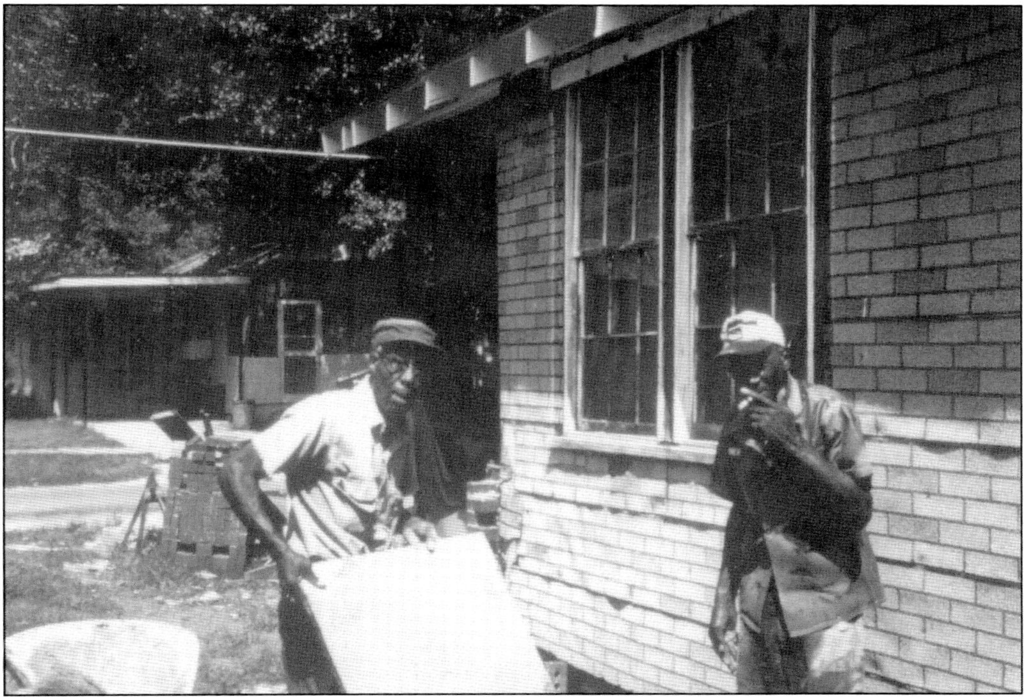

Carpenters, 1970. Alex Coner and Ed McCormick worked in home construction. Coner worked as a bread maker at People's Bakery, as a dogger (a carriage rider pulling logs at the sawmill), and as an electrician, often working all three jobs weekly. He and his wife, Mable, had four sons: Hilton, Jerry, Bobby, and Christopher. (Courtesy of Jerry Coner.)

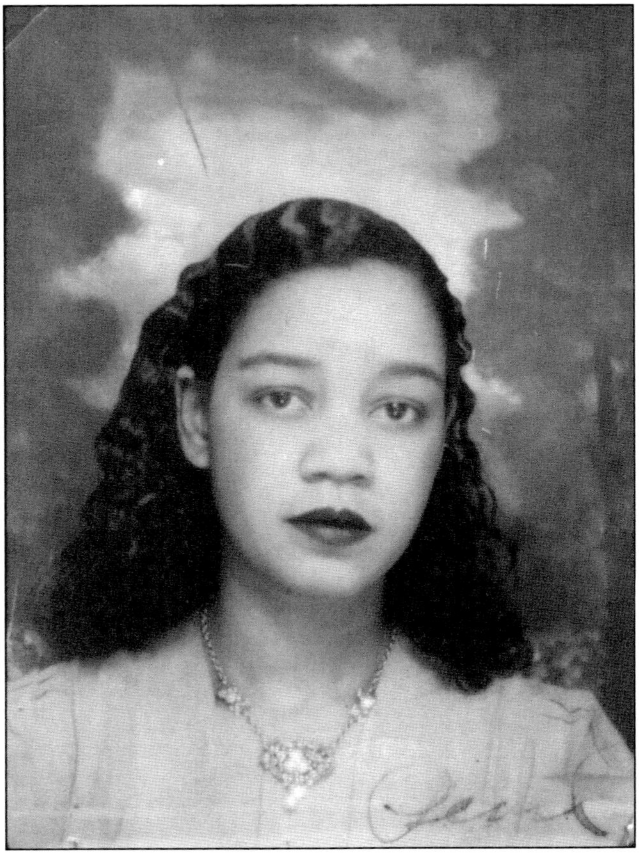

Pearl Randle Jacobs. Young women began domestic work very early in their lives. Pearl Jacobs lived on the premises as a servant for many years at an estate called Green Gates, just off Highway 190. She represents a majority of African American women who worked as maids in the homes of white Covingtonians. She was first cousin to Alphonse and Luteal Thomas. (Courtesy of Ida Thomas James.)

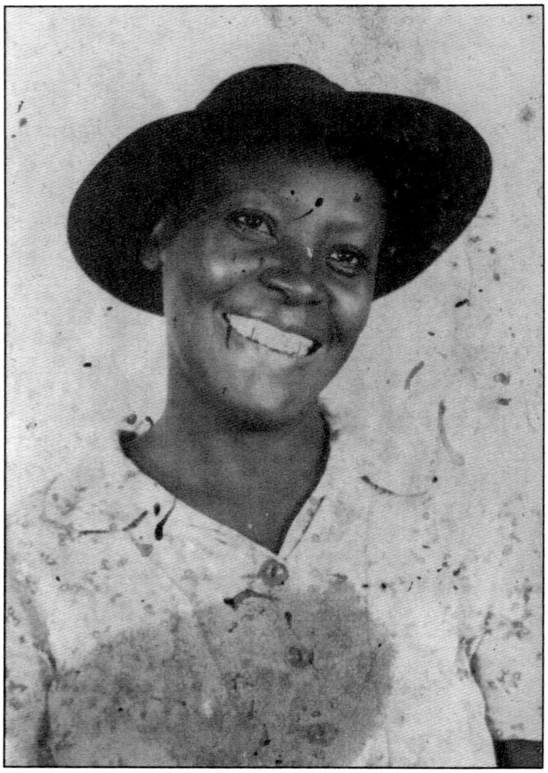

Clotilde Callahan Davis, c. 1940s. Willie Walter Lewis Davis Sr. worked as a cement finisher and was known as "the medicine man" because of his curative abilities. Clotilde Davis worked as a domestic. Her family is rooted in St. Tammany Parish; her mother was from Lacombe, and her father was from Covington. (Courtesy of Ella Selmon.)

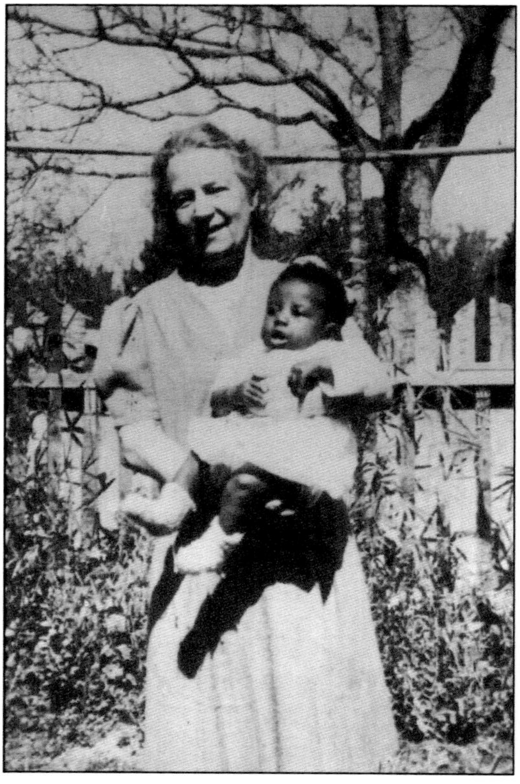

Poole and Davis, c. 1944. While Clotilde Callahan Davis cooked inside for the Wallace Poole family, Alice Poole played with baby Ella. The Poole family's history dates to the late 1800s in Covington's business community with the Poole Lumber Company. Both Ella's mother and godmother worked as domestics for the Poole family. (Courtesy of Ella Davis Selmon.)

Ten

MOVING FORWARD

Perhaps the pastor, his church members, and African Americans in Covington might say that it was divine intervention when he refused a transfer to another location. Rev. Peter S. Atkins's congregation followed him to a newly created church, Bethel Reform Methodist, in 1949, and he remained in Covington until his death in 1986. Between those years, Reverend Atkins's activism led to social and political progress.

Although passage of the 15th Amendment prohibited voter discrimination, it left options for disenfranchisement. One example was the poll tax. The *St. Tammany Farmer's* 1935 front page announced that 7,000 poll tax receipts were issued, and it was likely that no African American could vote. (The Supreme Court ruled the poll tax unconstitutional in 1966.)

To counter injustices, Reverend Atkins founded the NAACP Covington branch in 1963 and led a protest against segregation at the bus station in the old Southern Hotel. For his labor, vigilantes burned a cross at his home and his church in 1966. Violence did not deter him, and he formed the Black Voters League and left a framework that others followed.

Leroy and Helen Simon Frick found an activist for human rights in Walker Percy. As Leroy recalled, Percy was "interested in trying to help the colored people of this community." Helen Frick, who, according to daughter Rosetta Silvan "was into everything," teamed with Percy, a group of doctors, a law firm, and African American citizens, including Rev. Lawrence Tyson. Their focus was better jobs and better housing for African Americans. They created a credit union because African Americans could not bank in Covington, Head Start at Regina Coeli, and public housing, all of which focused on improving African American quality of life.

Other groups, the Human Relations Council and the Bridge, aided in the transition between segregation and integration. The Covington Civic League, among many efforts, spearheaded a successful drive in 1988 to name the community park after Reverend Atkins and initiated an annual Juneteenth festival. Civic fights and cooperation, although still challenging, resulted in integrated schools, elected African American officials, workplace opportunities, upward mobility, and a city different from its beginnings.

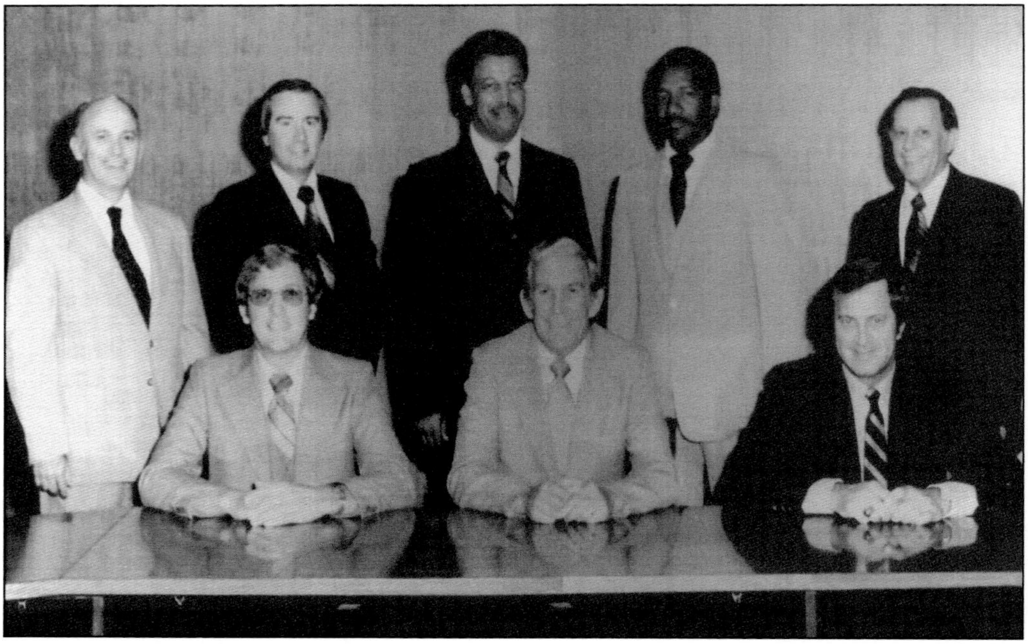

Covington City Council, 1979. The first African Americans elected to the city council posed with the full council for their official portrait. From left to right are (first row) Lee Alexius, Mayor Ernest Cooper, and unidentified; (second row) Ronnie Pogue, unidentified, Earl Christy, Freddie Primus, and unidentified. (Courtesy of Jerry Coner.)

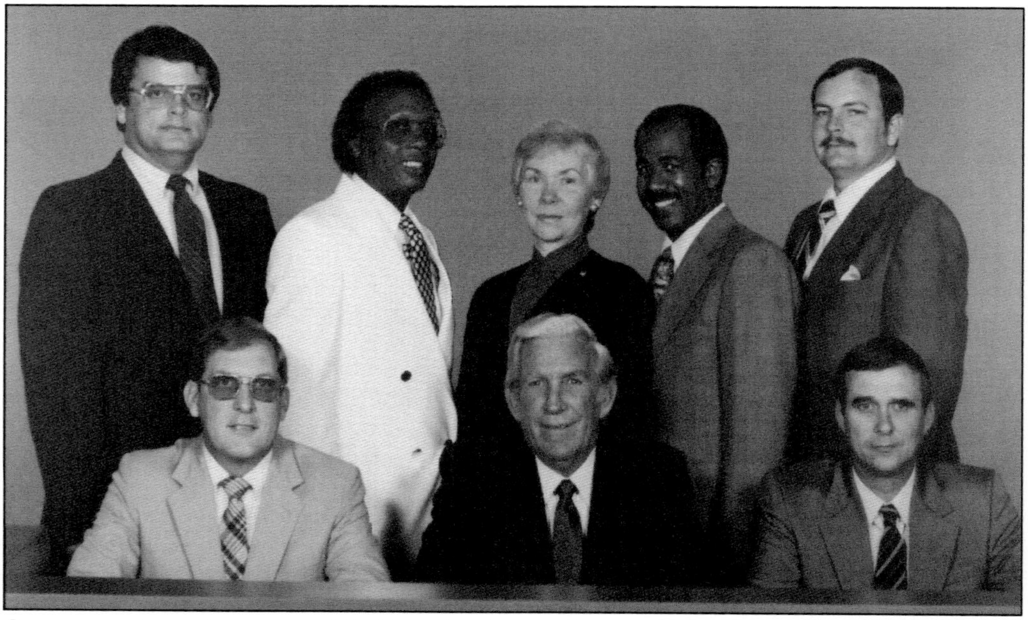

Covington City Council, 1987. By 1987, the novelty of African American council members had lost its shine, but not its interest. Other African American candidates threw their hats into the ring. Edward Conerly ran but lost against Lonnie Boykin's first effort. Pictured here from left to right are (first row) Leroy Jenkins, Mayor Ernest Cooper, and Jerry Sharp; (second row) Lee Alexius, Lonnie Boykins, Patricia Clanton (first woman elected), Jerry Coner, and Sammie O'Keefe. (Courtesy of Jerry Coner.)

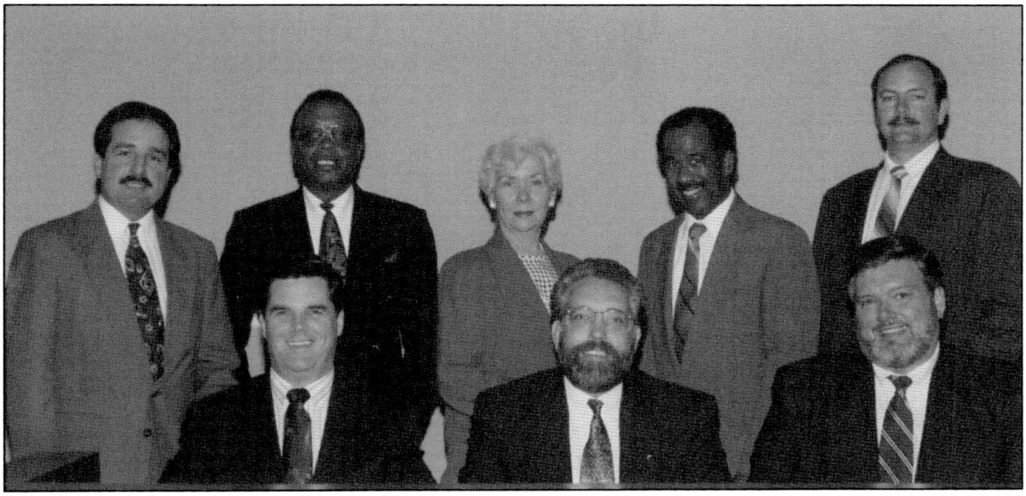

Covington City Council, 1991. In this photograph are, from left to right, (first row) Donald Primes, Mayor Keith J. Villere, and Robert J. "Bob" Champagne; (second row) Matt Faust (District E), Lonnie Boykins (District A), Patricia Clanton (District D), Jerry Coner (District B), and R.S. "Sam" O'Keefe (District C). (Courtesy of Jerry Coner.)

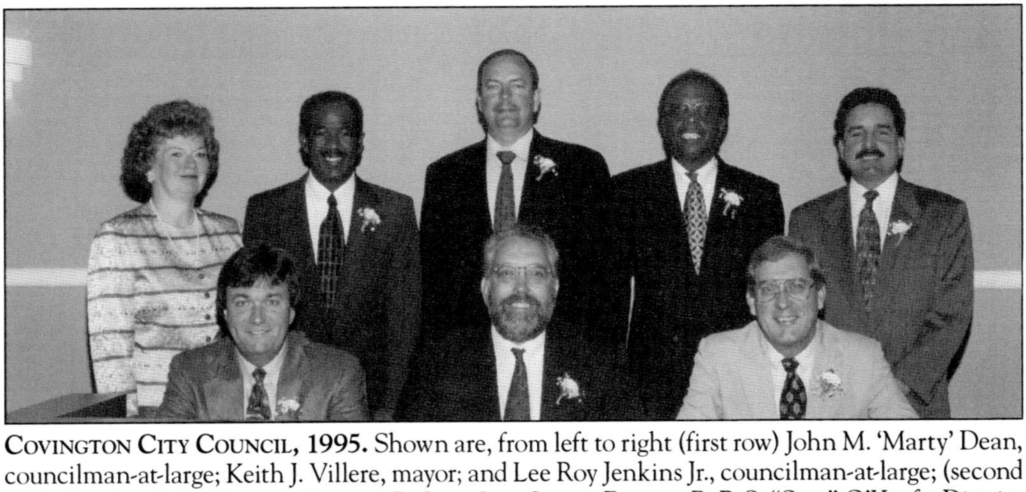

Covington City Council, 1995. Shown are, from left to right (first row) John M. 'Marty' Dean, councilman-at-large; Keith J. Villere, mayor; and Lee Roy Jenkins Jr., councilman-at-large; (second row) Carolyn Talley Pearce, District D; Jerry Lee Coner, District B; R.S. "Sam" O'Keefe, District C; Lonnie Boykins, District A; and Matt Faust, District E. (Courtesy of Jerry Coner.)

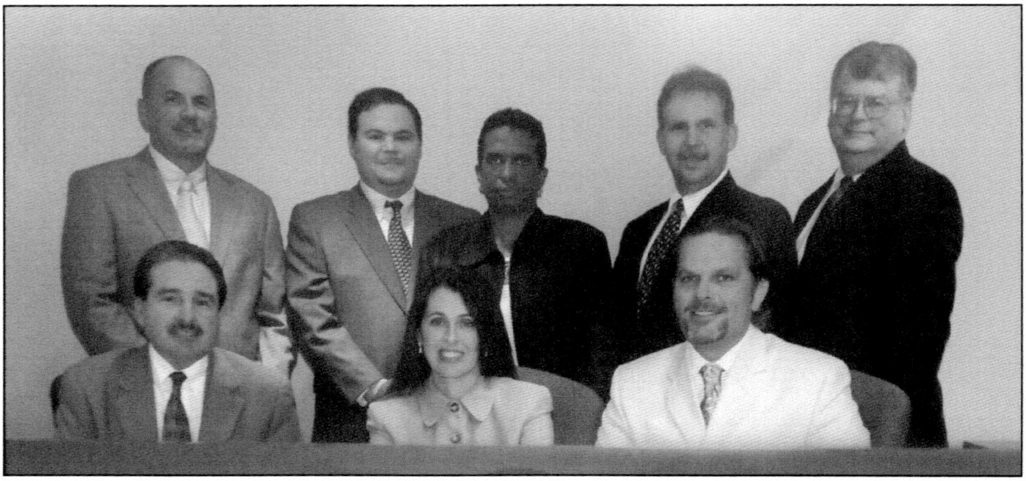

Covington City Council, 2007. Frances Dunn, the first African American woman elected to the City Council, stands at center. She served until 2011 and remained active in community work. Seated at center is the only woman elected mayor, Candace B. Watkins (2003–2011). From left to right are (seated) Matthew Faust (at-large), Watkins, and W.T. Blackall III (at-large); (standing) Clarence Romage (District B), Mark Sacco (District A), Dunn, Martin Benoit (District D), and Lee Alexius (District E). (Courtesy of City of Covington)

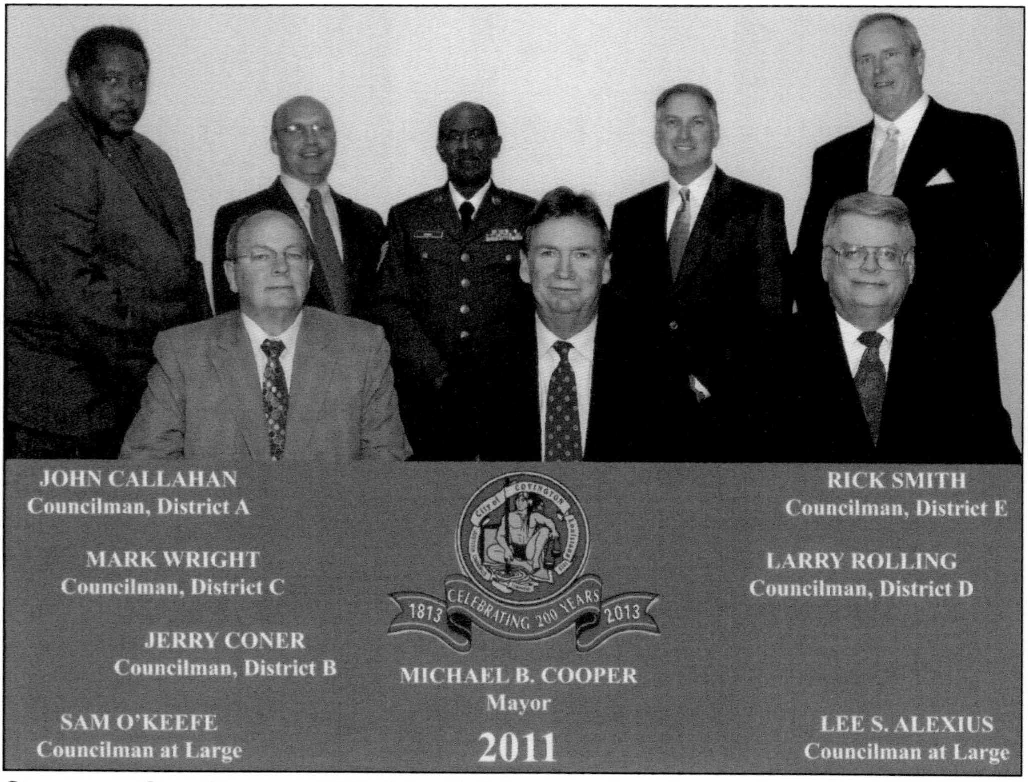

Covington City Council, 2011. John Callahan was elected council member for District A, replacing Lonnie Boykins. Other noticeable changes on the council include the lack of women and the addition of new members Mark Wright, Rick Smith, Lee Alexius, and Sam O'Keefe, returning after sitting out for a term. (Courtesy of Jerry Coner.)

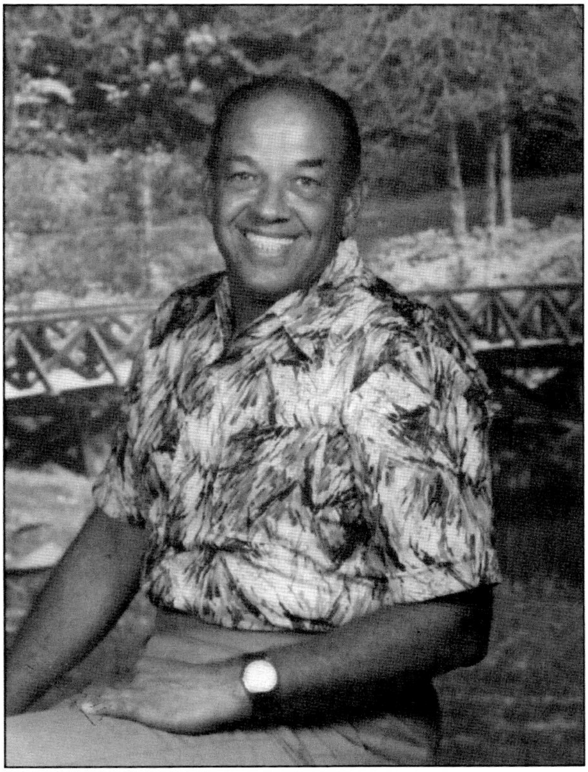

Leroy Frick, c. 1960s. Frick and his wife, Helen, were active participants in many facets of African American life in Covington. He was a native and recalled poor housing, no plumbing in his part of town, and a two-hour commute (pre–Causeway Bridge) to New Orleans to work at the Higgins Plant. The couple's hard work paid off as they built their home in 1958. (Courtesy of Rosetta Frick Silvan.)

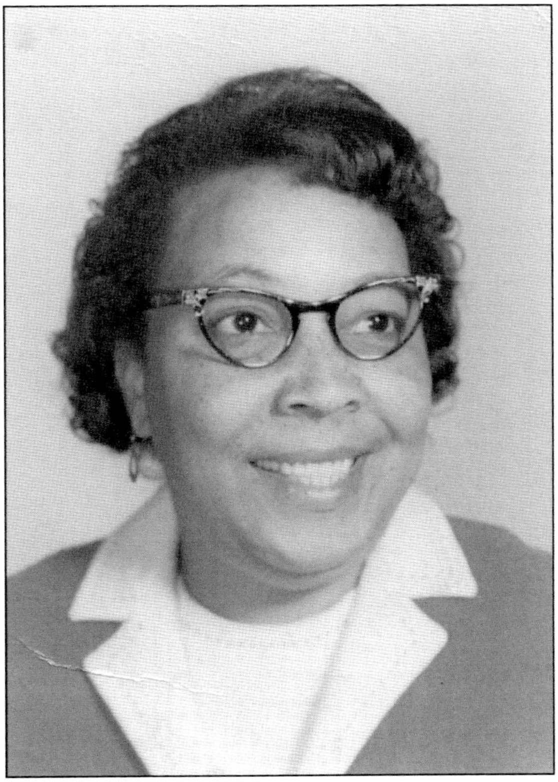

Helen Simon Frick, c. 1960s. Helen Frick's husband said she was the activist. She had a long resume of civic, civil rights, and educational work. She was the first president of Regina Coeli Head Start and worked with Walker Percy in its founding. She also is the namesake of Helen Frick Village of HUD, the 1983 Citizen of the Year, the first African American member of the League of Women Voters, and a teacher. Also, the city proclaimed April 15, 1993, in her honor. (Courtesy of Rosetta Frick Simon.)

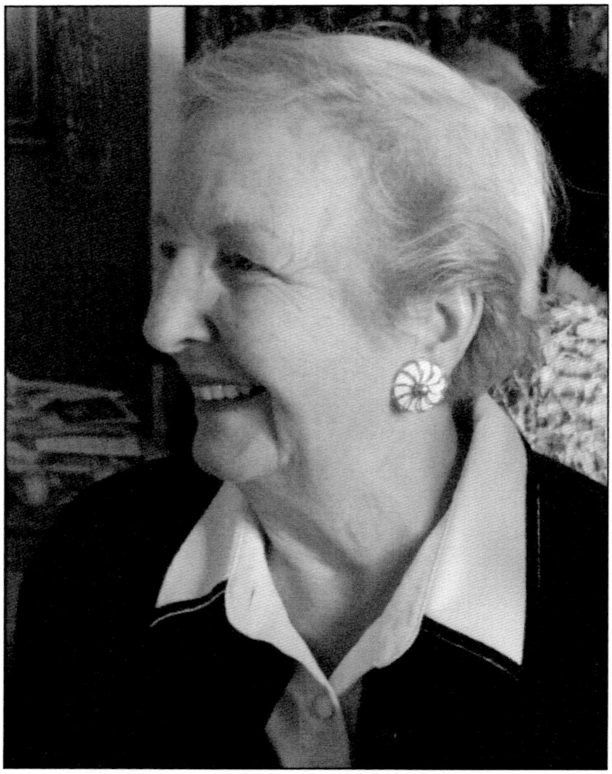

Emily Diamond. Emily Diamond was an integral part of the African American community. She was a member of the Human Relations Council and a cofounder of the local chapter of Habitat for Humanity (walking 100 miles to raise funds for it). She also worked for years without pay at a federal credit union, created to provide banking for African Americans, and volunteered at Faith Bible Church's residential rehabilitation center. (Courtesy of Stanley Diamond.)

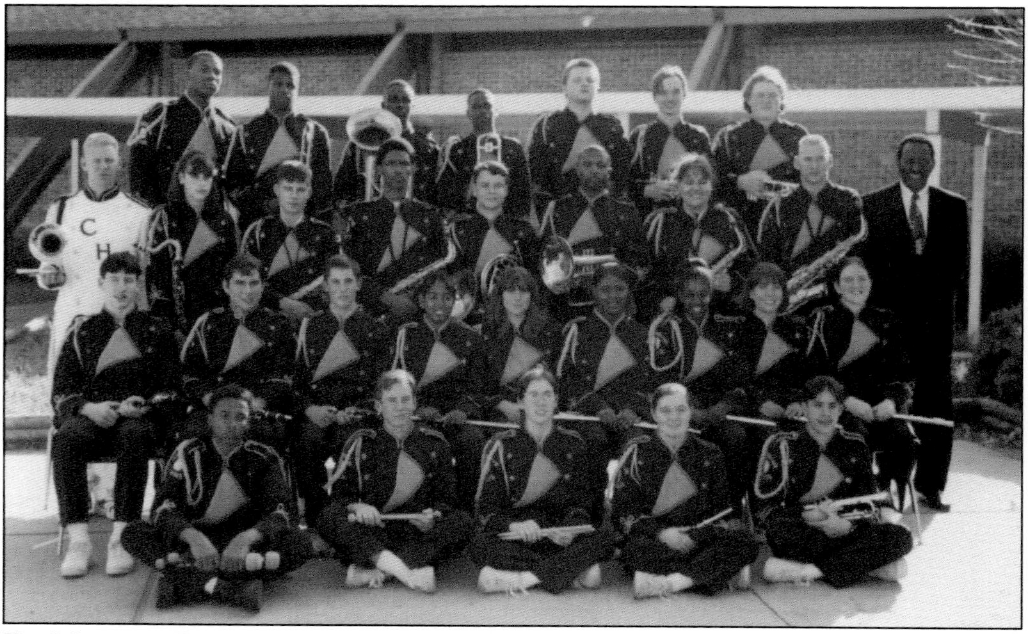

The Marching Band, 1986–2004. Roy Mouton directed St. Paul's Marching Band for 13 years. According to his wife, Alfreda Mouton, he was asked to teach and lead the band at Covington High School in 1986. He left St. Paul's, although not without having a great influence on some students. Students named a scholarship in his memory in 2011 at St. Paul's. He passed away in 2007. (Courtesy of Alfreda Mouton.)

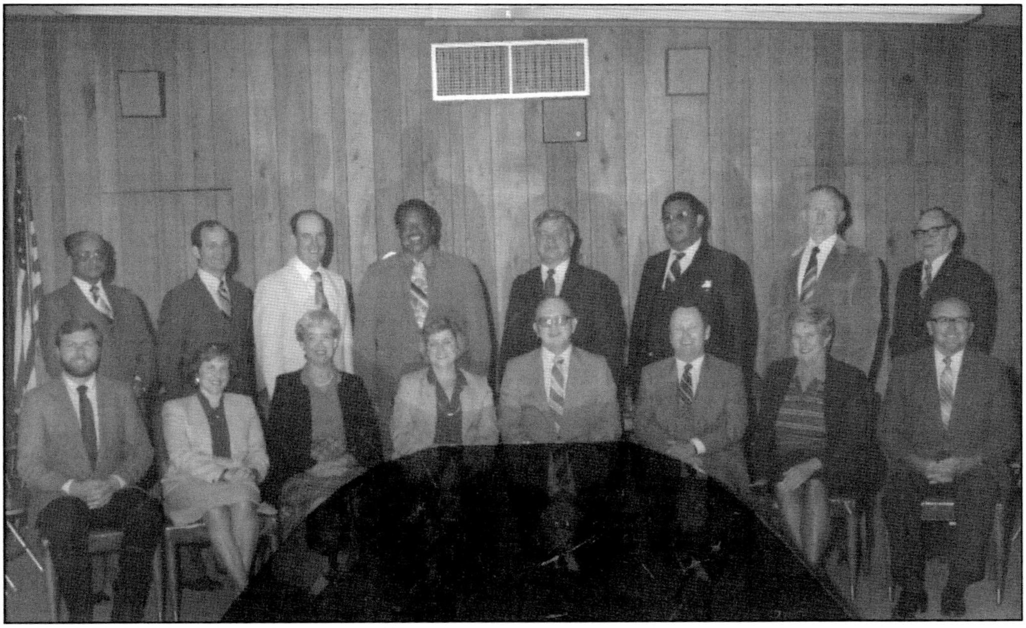

St. Tammany Parish School Board, 1983. Prior to 1979, no African Americans served on the School Board. Otis Campbell of Slidell (standing third from right) became the first such elected official. In 1980, Albert "Smitty" Smith (standing fourth from left) became the first elected from Covington. He served through 1998. The Albert R. "Smitty" Smith scholarship is an annual award to top students from Covington High School. (Courtesy of STPB.)

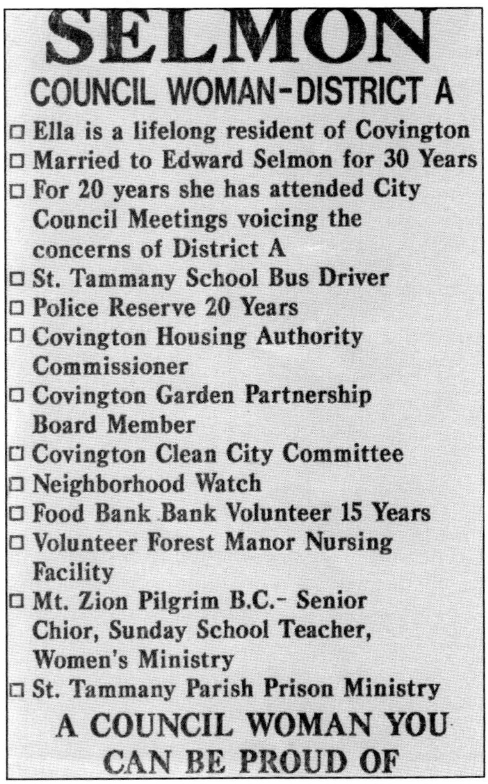

Campaign Flier, c. 1987. This is the reverse side of Ella Selmon's campaign flier. Selmon lives in the heart of the African American community and was involved in many civic, social, and political organizations. Although her activism was well known, Lonnie Boykins won the district. (Courtesy of Ella Selmon.)

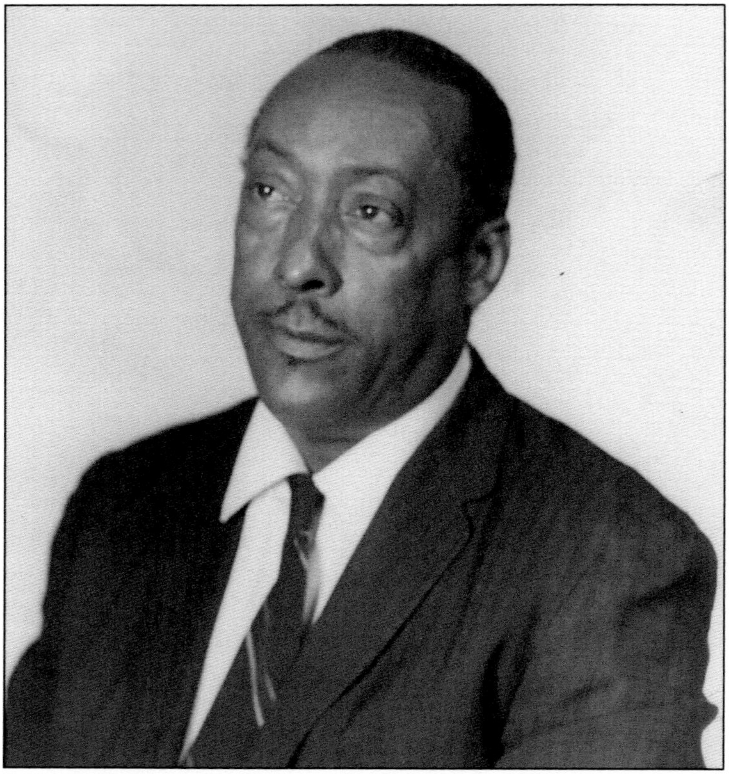

Police Officer. Clarence Marigny served as one of the first African American police officers in Covington. He could neither accost nor arrest any white person. He could only patrol the African American section of town, and was limited to using his police powers for or against African Americans. (Courtesy of the Randle collection.)

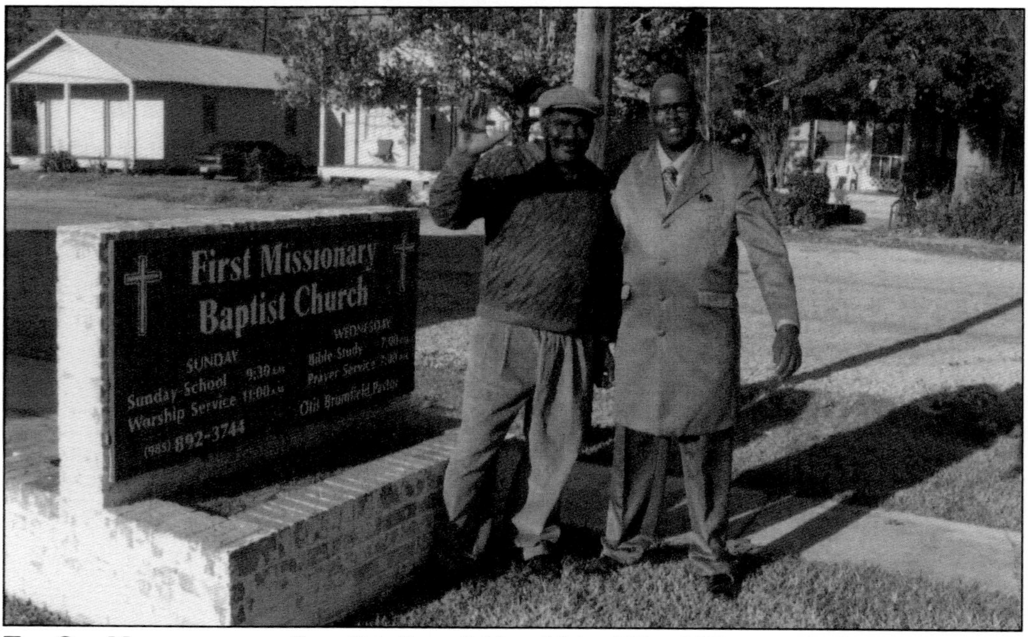

The Old Neighborhood. Rev. Otis Brumfield and friend Harold Ramsey Sr. share greetings in front of the church, which captures the neighborhood before much of the land surrounding the church was sold to St. Tammany Parish. The houses shown here have since been demolished, replaced by a parking lot. The only building standing in the block is the First Missionary Baptist Church. (Courtesy of Rev. Otis Brumfield.)

GENEVIEVE BAHAM JOHNSON. Young mother Genevieve Baham Johnson's husband Henry died and caused the family to move from New Orleans back to their family home in Covington in 1958. Their home, passed down from Genevieve's mother, Edor Reed Baham, stood across the street from what is now the St. Tammany Parish Justice Center. Johnson's children attended both segregated and integrated schools. (Courtesy of Victoria Johnson Trevigne.)

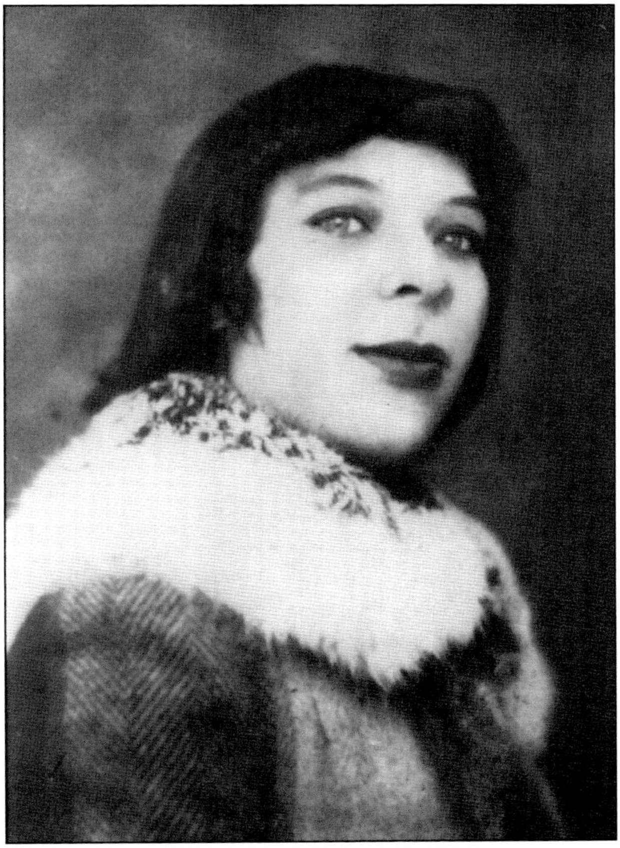

THE NEIGHBORHOOD GROCERY STORE, C. 1950S. Ivery James Sr. sits in front of his store on Thirtieth Avenue. Covington Rosenwald High School students recalled sneaking away to buy snacks at Ivery's store. He owned rental properties, as well. African Americans owned businesses that helped them to live independently from the larger Covington population. (Courtesy of Ida Thomas James.)

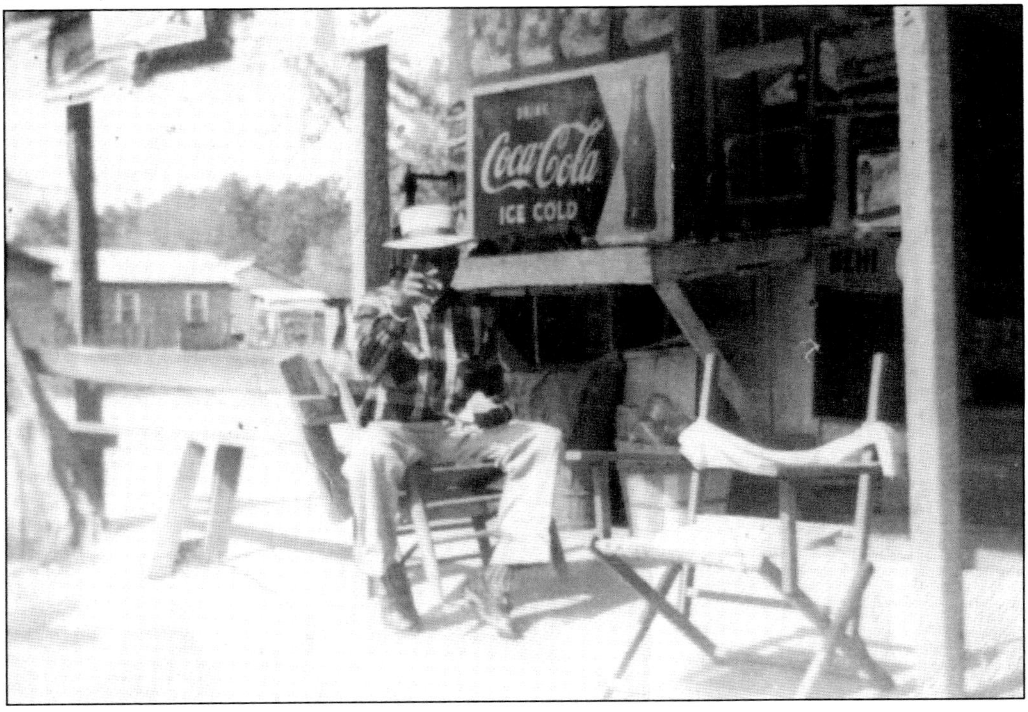

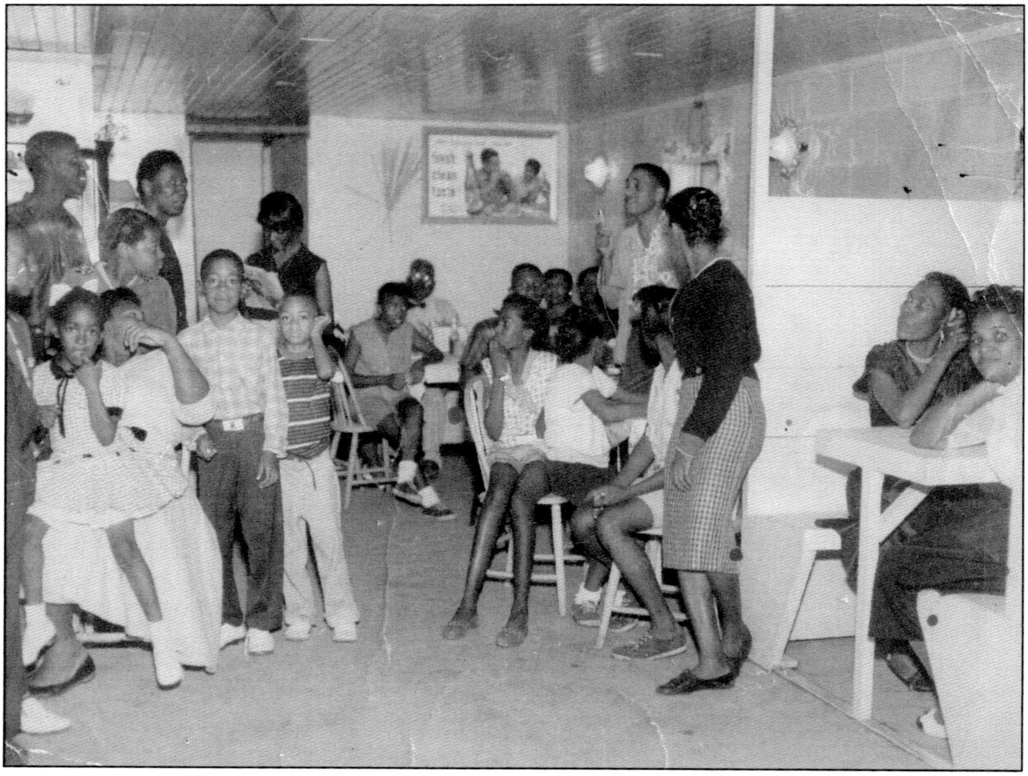

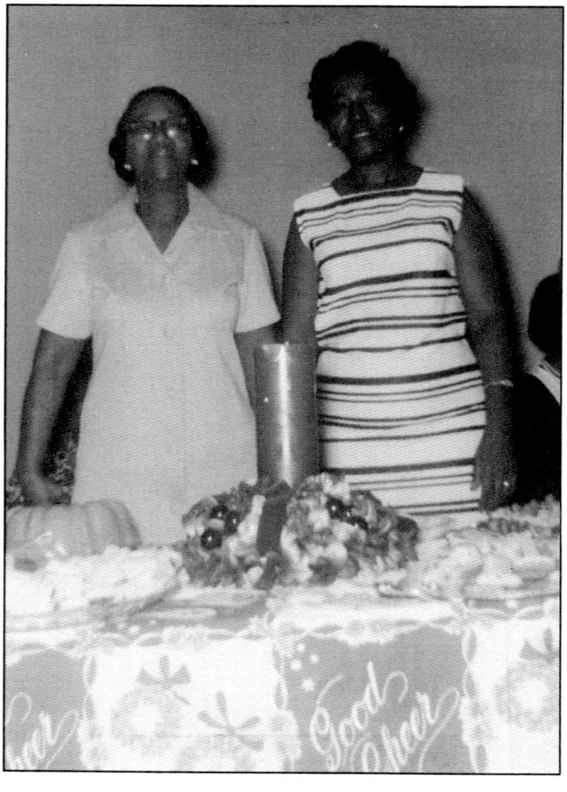

TEENAGE PLACE. Much of teenage life in Covington involved the school or the church. There were places to dance, however, and just to hang out and visit. Palmetto's provided that respite for youth. It was wholesome, allowing Deacon Raymond Zoll of Mount Pilgrim (seated at rear) and Ellison Gordon (standing at right) to host an event. (Courtesy of Ella Selmon.)

HOLIDAY TEA. "Ms. Honey" (Eula Mae Thomas) and Doretha Silvan host a table. "Teas" are fundraisers that highlight certain themes. Some are seasonal, monthly, or holiday-focused, with hosts decorating and providing catering for their table. This event is commonplace within the African American community, both as a fundraiser and as fellowship. (Courtesy of Ida Thomas James.)

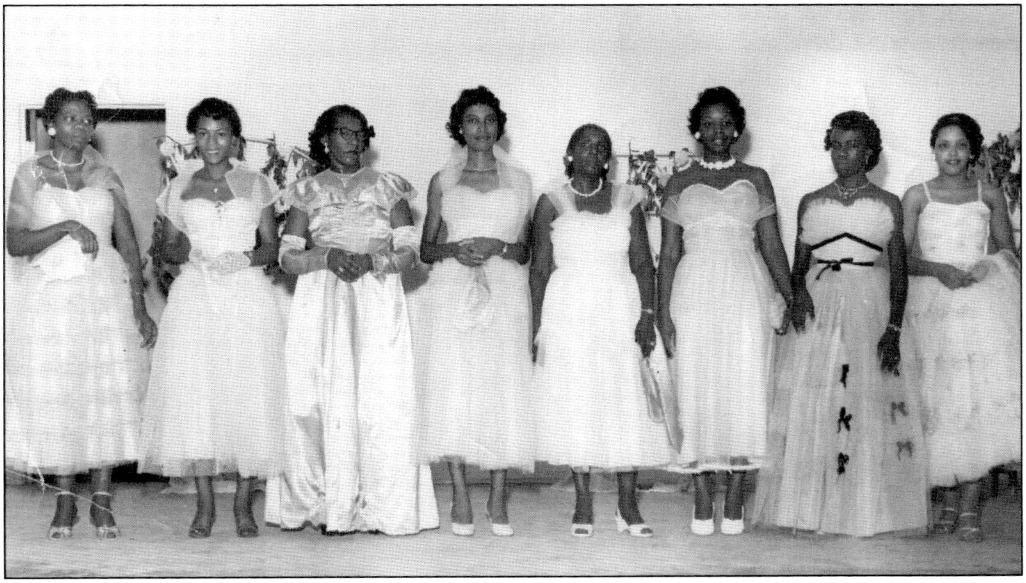

Society Ball, c. 1950s. Covington had a lively social scene for adults, where membership in organizations and invitations included people who were domestics, laborers, shift workers, porters, homemakers, hairdressers, barbers, and sawmill and shipyard workers. From left to right in this image are Ruth Weber, Dorothy Washington, Mary R. Bell, Thelma Brown, Gladys Marigny, Myrtle Lee Smith, Johnnie Mae Russell (Gordon), and Rosetta Frick Sylvan. (Courtesy of Ella Selmon.)

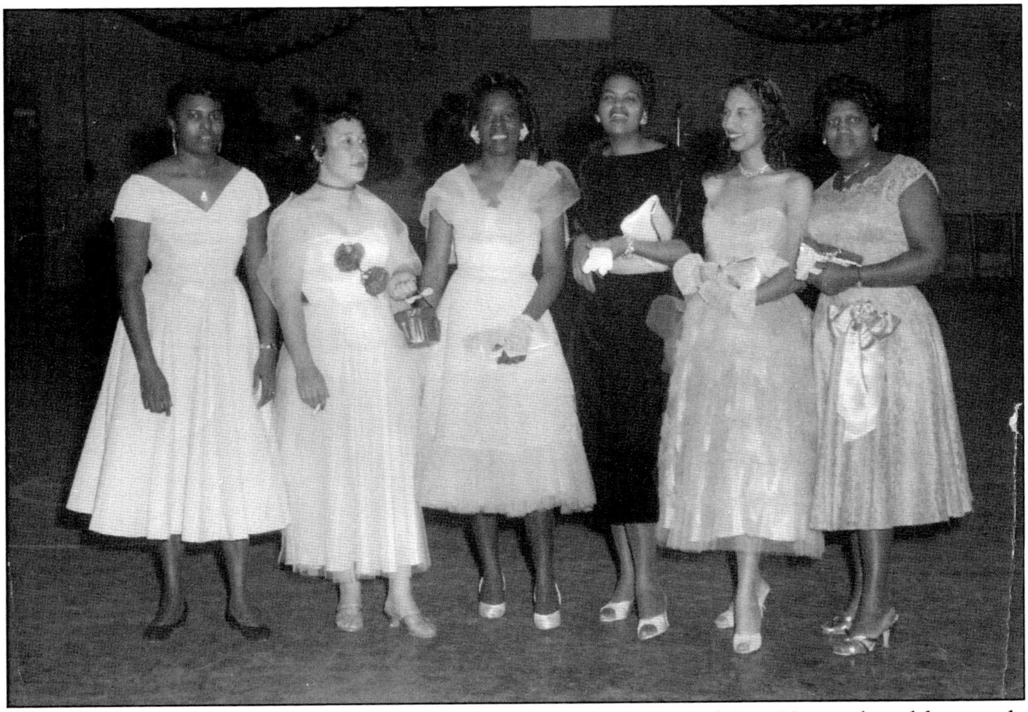

Society Ball, 1951. These ladies worked for the same employer, SouthEast Hospital, and frequently socialized together. Some of the ladies in this group, as well as others in the organizations, lived in nearby towns. From left to right are Leona Pierre, Leona Casborn, Grace Randle, Margie Wright, Ella Mae Doyle, and Jeanette Dunn. (Courtesy of the Randle collection.)

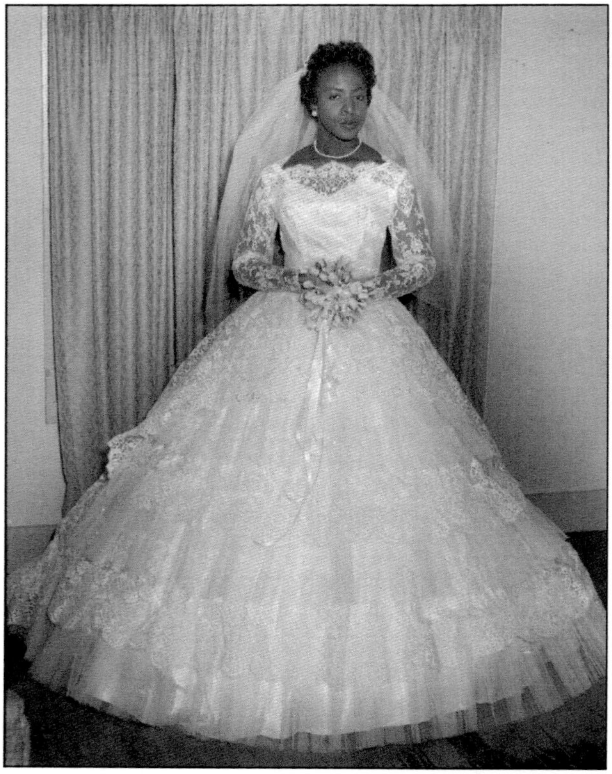

Beautiful Bride, c. 1950s. Geraldine Edgerson is prepared to wed Clarence Washington. She taught at Covington Rosenwald. Her finely tailored gown is likened to those made by local seamstresses. Local women recall rarely buying formal gowns and holiday ensembles from stores, where they either could not have a fitting or could not afford the merchandise. Fabric shops, however, had a brisk business. (Courtesy of the Randle collection.)

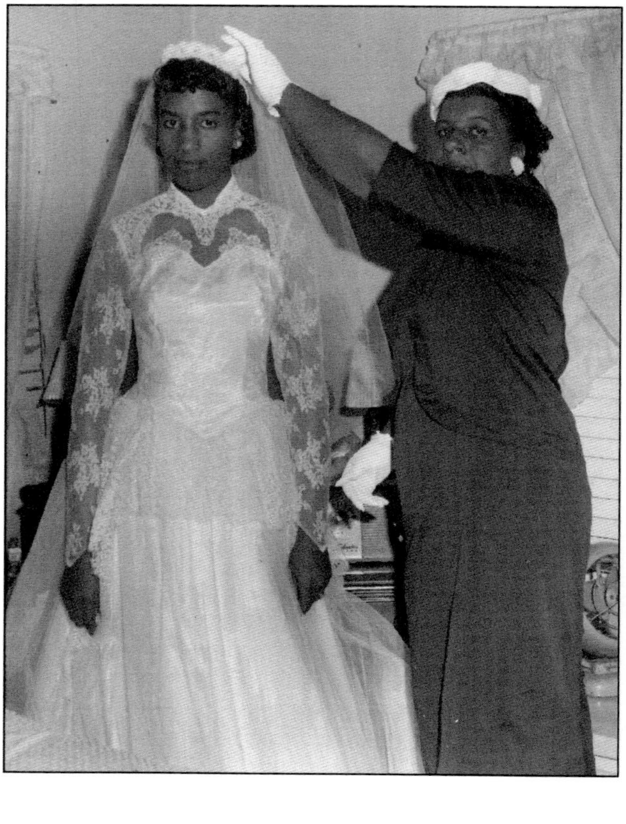

Mother and Bride, c. 1960s. Jessie Neal assists her daughter, Ruth, prior to her marriage to John Baham. Ruth's father, George, and Jessie both worked in various jobs, but George retired as a courier for First National Bank. Jessie was a housekeeper for several families. Their passion was in their business, Neal's Catering Service, the first such African American company in the area. They reared three children. (Courtesy of the Randle collection.)

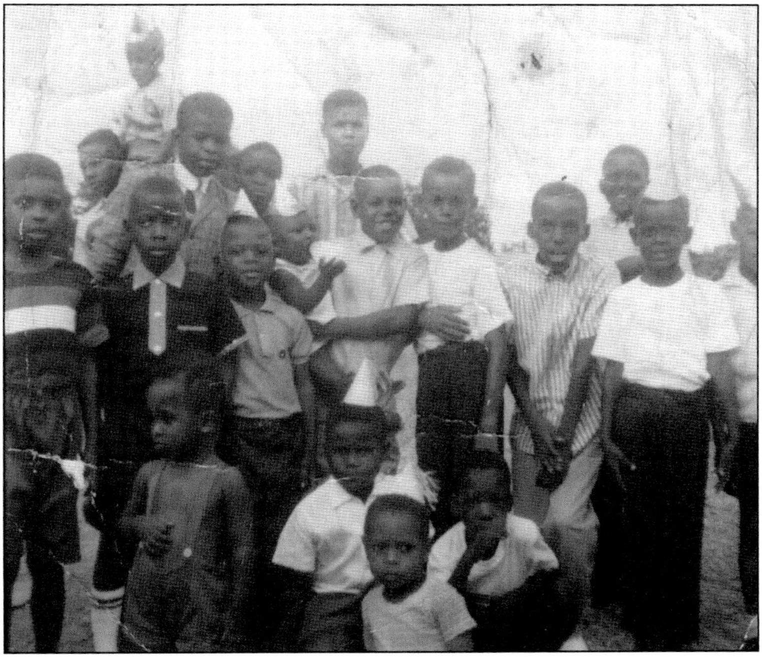

Demetrus Herbert's Birthday, c. 1960s. This is the boys' photograph at Demetrus Herbert's party. Living on West Twenty-seventh Street meant that all neighborhood children came to the celebration. No one was turned away, according to one of the attendees. (Courtesy of Victoria Johnson Trevigne.)

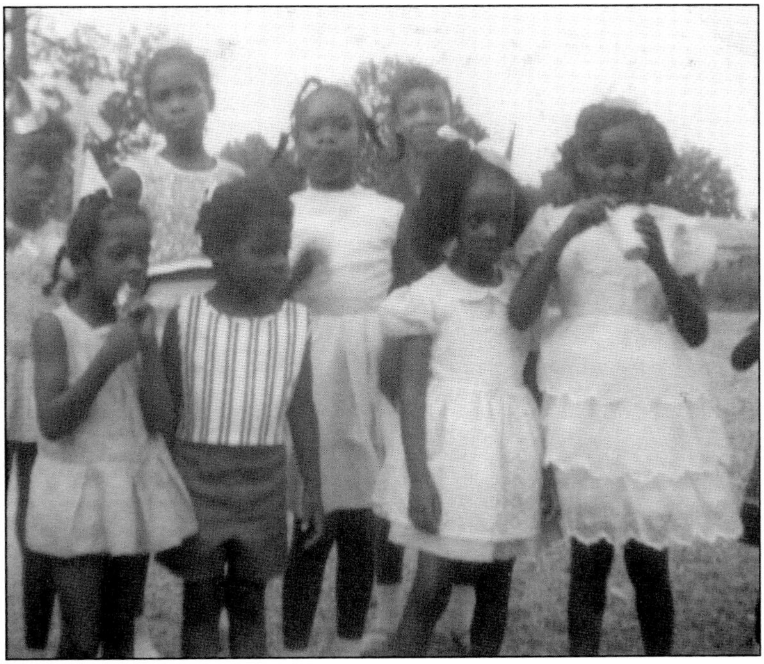

Birthday Party, c. 1960s. The photographer took the girls' photograph as their attention moved elsewhere. Invited or not, birthday parties meant dressing up. Often, the entire neighborhood, which could extend for blocks, of parents and children attended such events. (Courtesy of Victoria Johnson Trevigne.)

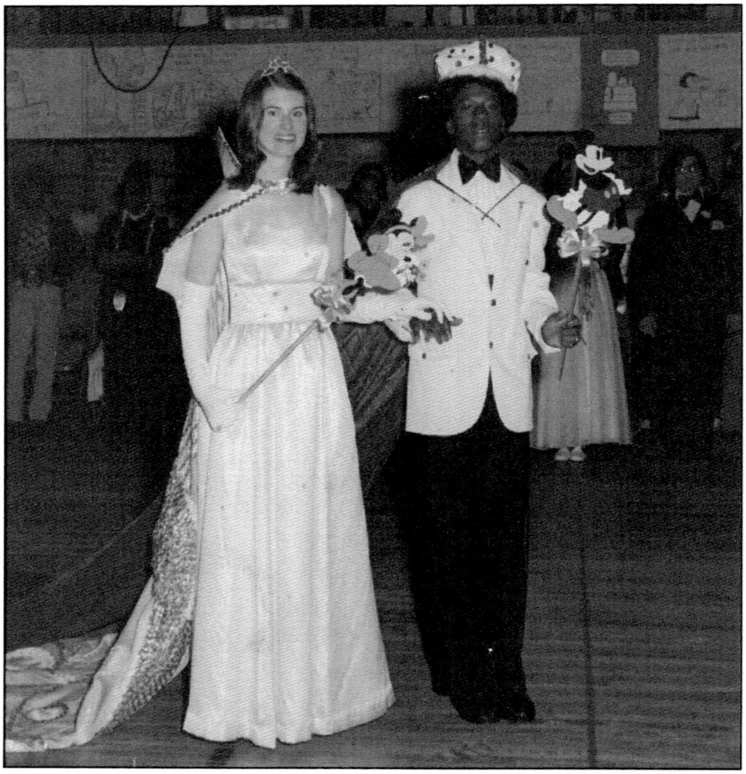

Mardi Gras Royalty. Henry Randle Jr., selected as king of the carnival ball at Covington High School, escorts the queen. In a move toward progress, students and faculty staged this event. It represented a big step from the anxieties surrounding integration, which was initiated in 1969. (Courtesy of the Randle collection.)

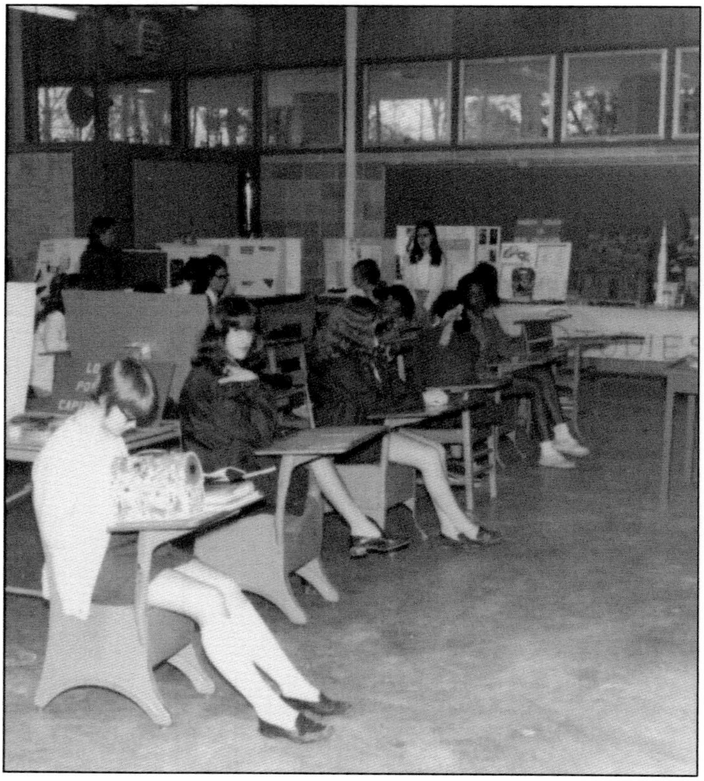

Gender Bender, c. 1970s. A remedy for integration of African American and white students rested on gender segregation. Girls and boys attended separate middle schools for 11 years. Covington High School had dabbled with integration when four African American students attended in the mid-1960s Freedom of Choice program. (Courtesy of the STPSB.)

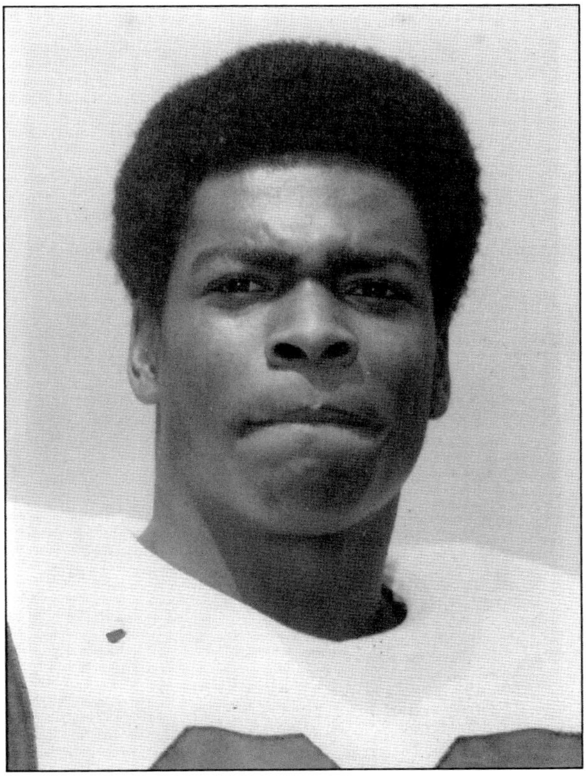

MIKE WILLIAMS. Mike Williams was one of the first two African Americans to integrate the Louisiana State University football team in 1970, on scholarship. The former Covington High School cornerback played with the San Diego Chargers and the LA Rams. (Courtesy of Mike Williams.)

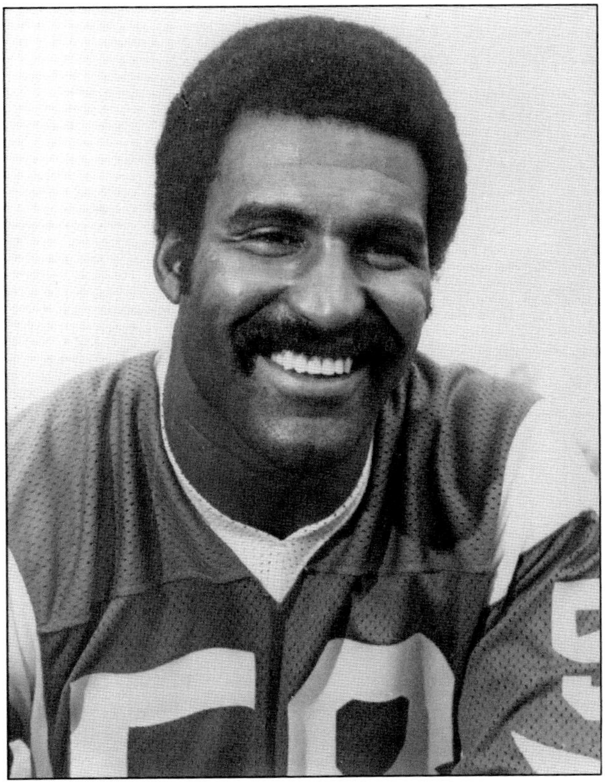

ISAIAH ROBERTSON JR. A native of Covington and son of Sonny and Doris Robertson, Isaiah says that he had "great teachers, role models and older black people that were a support group," in the town. He played at Southern University and for the Los Angeles Rams and the Buffalo Bills. (Courtesy of Isaiah Robertson.)

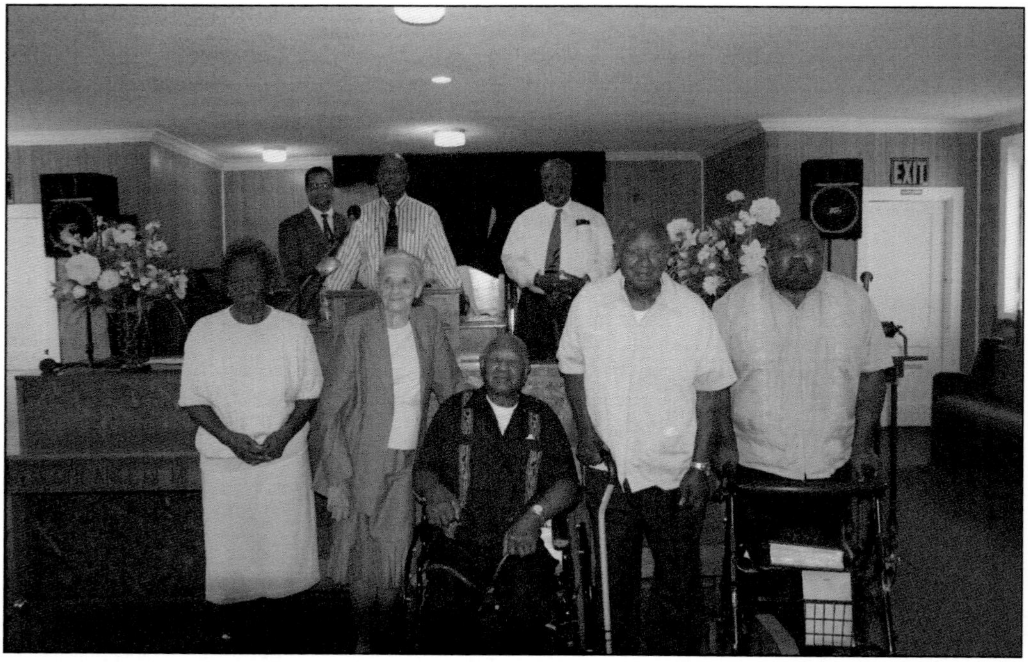

FIRST MISSIONARY BAPTIST CHURCH, 2013. Members whose families are rooted in the earliest years of FMBC and who were among the oldest included Jacob (wheelchair) and Joseph Kelly (with cane), along with Alberta Lambert and Dorothy McElveen Pouncey, who at the time of this photograph was 89. (Courtesy of Les Baham.)

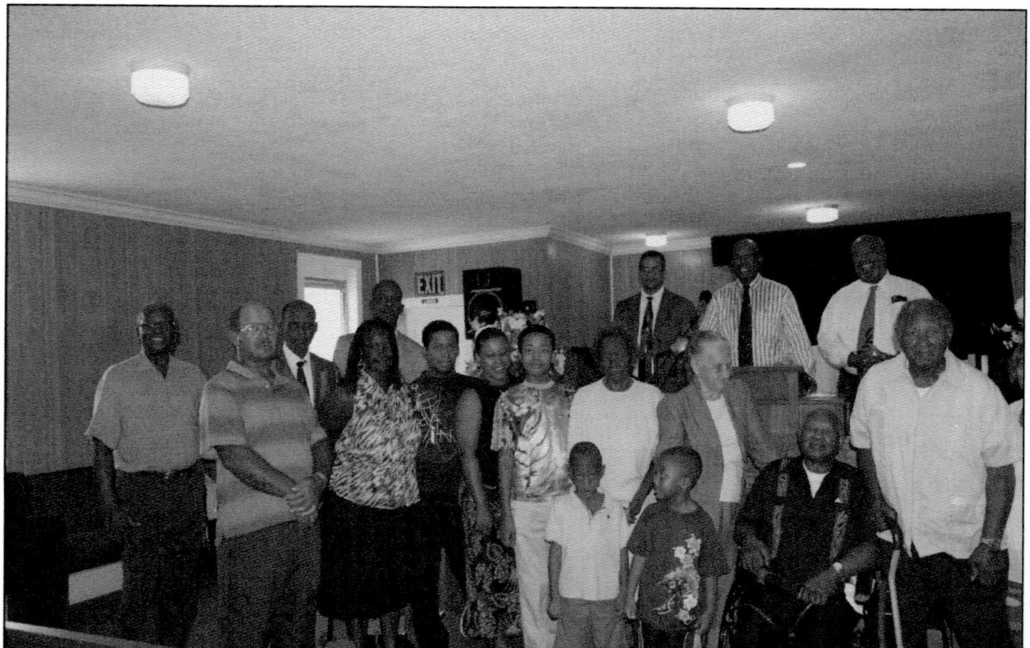

CHURCH MEMBERS, 2013. Members of the First Missionary Baptist Church joined in recognition of the church's oldest members, twins Jacob and Joseph Kelly, Alberta Lambert, and Dorothy Pouncey. Pastors Otis Brumfield and Kenneth Robertson stand in the pulpit. (Courtesy of Les Baham.)

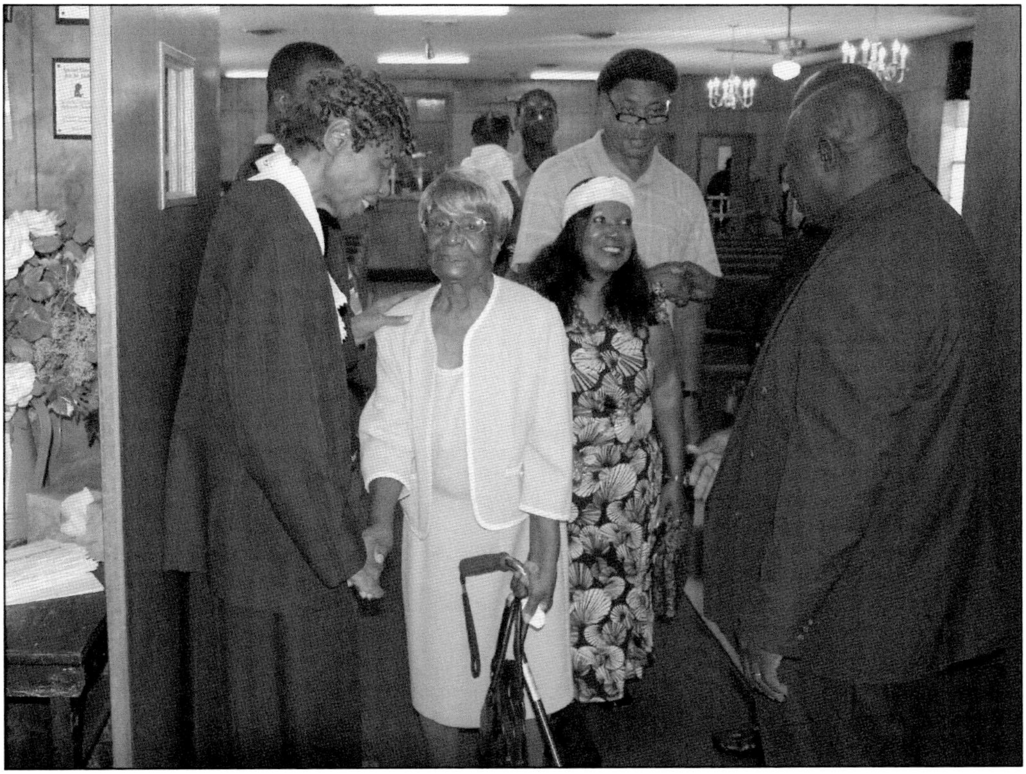

Bethel Reform Methodist, 2013. Greeting Mamie Martin after Sunday morning services is youth minister Rev. Joyce James. Behind her are Dionne James and Carl Spicer. Minister Lee stands with his back turned but facing the pastor, Rev. Wesley Cyprian. (Courtesy of Les Baham.)

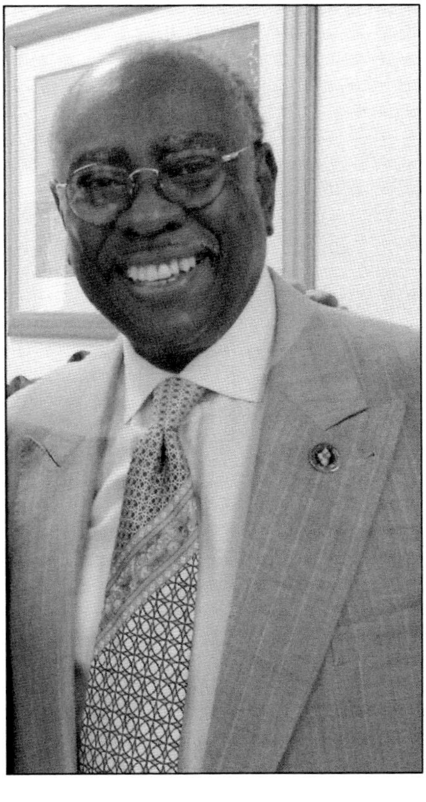

Rev. Mallery Callahan, 2013. Callahan is only the fourth pastor of Greater Starlight Missionary Baptist Church in its 83-year history. He also pastored Hopewell and Sweet Rest Baptist Churches. During the summer of 2014, he became the ninth president of the Louisiana Home & Foreign Missions Baptist State Convention. (Courtesy of Greater Starlight Missionary Baptist Church.)

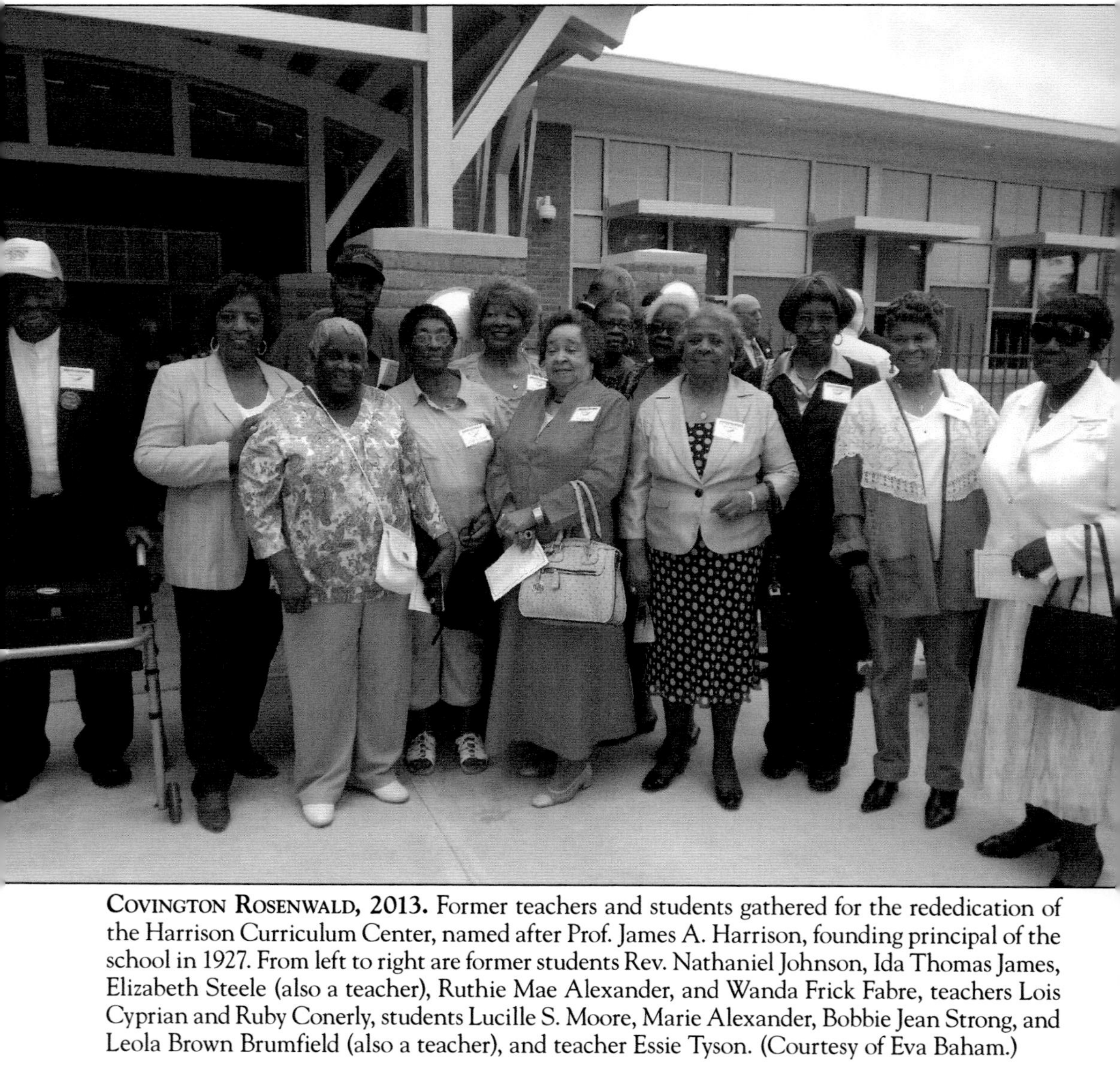

Covington Rosenwald, 2013. Former teachers and students gathered for the rededication of the Harrison Curriculum Center, named after Prof. James A. Harrison, founding principal of the school in 1927. From left to right are former students Rev. Nathaniel Johnson, Ida Thomas James, Elizabeth Steele (also a teacher), Ruthie Mae Alexander, and Wanda Frick Fabre, teachers Lois Cyprian and Ruby Conerly, students Lucille S. Moore, Marie Alexander, Bobbie Jean Strong, and Leola Brown Brumfield (also a teacher), and teacher Essie Tyson. (Courtesy of Eva Baham.)

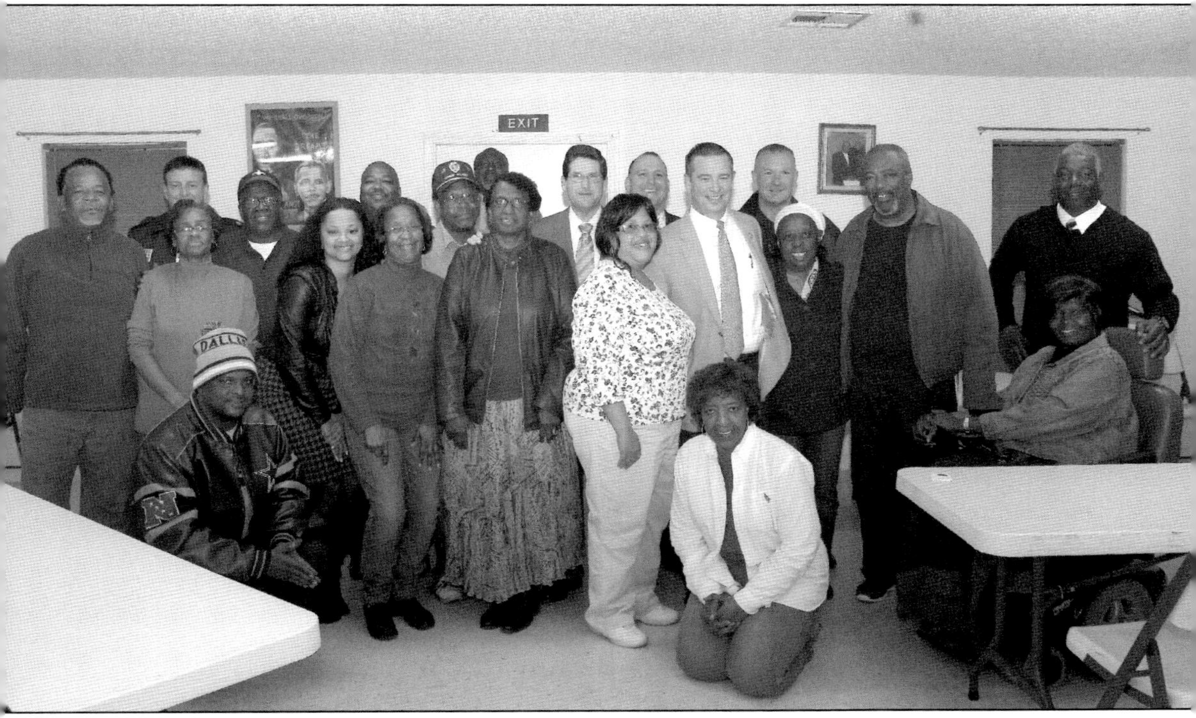

Unity Meeting, 2015. The NAACP convened a community meeting to foster goodwill between citizens and law enforcement. Kneeling are Ivory Celestine (left) and Ida James. Seated is Alfreda Smith. Standing from left to right are (first row) Robert Laurent, Diane Davis, Ariel Fabre, Gaynell Perry, Frances Dunn, Norma Weary, Covington police chief Tim Lentz, Ella Selmon, Rev. Kenneth Robertson, and facilitator Michael Rusk; (second row) Maj. Doug Sharp, Jerome Elzy, Covington warden Greg Lougino, Gus Davis, Monroe Rheems, Sheriff Jack Strain, Maj. Danny Culpeper, and Doug Arrowood. (Courtesy of Les Baham.)

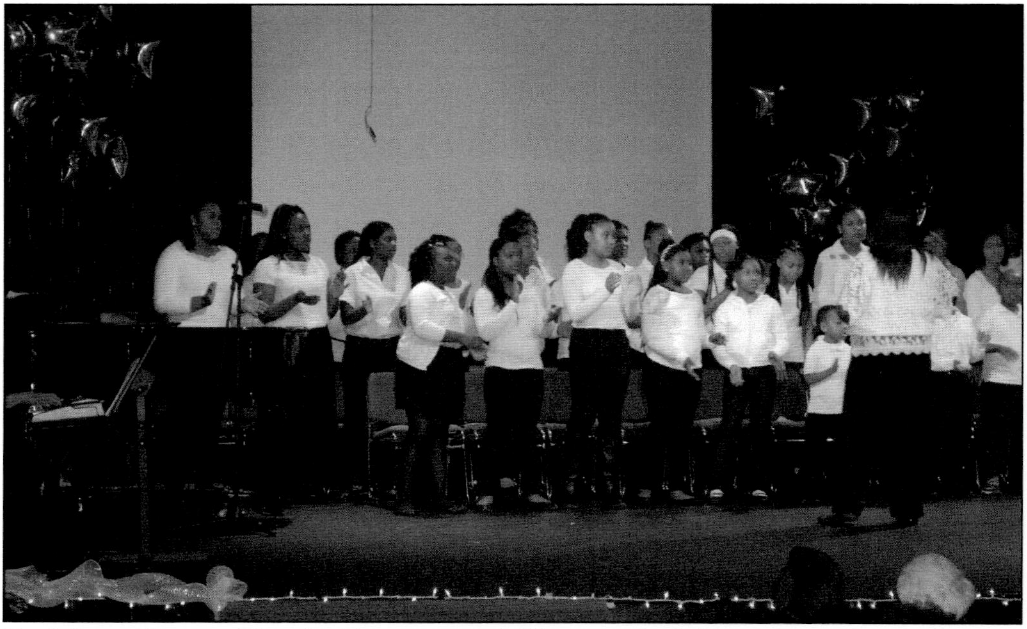

Dr. Martin Luther King Jr. Tribute, 2015. The citywide children's Mass Gospel Choir was directed by Rev. Rodney Barney, Erica Moses, and Dorothy Pennington, with musicians Robert Jones and Leon Payton and coordinators Gaynel Perry and Beatrice Penn. The poster and essay committee reviewed more than 300 submissions from students. Winners included both white and African American children, whose works were judged anonymously. The program was the culmination of months of planning, sponsored by the NAACP, local churches, area merchants, the school board, the mayor, city council, city agencies, schools, and individuals. The weekend was marked by community-service projects and a parade, ending with a fun day in Atkins Park with food and activities. Dominic Davenport, a high school student, served as master of ceremonies. (Both, courtesy of Deacon Kenneth Reeves.)

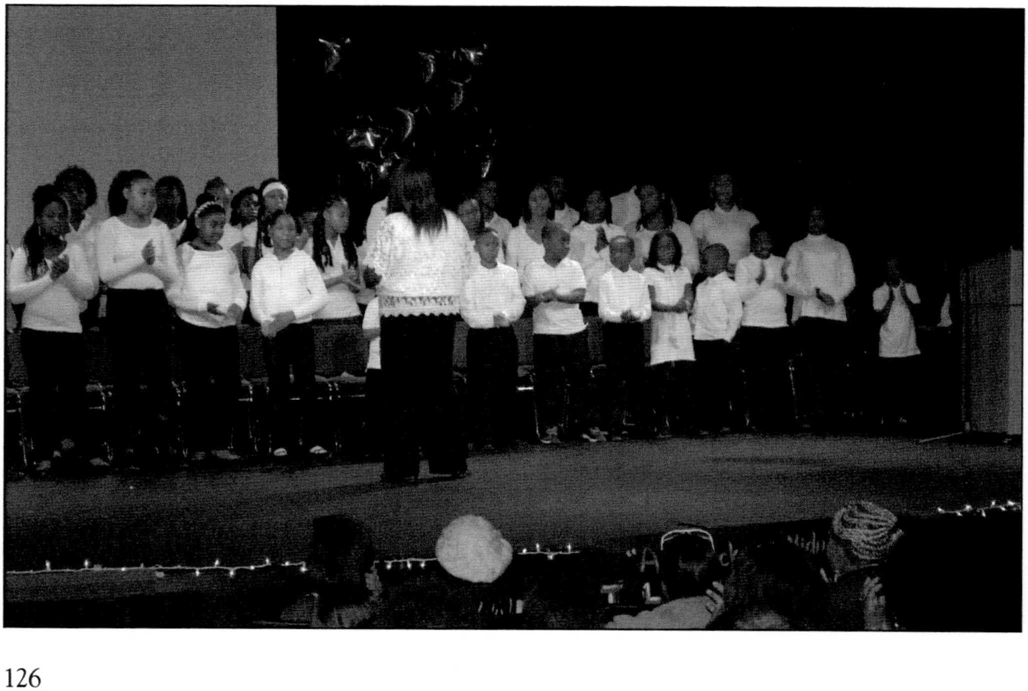

Bibliography

Dew, Charles. "Who Won the Succession Election in Louisiana?" *The Journal of Southern History* 36, no. 1 (1970): 1,832.

Ellis, Frederick S. *St. Tammany Parish: L'Autre Côté du Lac*. Gretna, LA: Pelican Publishing Co. Inc., 1981.

Fairclot h, Adam. *A Class of Their Own: Black Teachers in the Segregated South*. Cambridge, MA: The Belknap Press of Harvard University Press, 2007.

Fickle, James E. "Comfortable and Happy? Louisiana and Mississippi Lumber Workers, 1900–1950." *Louisiana History: The Journal of the Louisiana Historical Association* 40, no. 4 (1999): 407–432.

Hall, Gwendolyn Midlo. *Africans in Colonial Louisiana: The Development of Afro-Creole Culture in the Eighteenth Century*. Baton Rouge, LA: Louisiana State University Press, 1992.

Harwell, David Horace. *Walker Percy Remembered: A Portrait in the Words of Those Who Knew Him*. Chapel Hill, NC: University of North Carolina Press, 2007.

Hyde, Samuel C. Jr., ed. *A Fierce and Fractious Frontier: The Curious Development of Louisiana's Florida Parishes, 1699–2000*. Baton Rouge, LA: Louisiana State University Press, 2004.

Jones, William P. *The Tribe of Black Ulysses: African American Lumber Workers in the Jim Crow South*. Urbana, IL: University of Illinois Press, 2005.

Schwartz, Adrian. "A Brief Outline of St. Tammany Parish History: In Celebration of the Louisiana Purchase, 1803–1953." Pamphlet of the St. Tammany Parish Fair Assn. Louisiana Purchase Sesqui-Centennial Committee, 1953.

———. *Sesqui-Centennial in St. Tammany: The Early Years of Covington, Madisonville, Mandeville & Abita Springs, Louisiana*. Covington, LA: Covington City Council, 1963.

Schweninger, Loren. "Free Persons of Color in Postbellum Louisiana." *Louisiana History: The Journal of the Louisiana Historical Association* 30, no. 4 (1989): 345–364.

Swett, M. Philippine. "Origin and Development of Catholic Education in St. Tammany Parish, Louisiana." Unpublished, 1952.

Usner, Daniel H. "From African Captivity to American Slavery: The Introduction of Black Laborers to Colonial Louisiana." *Louisiana History: The Journal of the Louisiana Historical Association*. 20, no. 1 (1979): 25–48.

Vincent, Charles. *Black Legislators in Louisiana during Reconstruction*. Carbondale, IL: Southern Illinois University Press, (1987) 2011.

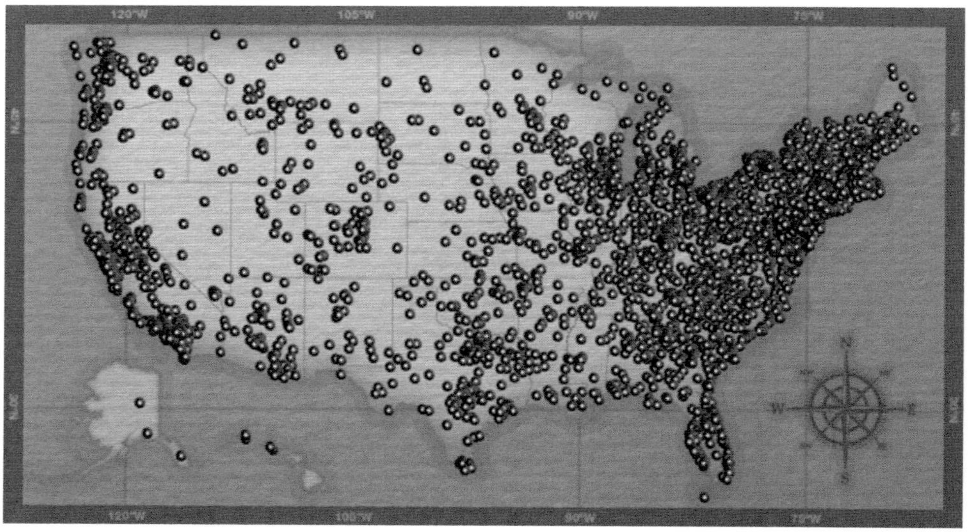